The
Girls in the
Back of the Class

Nedra —

Thanks for "excusing"
me from breakfast.

John Johnson

ALSO BY LOUANNE JOHNSON

Making Waves

My Posse Don't Do Homework

The
Girls in the
Back of the Class

LouAnne Johnson

ST. MARTIN'S PRESS
NEW YORK

Design by Sara Stemen

LIBRARY OF CONGRESS CATALOGING-IN-PUBLICATION DATA

Johnson, LouAnne.
    The girls in the back of the class / LouAnne Johnson.
        p.   cm.
    ISBN 0-312-13081-3
    1. Johnson, LouAnne. 2. High school teachers—United States-
-Biography.   3. English teachers—United States—Biography.
LA2317.J62A3   1995
373.11'0092—dc20
    [B]   95-1553
                                                            CIP

First edition: June 1995

10 9 8 7 6 5 4 3 2 1

Acknowledgments

Thanks to Reagan Arthur, Bob Hunter, Monica Howe Khoury, Ruth Nathan, Jim Ryan, and Zohreh Worth for much-needed moral support and patience. My love and gratitude to Simoa Alipate, Isabel Carrillo, Miguel Chacon, Oscar Guerra, Isabel Jimenez, Jose Jimenez, Juan Ortiz, Omar Hernandez, and Juan Sanchez for sharing their dreams with me. And thanks to Ron Bass, Jerry Bruckheimer, Lucas Foster, Margery Kimbrough, Elaine May, Michelle Pfeiffer, Don Simpson, Sandy Rabins, and John N. Smith for making so many dreams come true.

Author's Note

This book is based on actual incidents and real people. All names of people and places have been changed to protect the privacy of the individuals concerned. In some cases, characters in this book are composites of two or more people, either to protect individual privacy or to prevent confusion on the part of the reader (and author).

Introduction

I will be forever grateful that I had the opportunity to be part of a "school within a school," where I worked with a team of truly dedicated teachers and administrators in a program for at-risk teens—students who had the intelligence to succeed in school, but lacked the motivation or means to do so.

Our Academy program was based on the model created by a team of educators that included Dr. Marilyn Raby. Academy students enter the program as sophomores and remain with the same teachers and the same group of students for their junior and senior years. Juniors are assigned mentors from the local community, and seniors participate in a work-study program with local businesses, which range from family-owned markets to major corporations such as Sun Microsystems. A federal grant allowed us to limit class size to a maximum of twenty-five students and to establish a modern computer laboratory with IBM PCs, which we used to provide each Academy student with three years of training in computer applications such as word processing, spreadsheets, and desktop publishing.

I was part of the original Academy teaching team at Parkmont High, and our team held high expectations for our students—too high, many people said. Don't ask for too much, they warned. Passing grades and graduation would be good enough.

But we wanted more. We asked our students to come to school every single day, to stay away from drugs and alcohol, to change their bad habits, to complete every classroom and homework assignment, to resist the pressure to join gangs, to give up their bad attitudes and clean up their language. We asked for everything we could think of, and they gave us everything they had. They gave us good attendance and honest effort and excellent grades. They gave us headaches and heartaches and sleepless nights. They gave us trust and respect and love. They opened their tender hearts and shared their precious dreams. They taught us to believe in our own dreams. They stole my heart and kept it forever. Too little payment for so great a debt.

Chapter 1

A Deal's a Deal

Y ou better take this while I got it, Miss J." Raul Chacon sauntered toward my desk, his black eyes twinkling, his baseball cap
turned sideways and jammed down over his slicked-back hair.
He stuck out his fist, which held a bouquet of twenty-dollar bills.

I waved the bills away. "The deal was, you couldn't pay me
back until graduation day," I reminded him.

"What's the matter? You afraid I'm going to drop out of
school in the next five days?"

"No, but a deal's a deal. When you graduate, you can pay me."

"No sweat. I got all A's and B's right now. I could flunk all my
finals and still graduate." Raul slapped the bills down on my
desk. I picked them up and held them out to him. He pretended
to take them, then suddenly thrust them at me and took off running for the door. I grabbed the twenties, raced around my desk,
caught one sleeve of Raul's bulky, black Oakland Raiders jacket,
and pulled him back into the room.

"I told you I won't accept one penny until graduation day." I
stuffed the money into the back pocket of his baggy jeans. "Now
get out of here."

"Aw, Miss J." Raul reached for his back pocket, but I grabbed
his hand and pushed him out the door. After I shut him out of
the room, he ran along the row of windows that stretched the

length of my classroom, pressing his hand against the panes until he found one that was unlocked. He pushed it open as far as it would go and tried to crawl in, but the opening was too narrow, even for his wiry ninety-five-pound frame. He pressed his nose against the glass and yelled, "I'm gonna graduate and you know it!"

Raul grinned at me through the window, a wide, wicked grin that transformed his thin, sad face into a round, shining sun. When he realized that I had no intention of relenting and accepting his early payment, Raul shouted, "See you Monday!" and took off down the sidewalk.

There are certain memories that etch themselves in my mind so perfectly and permanently that I can see them as clearly as though they were photographs in an album. My first glimpse of Raul Valdemar Muñoz y Chacon is a full-color, eight-by-ten glossy in my memory album. The original four Academy teachers—Bud Bartkus, Don Woodford, Jean Warner, and I—were huddled inside our tiny office in the back of room T-1, taking turns peeking at our first group of fifty "at-risk" sophomores. Since the upper half of the office walls were glass, we had taped several large, colorful posters against the windows of our office, giving the students something to look at and us something to hide behind. We peeked between posters as the students milled around the room, waiting for the Academy orientation to begin.

Bud Bartkus, the Academy computer teacher and department chair during that year, took the first look. After a few seconds, he sighed and stepped aside, motioning for Jean to go next. A short, round woman with bright blue eyes and a baby face, Jean was the only teacher from the Social Studies Department willing to give our project a try. Although she was nearly fifty years old, it was her first year as a classroom teacher, and she wasn't confident that she could handle the discipline problems we all knew were waiting to test our idealistic enthusiasm.

"They look like regular kids to me," Jean said, obviously relieved, "but I didn't expect to see so many white faces in a class of potential dropouts." I hadn't either, although my own adolescence should have been reminder enough that white kids have problems, too. About one-third of the Academy students were white teenagers from the local neighborhood; the rest were black and Hispanic students who were bused in from the other side of the Bay Area.

Don Woodford tapped Jean on the shoulder. "My turn."

"See the one with the red ball cap?" Bud Bartkus whispered over Don's shoulder.

"I see three red ball caps," Don said.

"The little guy. Short, skinny, black hair."

"Yeah, I see him. What about him?"

"He looks like trouble to me. I've seen his kind before." Bud believed in the program, but he never got over his nervousness at dealing with "street kids." He ended up resigning from the Academy at the end of that year.

"Let me see," I poked Don in the ribs. He moved over and I squeezed closer to the window and pressed my nose to the glass so I could see through the narrow slit between an action shot of Michael Jordan and a portrait of Martin Luther King, Jr. A group of black boys huddled in one corner, trying to look like they weren't nervous. Most of the girls sat at desks, some checking their makeup or combing their hair, but most just sitting, looking resigned. In the front of the room, four tough-looking Hispanic boys stood watching a fifth boy, small and thin, who was drawing gang-style graffiti on the chalkboard, stepping back frequently to admire his work and accept high fives from his pals. Strands of shining black hair escaped from under the brim of his ball cap. His pants looked strangely misshapen, until I realized he had belted them far below his natural waistline, so that the crotch hung halfway to his knees, in what I soon learned was the popular "sick sag" style.

As I watched, Raul added some shading to his drawing of a

man's face, tossed the chalk into the air, and spun around, catching it behind his back. He dropped it immediately, though, and as he bent to pick it up, his gaze fell on the window in the back of the room. I must have moved just as he looked, because he pointed straight at me, winked, and grinned, revealing a row of crooked, slightly discolored teeth so small that I wondered briefly whether it was possible for a teenager still to have his baby teeth.

Later, much later, after Raul and I had become fast friends, I realized that his teeth, and his size—five feet tall and ninety-five pounds—were a result of eating only beans and rice three times a day for most of his difficult young life.

At seventeen, Raul was two years older than most of the other sophomores, but he had missed so much school and failed so many classes that he still didn't have enough credits to move up to junior status. Because of his size, none of the other students, except the members of his "posse"—Gusmaro Guevarra and Victor Rodriguez—were aware of Raul's age. If he graduated, *when* he graduated, he would be nearly twenty years old, but he would also be the first person in all the generations of the Chacon family to finish high school. His parents, migrant farm workers, had been allowed the luxury of attending first and second grades before joining their families as full-time fruit pickers and planters.

Raul often considered quitting school, but I knew he would never do it. He had given me his word of honor when I lent him a hundred dollars cash on a handshake to pay off a thug who had sold him a stolen jacket.

"You gotta charge me interest," Raul had insisted when I offered him the loan, but he hadn't expected the kind of interest I exacted. The terms of the loan were simple: He must repay the full amount, but he couldn't pay me back until his graduation day, two and a half years later. I knew Raul had been tempted many times since that day to quit school, but he had given me his word of honor, complete with five-part posse handshake, a complicated procedure involving finger locks and thumb presses, followed by knocking our knuckles together, fist against fist.

The jacket loan turned out to be an excellent investment. Raul's academic record at the start of his sophomore year consisted of failing grades, suspensions, and unexcused absences. Two years behind most of his classmates, Raul realized that turning over a new leaf wouldn't be enough. He cut down the tree and planted an entire new forest. He pushed himself harder than any teacher would have dared. By the start of his senior year, Raul had raised his grade point average from a dismal 1.0 to a respectable 3.2.

Raul wasn't the only success story in the Academy. More than half of those first fifty students surprised themselves and the school administration by earning enough credits to graduate, four with full college scholarships.

We made it, I thought, as I gazed out over the rows of lopsided wooden desks.

We made it through *Othello* and onomatopoeia and two thousand vocabulary words.

We made it through more than a thousand days of fistfights and knifings, gang bangers and babies, drugs and drive-bys.

I erased the chalkboards and cleared the papers from my desk, most of them last-minute makeup assignments from overly optimistic students. I stuffed the papers into my briefcase along with my gradebook and Raul's private journal, which he had offered to me as a memento.

"You can keep this so you don't forget me," Raul had said as he laid the battered red spiral notebook on my desk earlier that day.

"I could never forget you," I said.

Raul grinned and waved his hand. "I know that. I ain't that dumb. I'm giving you this because you always get such a happy look on your face when I write a whole bunch of stuff in my journal. And you're the only person who thinks my jokes are funny. I'm giving it to you so after I'm gone, in case you get sad, you can just read it and get a smile."

I did smile, as I clicked off the lights and locked the door. I smiled as I drove up the hill and under the I-280 overpass to my tiny apartment in Woodside. I was still smiling as I tucked myself into bed that night, the last Friday before the first Academy graduation. In exactly one week, I'd watch "my kids" walk across that stage, one by one, a diploma in one hand and a piece of my heart in the other. That night I slept smiling in a swirl of the sweetest dreams.

Monday morning, I hopped out of bed and hurried to school, eager to begin giving finals and get on to the postexam parties I'd carefully planned for each of my classes. If I had known what the following days held in store for me and "my posse," I might have stayed in bed.

Chapter 2

The Downhill Slide

The last entry in Raul Chacon's journal brought tears to my eyes, as so many of his personal essays did.

Dear Ms. or Miss or Mrs. Johnson,
I hate myself because I never take care of important stuff. My mom and dad always be telling me to do things and I never do them. Sometimes I tell myself I got to do things, but I don't even listen to myself. For example, I know I have to take care of business and register so I can go to community college this fall, but every day I don't do it. But I do make time for the dumb stupid shit like going to Great America every Saturday and Sunday to get drunk and act stupid at parties and hit on girls. And I got these three traffic tickets I owe and I want to pay them and they are just fix-it tickets, but I never take the time to take care of them, so I guess the police will put me in jail when they catch me because they'll find out I don't got no car insurance which I could get if I would just go and buy it after payday, but I never do. I just waste my money on stupid shit except you know I don't be buying no drugs or nothing like that. Sometimes I tell myself to change, but I think maybe it's already to late to change because I'm almost twenty years old al-

ready and I'm just the same as I always been. No matter what I do, I guess I will always be a ugly, lazy, hard-headed motherfucker. I try to say them positive affirmations like you told us to, like I'm smart and handsome and charming and I deserve to be successful and stuff and I say them but I don't think I really believe them.

—Raul

Raul's journal lay on my kitchen counter where I had dropped it Friday night after unloading my briefcase. I hadn't read it over the weekend because I hadn't assigned the seniors any additional writings since the last time I'd read their journals. Monday morning I glanced through it as I waited for my breakfast bagel to brown in the toaster oven. When I read the last page, I could have kicked myself for being so dense. Raul hadn't stopped by my room to give me money Friday afternoon; he'd stopped to get a hug and some reassurance that he could handle life after high school.

And what had I done? Kicked him out of my room and locked the door behind him.

I left Raul's journal near the phone to remind me to call him when I got home that evening, since the seniors weren't scheduled for exams in my class until Wednesday morning.

At school I finished arranging the seats and sophomore exam materials fifteen minutes early, so I decided to use the extra time to see whether I could remove the melted Gummi Bears from the fluorescent light fixture directly above Richie DiDonato's desk. I was standing on a chair, whacking at the petrified candy with a ruler, when, through the window, I saw Toshomba Grant chug around the corner of T-Wing and head up the sidewalk toward my classroom. Although my room is the last one in the wing, I could hear Toshomba clearly. He has one of those naturally booming voices; even when he tries to whisper, his voice ignores him and blares on, like a television set with a broken volume control. As he ran, Toshomba was chanting the same phrase repeatedly, the cadence of his voice rising and falling in rhythm with the pumping of his chubby arms and legs: "Rico socked the prin-ci-pal! Rico socked the prin-ci-pal! Rico socked the prin-ci-pal!"

When he reached T-1, Toshomba took a hard left through the doorway and screeched to a halt in front of me, his Nike high-tops squealing on the dingy gray floor tile. He glanced from side to side, as though he was about to be arrested for divulging important secret information, then leaned forward, cupped his hands around his mouth, and whispered melodramatically up to me, "Rico socked the principal, Miss J!" The kid was good. For a minute, I almost believed him.

"Oh, my goodness!" I said. I climbed down from the chair and grabbed a file folder from my desk to use as a fan. Waving the folder in front of my face, I batted my eyes and pretended that I was trying not to faint while I waited for Toshomba to grin at me and say "Psych," as he always did, delighted to have fooled me once again.

But Toshomba didn't say "Psych." He didn't say anything. He just stood there, panting, his chubby brown cheeks working in and out, in and out, as he stared at me.

"Psych?" I prompted.

Toshomba shook his head. "I ain't lying, Miss J. Come on. Check it out for yourself." He started for the door, but stopped when he looked back over his shoulder and realized I wasn't following. He studied me for a moment. "You all right?"

I nodded and waved one hand at him, indicating that he should go ahead without me. He hesitated. Usually I rushed to the scene of any emergency that involved one of my students.

"I'm fine," I assured him, trying to not to smile at his fat little frown. "But the first bell's going to ring in a minute. I have to start my exam exactly on time and you need to get to class so you won't be late for your first-period exam. You go check it out for me and come back at lunch to let me know what happens. But be discreet—kind of like a secret agent, okay?"

Toshomba's frown disappeared, replaced by his usual gap-toothed grin. Delighted to be assigned as my official agent of espionage, he spun around and took off down the hallway.

I wasn't worried. I didn't believe Toshomba's story for a minute, although if any student had the temerity to tackle the principal of Parkmont High, Rico Perez was that student. In a school where tough-talking, hard-hitting boys abound, where gang graffiti and broken windows advertise the attitude of a generation, Rico stood out from the crowd. At five foot six, he wasn't the biggest or the meanest boy at Parkmont. Unlike the self-proclaimed gangsters who strutted around campus, flexing their biceps and displaying their disrespect through loud, foul language, Rico walked quietly and spoke softly. Although he spent hours in the weight room and occasionally broke dress code during the hot summer months by wearing a tank top that revealed his thick, muscular chest and arms, he never flaunted his physique, and I never once heard him curse.

When I first saw Rico, I assumed he was just another wannabe gangster punk. He certainly had the look—black jeans, baggy black Raiders shirt, black high-tops with untied laces, thick black hair slicked straight back from a deep widow's peak that dipped almost to his eyebrows, framing his face into a small, hard, heart shape. When Rico walked into a room, people noticed. Much larger boys stepped quickly aside to let him pass, and Rico paused for a split second whenever he crossed the threshold, the way a high-ranking military officer does, to give the troops time to take note and jump to attention.

Rico wasn't the only tough kid at Parkmont, but he was the only one I would describe as absolutely fearless. Rico was also extremely intelligent, so I knew he wouldn't do anything as stupid as assaulting an administrator one week before the end of his junior year. At least, I didn't think he would. But when the first

exam period ended and lunch period passed without any sign of
Toshomba, I started to worry.

If Rico did hit Dr. Delgado, I reasoned, there was very little I
could do to help him until a wheelbarrow full of official forms
had been filed. Instead of rushing to the office or calling the
principal's secretary for advance information, I decided to wait
and let trouble come looking for me for a change.

Toshomba arrived just before the bell and whispered, "He's
coming," as he hurried past my desk to take his assigned seat.
Before I could ask who "he" was, Rico Perez strolled into the
room.

I was so relieved to see Rico that I didn't reprimand him for
wearing his T-shirt rolled up into his armpits, baring his entire
midriff. His face was flushed and his chest glistened, perspira-
tion giving his skin a sheen like highly polished mahogany. He
nodded silently at me, accepted the exam I handed him, and
took his seat in the far left corner of the room where he hunched
over his desk, avoiding eye contact until the dismissal bell rang.

Toshomba lingered behind the others but didn't get a chance
to file his report, since Rico also stayed. Toshomba hovered near
my desk, reluctant to leave.

"Thanks, honey, but—" I started.

"I'm her clerk," Rico interrupted. "If she needs help, I'll help
her." Toshomba started to argue, but one look from Rico sent
him scurrying out the door.

I sat at one of the student desks and motioned for Rico to sit
down near me, but he stayed where he was, in his corner of the
classroom.

"Bet you thought I was gonna cut out of the exam. Right?" he
asked.

"No. You've never stood me up."

"That's right. Because if I did, I'd be out of here so fast my
head would spin and I'm not kidding," Rico said with a sly grin,
repeating word for word the warning I'd given him on his first

day as a student clerk, back when I had believed tough talk was the best way to make my point. I had enlisted Rico to clerk during lunch periods to keep him from engaging in recreational head bashing off campus. Within the first two weeks of starting his junior year, he had been in three lunchtime fights, with a three-day suspension after each one. Since he never ate lunch, claiming it made his brain feel "too heavy," I figured that if he spent lunch hour with me, he might spend less time fighting and more time in class. It worked. Not only did Rico's grades improve, but he turned out to be the best student clerk I ever had. If I could have cloned him, I would have. But on that particular day, I felt more like clobbering him.

"I heard a crazy rumor about you and Dr. Delgado," I told Rico.

"Yeah," Rico said. "Sorry about that. We had a little trouble." He unrolled his T-shirt and bent his head, using the front of his shirt to wipe the sweat from his face. "Don't worry, I took care of it," he mumbled into his shirt. When he finished wiping his forehead, he kept his shirt up in front of his face for a few seconds, then lowered it to reveal just his eyes, peeking at me between his fingers like a little kid.

"You didn't hit the principal," I said. He couldn't have. If he had hit Dr. Delgado, or even threatened to, Rico wouldn't be in my classroom; he'd be on his way to juvenile hall.

"Naw, I didn't hit him." Rico dropped his T-shirt.

"Good. I knew you wouldn't do such a dumb—"

"I tried to, though," Rico interrupted me. "But Casey grabbed me."

I covered my face with my hands. Casey, the head of security, wore mirrored sunglasses, even indoors, and carried his walkie-talkie in a hip holster. If Rico had assaulted him, I knew a suspension notice, or at the very least a week's detention, was en route. That meant Rico would miss half of his exams, which would lower his GPA and hurt his chances for a scholarship in his senior year. I think I was counting on that scholarship more than Rico was. I got up and walked to my desk to get a tissue, keeping my back turned so Rico wouldn't see the tears in my eyes. "I can't believe you hit Casey. What a dumb move."

"I didn't hit him. I just flipped him."

I turned around to look at Rico's face. He was serious. I sank into the nearest seat and closed my eyes. For two years, I had worried and pleaded and prayed for this boy to make it through high school alive. One by one, during the past two years, all but a few of his friends had been expelled from school, then either arrested and imprisoned or shot to death on the street. Rico had the brains to make it through college if he could just survive his adolescence.

"Don't cry, Miss J," Rico said. "Come on. Open your eyes. Look at me." I did. He grinned sheepishly and sat down next to me. He scooted his desk until it bumped into mine and put his feet onto the wire book rest beneath my seat.

"Honest, it's gonna be okay," he said. "I handled it."

"What happened?" I asked, not at all sure I wanted to hear his story.

Rico explained that he and some friends had sneaked off campus during lunch to go to Taco Bell, and when they came back to Parkmont, Dr. Delgado spotted them sneaking through a hole in the fence behind the school.

"Dr. D yelled at us to stop," Rico said, "but the other guys all ran up in the hills behind the school and got away. Dr. D couldn't run that fast."

"Why didn't you run, too?"

Rico drew back his shoulders. "I don't run from nobody."

"Of course."

"So I kept walking up here to your room because I didn't want to be late—because it is selfish and inconsiderate to keep other people waiting for you," Rico said, another letter-perfect imitation of my own much-repeated reminder. His smile widened for a second, then disappeared as he added, "But Dr. Delgado kept yelling at me to stop."

"So, why didn't you stop?" I asked. "He's the principal, for Pete's sake."

Rico gave me a pained expression that implied my question was too silly for words. I returned his look. Rico sighed.

"Nobody yells at me," he explained with exaggerated patience. "So I kept walking. The next thing I know, Dr. D runs up and starts yelling right in my face." Rico stood up, pushed his desk aside, and started pacing the room, fists clenched.

"I told him nobody yells at me and I was going to my class and he should leave me alone."

I could see it clearly in my mind, and I didn't like the picture.

"He said, 'I'll yell at you if I want to!' Then he grabbed my arm and I told him to back off because nobody grabs me, but he wouldn't let go. He started yelling at me. Right in my face. So I told him nobody yells at me, neither, but he wouldn't listen. So I drew back on him like this—" Rico cocked his right arm. "And—"

"You said you didn't hit him," I interrupted.

"I didn't. I would of, but Casey grabbed me from behind, so I flipped Casey onto the ground and put him in a neck lock." He went through the motions of flipping somebody over his back onto the floor, pressing his knee onto the chest of his imaginary foe, throttling the man's neck. "Just like that."

"Oh, my God," I put my head down on my arms and spoke into the desktop. "You beat up the chief of security?"

"Naw, I didn't even hurt him a little bit," Rico said. I raised my head. Rico looked me straight in the eye. He was telling the truth. He stood up and dusted off the knees of his jeans. "I just put Casey down on the ground and explained that he shouldn't grab me."

"But, Rico," I cried, "you can't afford to get suspended now, right in the middle of finals!"

"I'm not *getting* suspended," Rico reassured me.

"You're not?"

"I *told* you." Rico looked at me as though I were too dense for words, as he perched on the top of the desk next to me. "I explained to Casey, and Dr. Delgado, too. I told him how does he expect me to respect him if he doesn't respect me. Now we understand each other. We shook hands, man to man, and everything's cool."

Cool is an important thing to be, according to Rico, who has frequently explained that people have to be violent, have to create a reputation as ruthless and cruel, to survive in today's world, especially in his neighborhood of East Palo Alto, California, which has been described by national news media as the "homicide capital of the country."

"You have to get respect on the street, any way you can," Rico had explained during our first class discussion on the topic of violence. "If you don't get respect, you're a dead man." From the looks on the faces of the other students in class, I could see that most of them agreed with Rico. They think I'm hopelessly idealistic and old-fashioned for believing that education is the ticket that will enable them to move out of their poverty-stricken and dangerous neighborhoods, into a safer, calmer world. Rico insists that most of the people he knows would stay even if they had the opportunity to leave, because they thrive on excitement and danger.

"It's like we're hooked on that high you get when you know you could get arrested or hurt or even die any second," Rico told me during one of our many lunchtime conversations.

Recalling that conversation, I asked Rico if he had been afraid, even for a split second, during his scuffle with Dr. Delgado and Casey.

"No," Rico shook his head firmly. "I wasn't scared a bit. It was kind of fun. You probably won't believe this, but it feels good to get in a fight or mug somebody." He was right, I didn't believe it, but I tried not to show any expression of disapproval or shock. When Rico, or any of my students, revealed private thoughts and personal lives to me, I tried to remain nonjudgmental, so I could learn to understand them—and perhaps help them.

I stood up and walked to my desk, where I shuffled the exams into piles, so Rico couldn't see my face.

"Whom did you ever mug?" I asked.

"There was this white guy on my street one day," Rico said. "He was probably looking for a buy or something; otherwise he wouldn't have been in my neighborhood. So I knew he was probably nervous. I went up to him and asked him what time was it. He told me. Then I said, 'Thanks. Now can I have your jacket?' And he gave it to me. Just like that." Rico snapped his fingers. "It was a nice leather jacket, too."

Rico, perceptive as usual, stood up and walked casually around to the other side of my desk so that we were facing each other again. He didn't always look at me while he was talking, but he liked to be able to see my face, and my reactions, if he wanted to.

"What were you wearing when you asked this guy to give you his nice leather jacket?" I asked.

"Just a T-shirt and jeans," Rico held his arms out, palms up. "Just like what I got on right now."

"Did you have a gun or a knife or anything?"

"No. And I kept my hands right out where he could see them so he'd know I was clean." He squinted at me. "I know what you're thinking, but I didn't steal that dude's jacket. I asked him for it, real polite, and he gave it to me. He could have said no, but he didn't."

"And why do you think he gave you the jacket?" I knew, but I hoped Rico didn't.

"He gave it to me because he thinks all Mexicans are low-life criminals who carry guns and knives and go around killing people," Rico said. So much for hope. "He gave me that jacket because he was stupid and prejudiced and ignorant. He deserved to lose it." I couldn't argue.

"After that, I did it a few more times." Rico said. "I got four jackets. Gave one to my little brother and the rest to my homies."

Always the teacher, I couldn't resist asking Rico if he might have felt better about himself if he worked and saved his money to buy a leather jacket.

"Why should I work for minimum wage at a shitty job to buy something when I can just ask some guy and he gives it to me for free because he's stupid?" Rico asked with a shrug.

I was tempted to ask him what his mother would say, but it's dangerous to mention a man's mother, even if the man is only seventeen. Rico wouldn't have told me the story if he didn't trust me, and I didn't want to risk losing that trust just to make a point. Besides, I didn't have to remind Rico that his mother would disapprove, because he already knew that, and he would make sure she never found out. When he spoke of his mother, which he often did, Rico's voice softened and so did his face. I could see the shadow of the sweet, kind little boy he must have been before he decided that a strong punch carried more weight than kindness ever could.

"You wouldn't believe this, probably," Rico said, in that same soft voice he used whenever he spoke of his mother, "but I used to be a good little kid. I had the best grades in the class. Then, when I was in the fourth grade, I looked around and realized nobody liked me anymore. Nobody respected me for being a good student, a nice little boy. So I changed. I made everybody respect me."

"And now everybody respects you?"

"If they don't, I make 'em. Just like Dr. D and Casey."

"Don't forget me," I said. "I respect you."

"I could never forget you." Rico looked straight into my eyes for as long as he could stand to be vulnerable. Then he slapped both hands down on my desk, breaking the tension and the mood. "I better get going."

"Are you sure you're not going to get suspended or detention or anything?"

Rico shrugged. "I'm pretty sure, but I guess we'll find out tomorrow."

"Could you do me a favor?" I asked, as he headed out the door.

"Name it."

"Would you give me your word that you won't hit, threaten, flip, kick, or put a neck lock on anybody for four more days? Just three school days and the ceremony on Friday. Do you think you could do that for me, so you'll be allowed to come back to school for your senior year and I won't have a nervous breakdown before graduation?"

Rico gave me a thumbs-up, tucked in his T-shirt, and sauntered out of the room. I knew he'd keep his word. I just hoped the other 149 Academy students would also stay out of trouble. Four days.

"That's not too much to ask, is it?" I asked out loud.

"Talking to yourself again," Hal Gray said, peering around the edge of the doorway. "Tsk, tsk." He shook a warning finger in my direction. "Better watch it. If they catch you doing stuff like that, they'll make you an administrator."

"Four days," I said to Hal. "Is that too much to ask?"

"Yes," Hal said.

"But you don't even know what I'm asking for."

"No. And I don't want to know. And I know something you probably don't want to know."

"You're right, I don't. Tell me tomorrow."

"Okay." Hal ducked back out the door and disappeared. I waited a few seconds, certain that he'd return to tell me whatever it was he had stopped to tell me. After a minute I realized he wasn't coming back.

"Hey! Wait a minute," I called as I ran out the door. Hal, a speed walker, was already at the end of the sidewalk that connected to the main entrance driveway by the time I caught up with him.

"I changed my mind," I told Hal. "Tell me now."

Hal had to shout his answer above the sound of sirens as three black-and-white police cars screamed through the main gate, spraying gravel as they swerved through the turn and sped up the drive toward us. "Emilio Lopez just threatened to dissect one of our biology teachers."

Chapter 3

Lydecker vs. Lopez

Emilio Lopez had a hard-earned reputation as a fair but furious fighter. Other boys used him as a benchmark—when a boy wanted the world to know he was tough, he challenged Emilio. Winning wasn't the issue. It wasn't even a hope in most cases, because Emilio was bigger, stronger, faster. Nobody beat Emilio in a fair fight, but Ken Lydecker wasn't interested in fair. He was interested in winning.

Ken Lydecker had the thick, doughy look of a professional wrestler well past his prime, and his pugnacious personality enhanced that image. He had been at Parkmont for thirty-five years, longer than any other teacher on the staff, and everybody from the superintendent to the students had learned to accept his teaching style, a mixture of sarcastic stand-up comic and demented drill sergeant. His idea of encouraging students, particularly boys, was to refer to them by an assortment of colorful nicknames, such as "worthless slime bags" and "butt-ugly dickweeds." An equal-opportunity bully, Mr. Lydecker added an *"estupido"* or *"chollo"* in the case of Hispanic students.

Occasionally, a student took offense at Lydecker's remarks and fired one back at him. Then the race was on. The first time one of my students sped around the corner of the building and hurtled into my room, with Mr. Lydecker hot on his heels, I was too surprised to do anything except stare. I was doodling on one of the student desktops, trying to camouflage a "fuk u" that was permanently carved into the wood, when Richie DiDonato ran into the room and crouched down on the floor behind me. A few seconds later, Ken Lydecker lurched through the doorway, scarlet-faced and gasping, one oversize index finger aimed at Richie, a loaded pistol to hold the boy in place while the man caught his breath. As soon as he could talk, Mr. Lydecker blasted Richie with a string of adjectives that were not in our vocabulary workbook.

Richie had spent his entire sophomore year on Academy probation for one offense or another, so it wasn't hard to believe that he had devised some clever and creative way to exasperate Mr. Lydecker. Still, I was shocked by the man's outburst. After he finally shouted himself hoarse and stomped out of the room, Richie sank into a seat near my desk and slumped down as far as he could.

"Don't worry about it," Richie said. "Nobody pays any attention to him when he gets like that."

I gave Richie a skeptical look. How could you not pay attention?

"You know what I mean," Richie said. "Sometimes we even do stuff on purpose, just to watch the veins pop out in his head."

"Oh, that sounds like a peck of fun," I said. Although I was being sarcastic, I could almost understand why Richie and his classmates enjoyed testing Ken Lydecker's limits.

"Last year, Lydecker had a stroke. Right in class." Richie jumped to his feet and paced back and forth, puffing out his cheeks and chest, pretending to be Mr. Lydecker. "Right in the middle of yelling, he fell over, smacked his face on one of the desks. *Whap!* It was so cool."

Richie flopped, facedown, smacking his hands against the desktop to simulate the sound of Mr. Lydecker's face hitting the wood. He dramatically "died" for a few seconds, then glanced up at me. "You shoulda been there. It was awesome."

If I hadn't just witnessed the man's tirade, I might have been more sympathetic, assuming that Richie's stroke story was true. But given the circumstances, I decided to check with Dr. Norton, the principal at that time, to see what was what. I expected a lukewarm reception from Dr. Norton. A former football player and Marine Corps officer, Chet Norton was a straight shooter, ultimately fair in dealing with staff, but he didn't waste his time or sympathy on students who ended up in his office, regardless of their reasons. Chet stood behind his teachers 100 percent, so I was more than a little surprised when he started nodding before I finished my first sentence.

"I've got a file this thick on Ken." Chet held up his right hand and measured four inches with his thumb and index finger. "But the man's been here for thirty-five years. He has tenure—"

"So that's it—" I interrupted.

"—and he helped a hell of a lot of kids before he burned out," Chet kept on talking. "Took kids into his own house, fed them, bought them clothes, paid for their glasses, found them jobs after school."

"That's admirable," I said, "but I'm talking about now. You should have heard the language he used—in front of a student, I might add."

"Nothing they haven't heard before, I'm sure," he said.

"That's not the point," I insisted. "It amounts to child abuse."

Chet opened a desk drawer, pulled out a sheet of paper, and handed me a pen. "Go ahead. Write it down. I'll add it to the file."

I didn't bother to write it down, but I did bother to go and talk to Mr. Lydecker when his complexion was a more normal color. He assured me that the kids didn't take him literally.

"Aw, those knuckleheads know I love 'em," Lydecker said. "Some of them even get a kick out of me yelling and hollering at them. They're probably hoping I'll drop dead right in front of them, provide a few minutes of free entertainment."

Not fully convinced, but not unduly concerned any longer, I decided to wait and see what happened. Three or four times during the next months, I saw Lydecker chasing one of my students around the back of T-Wing, but they both seemed to be enjoying themselves. And the kids invariably returned to class the following day, which I interpreted as a sign that they didn't take the incidents too seriously.

But Emilio Lopez takes everything seriously. At the beginning of the school year, Emilio had been assigned to Mr. Lydecker's biology class, his girlfriend to Lydecker's general science class. The first day of class, Mr. Lydecker pretended to read "Beaneater Lopez" off the roll sheet, and Emilio walked out. He agreed not to kill Mr. Lydecker only if he could change to another teacher's class. I checked the schedule, found a seat in a section taught by Miss Pierre, an energetic new teacher, and filled out a small mountain of paperwork to make the change. The last piece of paper was a drop slip that required both teachers' signatures. I filled out the form and instructed Emilio to get Mr. Lydecker's signature first, then Miss Pierre's signature. Within five minutes, he was back.

"What are you doing here?" I asked.

Emilio held out the forms. The paper looked as though it had been caught in a blender. It was a mass of wrinkles, and the lower right corner was ripped off.

"He bit it." Emilio had to explain what happened several times before I finally understood that when he presented the form for his signature, Mr. Lydecker had grabbed the paper, crumpled it in his fist, and bit off the signature block.

"Why?" I wondered. Emilio insisted that he hadn't said or done anything except hand the slip to Mr. Lydecker. I waited and called Mr. Lydecker a few minutes before the end of class, so that I wouldn't interrupt his lesson but would be sure to catch him before he left. As soon as I mentioned Emilio's name, Mr.

Lydecker screamed, "That worthless piece of dog meat!"

"Excuse me?" I winced as I visualized the class full of students sitting in Lydecker's classroom, undoubtedly listening closely to his end of the conversation.

"The kid's a short-timer," Lydecker said. "You're wasting your time on him."

"If you feel that way, then why didn't you sign his drop slip?" I asked.

"Hell, no!" Lydecker hollered.

"I'm taking him out of your class, like it or not."

"Not without my signature, you aren't."

"With or without." I hung up, filled out a new form, signed it, and sent Emilio to his new class. The next day, Mr. Cranston, the chairman of the Science Department, called me to ask why I changed Emilio's class without Mr. Lydecker's approval. I explained what happened. Mr. Cranston agreed to approve the change to Miss Pierre's class.

When Lydecker found out I had gone over his head to Mr. Cranston, he stopped me in the teachers' lounge. "You can't change a kid's schedule over a teacher's objection without department head approval," he said, stabbing the air in front of my face with his finger.

"Get that sausage out of my face before I bite it," I snapped. "And I *am* a department head, Pea Brain."

For Emilio's sake, if not my own, I should have held my temper and my tongue. But patience isn't one of my virtues.

Ken Lydecker snorted and stormed out of the lounge after I threatened to bite him, and he avoided me after that, ducking into the men's room or spinning into an abrupt about-face whenever he saw me heading his way in the halls. I liked to pretend he was afraid of me, although it was much more likely that he was afraid he'd be tempted to strangle me if he got too close. Either way, I was happy to have him on one side of the campus and me on the other. He seemed equally determined to maintain the maximum distance from my students, which he did until the last quarter of the school year. Then, with graduation four short days away, Ken Lydecker struck again—this time a TKO.

In a fair fight, my money would have been on Emilio, a six-foot-tall, two-hundred-pound would-be boxer with a trip-switch temper. But Lydecker vs. Lopez was one fight Emilio couldn't win. Emilio was already in handcuffs by the time two police officers led him out of the building. Hal Gray and I stood in the driveway watching, along with the crowd that had gathered when the police arrived, sirens wailing. As the trio approached the squad car, I pushed past the officer who was holding back the crowd.

"Wait!" I yelled. The two police officers with Emilio ignored me. I ran over and planted myself directly in front of Emilio, between him and the car. Both officers looked at me. Emilio stared at the ground.

"Ma'am, you're going to have to move," one of the officers said.

"Just give me ten seconds, please," I begged. The man glanced at his partner, who shrugged and nodded his head sideways at Emilio.

"What happened?" I asked Emilio.

"Nothing," he said, still staring at the pavement.

"You know I'll still love you, no matter what you did." I ducked down and tried to catch Emilio's eye, to make him look at me, but he shook his head and turned toward the police officer on his right.

"Let's do it," Emilio said.

"Excuse me, ma'am," the officer said. "The longer it takes to book Mr. Lopez, the longer it will be before he's out of jail."

"Jail?" I echoed. "Don't you mean juvi?"

"No," the officer said. "I mean jail. He's eighteen."

"Are you eighteen?" I asked Emilio.

He looked at me, his eyes unreadable, and nodded.

"Since when?"

"Since yesterday."

A few short seconds later, Emilio was a thousand miles away, locked inside the squad car, unable to hear me say, "I'm sorry I forgot." Even if he had heard my apology, it wouldn't have helped. Every year, I made a big deal of singling out each student on his or her birthday for a big hug and a goofy little gift—a neon-colored pencil or a package of animal crackers. Emilio could pretend he didn't care that I had overlooked his birthday, but we both knew better.

I stared at the back of Emilio's head as the squad car rolled down the drive, willing him to glance back at me, just for a second. Emilio sat as still as stone until the car disappeared through the front gate.

Rico Perez filled me in on the details. It seems that Mr. Lydecker had been needling Emilio for weeks, using Emilio's girlfriend, Silvia, as bait. Silvia was in Mr. Lydecker's fifth-period general science class.

"Every day, when Emilio walks Silvia to class," Rico said, "Mr. Lydecker be standing outside of his room, smiling at Silvia and looking at her, you know, like, one inch at a time." Rico rolled his eyes up at me. "You know what I'm saying, right?" I nodded.

"Okay," Rico continued. "So, this be happening just about every day. And when Emilio go to kiss Silvia good-bye, Lydecker always be standing right there, looking at them. Sometimes he says stuff. Like this one time, he says to Silvia, 'What you doing with a loser like that, baby? You can do better than that.' "

Rico shook his head and smacked the fist of one hand into the palm of his other. "That's cold, Miss J. Nobody shouldn't have to take that." He suddenly glanced around, as though he suspected somebody of eavesdropping, then looked deep into my eyes. "Don't tell Emilio what I said, okay, because he's like me. He likes to keep his business private. Okay?" I returned his look until he smiled at his own mistake.

"Okay," Rico said. "Don't get insulted. I know you wouldn't never tell anybody anything real personal. I just forgot who I was talking to for a minute."

I wished Emilio had felt the same trust in me as Rico did, so I could have helped him deal with Mr. Lydecker. But it was against Emilio's principles to accept help, much less ask for it. It also wasn't his style to accept insults without retaliating. If he hadn't been on permanent probation since his junior year, with the threat of immediate expulsion if he was involved in one more fight, Emilio most certainly would have confronted Mr. Lydecker sooner. But he managed to control himself, until the day after his birthday, when Mr. Lydecker had reached in front of Emilio as though he intended to touch Silvia's shoulder. In a heartbeat, Emilio grabbed Mr. Lydecker by his shirt collar, slammed him up against the building, and threatened to kill him then and there. Silvia convinced Emilio to let go of Lydecker, and the second he did, Mr. Lydecker ran to the office and called the police.

"Threatening a staff member is grounds for expulsion in itself," Chet Norton said, when I went to plead on Emilio's behalf. "But assault means jail time."

"It's not Emilio's fault," I argued. "You know how Mr. Lydecker treats kids. And he's been after Emilio ever since I switched him to another class. If it's anybody's fault, it's mine. Ken's using Emilio to get back at me."

"I'm sorry," Chet said, without one speck of regret in his voice, "but I have to follow district policy and the law."

So I took the matter to a higher court—Emilio's mother. A tiny, soft-spoken woman, Mrs. Lopez had taken an angry and bitter twelve-year-old refugee into her home, adopted him, and managed to keep him in school, away from drugs, and out of gangs for six years. We had met only once before, but I would never forget the day that a soft rapping interrupted my lecture on developing a thesis statement. I opened the door to find a man and woman, both of them a foot shorter than I. The man's hair was carefully combed, his suit a shiny blue. The woman wore a bright flowered dress and a matching pillbox hat, and clutched a black vinyl handbag with both hands. They looked freshly scrubbed and starched, like children dressed for Sunday school.

"You are the *maestra* of Emilio?" the man asked, his voice and manner as polite and proper as his crisp, white shirt.

"Yes, I am Emilio's teacher," I nodded. "Do you need to speak with him? He's right here in class."

"No," the man said. "I am Hector Lopez. This my wife, Flora. We are *padres de* Emilio. We like make you—" he turned to his wife and shrugged. She patted his arm and offered me a shy smile, revealing one gold tooth.

"We bring you our car for you use," Mrs. Lopez said, turning around to point at an ancient but well-cared-for dark green Pontiac station wagon. "Emilio say you little car go to shop for so many repair. We like you take our car. Drive as long as you want." She smiled again and reached to pat my hand. "You help our son many time. He tell. Now we help you."

"Do you have another car?" I asked. They shook their heads. Their house was twenty miles from Parkmont, yet they had been prepared to walk or ride the bus because I tried to teach their son. I assured them that I did not need their car but promised to call them if I ever needed to borrow it. They were gracious but clearly disappointed not to have the opportunity to show their gratitude.

Now, with Emilio up to his neck in bureaucracy, I was counting on that gratitude to overcome their respect for school authorities. I called Mrs. Lopez, explained the situation, and urged her to protest to the district office.

"What I should say?" she asked.

"It doesn't really matter," I explained. "Say he's a good boy. He has a part-time job after school. He's supposed to graduate in a week. Whatever you think of. But be sure to say 'civil liberties' at least once. All right?"

A few days later, Chet Norton walked into the staff mail room as I was leaving. In an instant, he had created a human barrier between me and the door. He reached over my head for the stack of papers in his mail slot.

"Civil liberties?" Chet said softly and scratched his head in mock bewilderment as he sorted through his mail. He pretended to be talking to himself, and I tried to pretend I didn't hear him, until he looked straight at me. "Mrs. Lopez doesn't speak very much English. I wonder where she learned that term?"

"Television, probably," I said, "but you never know. She's a smart woman, Dr. Norton, and she's working very hard to develop her vocabulary. You'd probably be surprised at how many English words she knows."

Emilio's expulsion papers disappeared, and his jail sentence was served after school and on weekends, so he could finish his final exams. Except biology. Ken Lydecker refused to allow Emilio to take the exam.

"Forget it, Miss J," Emilio said, when he found out he couldn't take the exam. "I got too much work to make up in that class anyway before I could've took the test. I'll never pass. And I can't graduate without that class. I'm screwed."

"We can always ask Mr. Cranston," I said.

Emilio rolled his eyes and shook his head. Mr. Cranston was the toughest teacher in school—no late work, no missing assignments, no unexcused absences were permitted in his class. Only a few Academy students had been brave enough even to attempt Mr. Cranston's biology class, but those few passed. And they admitted that he was one of the best teachers they'd ever had, that they'd learned more science in one year than in all of elementary and middle school combined.

"But I'll never pass," Emilio insisted when I suggested asking

Mr. Cranston if Emilio could take the exam in his class, if he finished the missing assignments first. "I'm not one of them smart kids. I'll never finish all that work. You know I read real slow."

"So what?" I argued. "Faster isn't always better. Maybe in sports, but I can think of a hundred things that are better if you do them slowly—eating ice cream, walking in the moonlight, kissing that pretty girlfriend of yours—"

"Okay, okay," Emilio interrupted, blushing. "Will you ask him for me?"

"You're not afraid of him, are you?" I teased.

Emilio didn't bite. He curled one lip, à la Elvis. "I ain't afraid of nobody and you know it. But I got a lot of business to take care of and I thought maybe you could talk to him for me. But if you're too busy—"

"All right. I'll ask him. You're pretty slick, you know that?"

"I had a good teacher," Emilio shot back.

I wasn't sure myself whether Mr. Cranston would agree to work with Emilio. I had had only two or three conversations with him, but that was enough to know that he took his responsibilities, both as teacher and as department chair, seriously. At staff meetings, he sat in front with the administrators, where he was called on frequently to provide background information and statistics. Tall and thin, he wore his bifocals and a frown the way some women wear hats and scarves—their accessories become an integral part of their character.

Mr. Cranston's frown did not waver as I explained Emilio's situation, aware that as Mr. Lydecker's supervisor, Mr. Cranston probably knew more about the incident than I did.

"I'm not asking you to give him a grade," I said. "All I'm asking is that you give him a chance to do the work and take the exam. He isn't the best student in the world, but he's a hard worker, and—"

Mr. Cranston reached into the chest pocket of his sports coat and pulled out a pocket planner. He paged through it, made a note, and replaced it in his pocket.

"Tell Mr. Lopez that I'll expect him in my office tomorrow morning at seven thirty sharp," Mr. Cranston said.

I grabbed his hand and shook it before he had a chance to reconsider. "Thank you, sir," I said. "He'll be there."

"I hope so," Mr. Cranston said. For a brief second, his frown lifted, and I knew then why he worked so hard to keep it in place. He had too soft a heart to survive any other way.

Emilio stopped by my classroom Wednesday morning, after his meeting with Mr. Cranston.

Emilio sighed. "Man, that guy 'spects me to outline the whole book and do the questions for every chapter. And I gotta do these worksheets, too." He dropped his backpack on the counter beneath the windows and pulled out a stack of worksheets, neatly stapled, in various colors, a different color for each chapter. "Plus, if I don't pass the exam, I flunk, even if I do all this stuff." We both stared, dismayed, at the three-inch-thick textbook and the mountain of worksheets.

"That's a lot of work," I said. I knew how hard it would be for him just to do the reading. Shortly after Emilio had joined the Academy program the year before, he had cut my class one morning and, to make up the time he missed, I had him come in after school to help me sweep the room, empty the trash cans, and file papers. There wasn't much filing to do, maybe five minutes' worth. I handed the papers to Emilio, pointed him at the file cabinet, and went to the duplicating center to copy some worksheets for the next day's class. When I returned, Emilio was standing in front of the file cabinet, staring at the folders in the top drawer.

"Earth to Emilio," I said, thinking that he'd been daydreaming.

He turned away, his face flushed with shame. "I don't know those alphabet letters," he muttered.

"Didn't you learn them in kindergarten?" I asked.

"I didn't went to kindergarten."

How could I have forgotten that Emilio had started school at age twelve, after being smuggled out of El Salvador, the only surviving male in his family? The others had been killed or jailed during political struggles. Emilio entered the ninth grade unable to read, write, or speak English, yet he had managed, through sheer determination, without any special classes or assistance, to pass his classes and make it through four years of high school.

For a second, I thought about relenting, giving Emilio a chance to back out. Not many people, including adults, could handle the amount of work Mr. Cranston had given him. He could always make up his biology credits the next year, or earn his GED. While I was trying to figure out how to phrase an excuse for him, Emilio looked at me and shrugged.

"It ain't like I got a lot of stuff to do in jail," he said. "I guess this will keep me busy. And I'll probably end up smarter than I would've if I took Lydecker's test."

I said a little prayer of thanks that I hadn't had a chance to open my mouth. What had I been thinking? This kid was not a quitter.

Emilio outlined all the chapters, did every worksheet, and earned a C on his biology final. He took his exams during the days and spent the nights in jail until school was out for the summer. Then he served the rest of his sentence.

Mr. Cranston was impressed by Emilio's determination. Emilio was proud of himself for passing all of his exams, particularly biology. His parents were grateful that their only child had been permitted to finish school.

I was the only one, it seemed, who couldn't let go of my anger.

Chapter 4

What's Your Prob?

I admit it. I had visions of one child, a shy kid who rarely spoke out, taking my hand and thanking me for teaching him. No, the boys were too cool; it would be a her—"right from wrong, weak from strong," a scene straight out of *To Sir With Love.* I needed that scene.

Perhaps if I hadn't planned a brief final exam to allow time for a party, and if I hadn't spent sixty-three dollars on a triple-layer chocolate mousse cake, and if I hadn't bought a single red rose as a memento for each of my seniors as an expression of my very real love for them, perhaps then I might not have been so upset that half of them—including Raul Chacon—cut class on the day of their English final.

On senior exam day, I arrived early and rearranged the desks in my room. Usually we sat in double rows, facing the center of the room so we could see who we were talking to, but during exams, I lined up the desks in what the kids called "real school" rows. I placed a red rosebud on each desk, gently, as though the roses were my precious students. Then I perched on a stool near the front of the room and waited.

And waited.

And waited.

Thirty minutes after exams were supposed to have started,

only fourteen students were present. LaTisha Wilson and Richie DiDonato, who were among the first to arrive, had taken seats in the front row. A few minutes after the late bell, they both escaped to the back of the room where the others had headed after one look at the expression on my face. Thirteen empty seats stared back at me from the front rows.

"Would somebody be so kind as to tell me where the rest of the class is?" I asked. Suddenly everybody was intensely interested in the ceiling tiles or the scratches in the wooden desktops.

"Richie?" I tried for a gentle smile, but from the wary look in his eyes, I could tell my lips weren't cooperating. He shook his head.

"LaTisha?" She bit her bottom lip, a sure sign that she knew. I walked to her desk and patted her shoulder as softly as I could. "Please?" She looked around. Most of the other kids ignored her, but a few shrugged their shoulders. Go ahead.

"Remember when you told us that you didn't think it was fair for the final exam to determine somebody's grade for a whole semester of work?" LaTisha asked me. I nodded. Yes, I had said that.

"Well, you said that you were really proud because we had worked really hard and everybody in our class had an A or a B. Remember?" I nodded, although I knew what was coming and didn't really want to hear it. "Well, a lot of kids figured that if they had an A or a B, then it wouldn't matter if they didn't take the final because since it was only fifty percent of their grade, the lowest they could get would be a D-plus and that's passing. So they cut—"

I didn't hear the rest of her explanation. Neither did anybody else, I'm afraid, because I pitched a fit that still makes me ashamed, three years later. I cried and stamped my feet, ripped all the test papers to shreds, smashed the erasers against the chalkboard until the teacher next door pounded on the wall. I took the roses off the desks of the absent kids and stomped them to pieces on the floor. None of the kids said a word, just watched, eyes wide, hands over their mouths to hide their expressions. When I calmed down, I apologized, they accepted, and we ate the entire cake. My heart wasn't in it, though, and the kids could tell. Instead of racing out of the room at the bell, they filed out, subdued and silent. Richie DiDonato stayed behind.

"Get out of here, you slime bags," he said, shooing the slowest to leave, the ones who lingered for a hug or a special smile. "Can't you see she's in an emotional state? Give her a break. You'll see her in a couple days at graduation anyway. Save it for the big day." After the others had left, Richie put his hands on his hips and cocked his head.

"So. What's your prob, Miss J?" he asked. "Afraid you're going to miss me too much?" Miss this kid who used to fit neatly under my arm and now stood a head taller than I did? This kid who used to throw his sophomore literature book on the floor and refuse to read, who as a senior had insisted he must read the role of Hamlet? Miss this kid who once leaped out of his seat, swooped me off the floor, and spun me around in circles because he thought I looked "too sad to teach anybody anything" that day?

"That must be it," I whispered.

Richie put his arms around me and held me while I cried, as I had done for him so often when his temper had overtaken him and gotten him grounded or suspended.

But that wasn't it. It was something else, something I couldn't name.

I sat in that classroom long after Richie left, staring at the empty desks, at the paper shreds and rose petals strewn across the gray tile floor. It took me several hours to figure out why I was so upset. It wasn't the cake or the roses. It wasn't the grades. Everybody had passed my class, just as LaTisha pointed out. What bothered me was that I had convinced myself that I had taken a bunch of kids who hated school, loathed books, worked harder at avoiding assignments than they would have had to do them—and I thought I had instilled in these kids a love of literature, of learning, of intellectual exploration that would stimulate them to continue learning and growing for the rest of their lives. I thought I had taken a tough bunch of teenagers and turned them into scholars. But I hadn't taught them anything. I wasn't the brilliant teacher I had thought I was.

I was still sitting in my classroom when the janitors came by to lock up. They didn't see me brooding in the shadows. When the street lights started to glow, and I finally trudged across the grass toward the parking lot, my master teacher, Hal Gray, came bounding out of the teachers' lounge, his battered leather briefcase bouncing against his thigh. He walked the three miles to and from work every day, claiming that the exercise canceled out his daily pack of Camels. Hal grinned at me and started to pass by, then stopped and put one hand on my forearm.

"What happened? Did you have to flunk somebody?" he asked. He knew how I hated to let one of my students fail, even when the student was as determined to self-destruct as I was to save him.

I told Hal about the thirteen kids who had cut my exam and taken a lower grade, just for an hour of fun. I told him about the roses, and the cake, and how ungrateful they were. He listened, nodding sympathetically, and shook his head.

"It's disgusting," he said.

"I know," I huffed, my energy recharged now that I had the support of a kindred spirit. "You'd think they would at least have a little gratitude."

"That's not what I meant," Hal said. "Teenagers are supposed to be ungrateful little brutes. They're supposed to trample your tender feelings, break your heart. It's their job." He motioned me over to one of the picnic tables provided for students to sit at during lunch. He sat me down on a bench and perched on the edge of the table beside me, looking into the tree branches over-head. He pulled a cigarette pack from his sock where he stashed it, navy style, and lit a match with his thumbnail. He inhaled slowly and shook his head sadly as he exhaled a cloud of smoke.

"What's disgusting is that every year I say I'm going to change, but I never do," Hal said. "Every year I decide I'm going to pay more attention to the students who come to school, learn to share, play nice with the other kids, do their homework, put away their toys, say please and thank you. And sometimes, for a day or two, I do that. I pat them on the back or give them a special smile. But at the end of the year, sure as shootin', I'm spending all my time and energy chasing after the ones I'll never catch. I'm so busy worrying about that one kid who just won't play fair that I forget all about the kids who do."

"It's nice of you to pretend you're the one who does that, Hal," I said. "And I thought you were tactless."

"Oh, I am," Hal insisted. He flicked his half-smoked cigarette onto the gravel drive and exhaled one last stream of smoke. "I was going to tell you that that new hairdo you have there makes you look like Harpo Marx in drag, but I never waste my time insulting somebody who's too busy feeling sorry for herself to appreciate my tactlessness."

Chapter 5

It's Hard to Say
Good-bye to Yesterday

To take advantage of the California climate, Parkmont High holds its graduation ceremony outdoors with the graduates seated on a wooden platform nestled among a grove of giant eucalyptus trees. Teachers are supposed to mingle with the parents and other members of the supporting cast, but I sneaked behind the ropes and stood in the shadows near the student seating area where I would be first in line to hug my shining stars as they stepped off the stage with their diplomas.

One forlorn folding chair sat slightly askew, alone and empty, in the middle of the Academy seating section, because Emilio Lopez's classmates refused to allow anybody to sit in his seat when he was sitting in a jail cell instead of celebrating his high school graduation.

Next to Emilio's empty chair, Victor Rodriguez slouched, arms folded across his chest, his legs outstretched, observing the ceremony from behind the mirrored sunglasses he insisted on wearing. I wasn't sure whether Victor would let me hug him when it was his turn. We hadn't talked much since the cold, rainy Monday in March when he had threatened to whip my butt.

Nobody, including me, had wanted to be in school on that particular day. The heater wasn't working, the roof was leaking, and the seniors were having a hard time working their way through *Othello* because the students who were reading the parts of the two main characters kept catching colds and missing school, and nobody else wanted to read in their absence.

"That's Lavel's part, Miss J," Curtis Lawson complained when I asked him to read the part of Iago. "Lavel's too good. I be sounding like a fool if I try and read like him."

Curtis was the fifth student that morning who had refused to read, and everybody was starting to get impatient and grouchy. When the moans and groans began to drown out the few reluctant readers, I sat down at my desk for a minute and closed my eyes as I considered the situation. I couldn't decide whether the kids were truly intimidated by reading, or whether they simply wanted to get out of working.

Sitting down during class is always risky, but closing my eyes was dangerous. Within seconds, personal conversations sprang up around the room—and so did Victor Rodriguez. When I opened my eyes, Victor was dancing down the aisles between two rows of desks, smacking all the boys on their arms and making eyes at the girls. When Victor reached Emilio's desk, Emilio raised one elbow as a warning.

"Victor," I said, "please sit down."

Victor squared his shoulders and pushed up his sleeves, his eyes on Emilio.

"*Vic*-tor," I warned. "Sit down. Now."

Emilio looked at me and shrugged to show that he didn't intend to fight, but Victor ignored me and started jabbing at the air in front of Emilio's face. Forgetting my rule about not letting the kids suck me into confrontations, I slapped my book down on the desk.

"Victor, sit down right now, or I will come over there and sit you down!" The second I said it, I knew it was a mistake, but it was too late.

Victor turned around, very slowly, and stared me straight in the eye. "I'm going to kick your ass," he said.

I had set myself up for it by making the first move, and Victor had called me on it. We were an even match—about the same height and weight, both of us with quick, hot tempers.

It didn't occur to me to apologize, although in retrospect I doubt that an apology would have resolved the situation. Victor had been looking for some way to vent his emotions, and I had offered the perfect opportunity.

I gave Victor one last chance to escape. "Excuse me?" I asked, as though I hadn't heard him.

If Victor and I had been alone, he might have backed down, but with more than twenty witnesses, he had to play his part. He crossed his arms and aimed his sunglasses at me. I couldn't see his eyes, but I could feel them. "I said I'm going to kick your ass," he repeated.

"Fine," I said. "Come on over here and kick my ass. If you think you can do it. I won't even tell the principal on you. In fact, I'll give you one free hit." I opened my arms.

Victor glanced sideways to check whether his "posse," Gusmaro Guevarra and Raul Chacon, was on his side or mine. Both boys were staring at the floor, unable to take sides between their friend and their teacher. Without their support, I knew Victor would falter. I hated to humiliate him, but it was him or me, and I couldn't afford to lose. If he lost, he'd get over it. If I lost, it was over. I didn't have the energy or inclination to fight the million little battles I'd have to win in order to establish control in my classroom where 150 troubled, angry teenagers faced me each day.

"Come on," I waved Victor forward and took up what I hoped was a convincing boxing stance. "Take your best shot. But it had better be damned good because if it isn't, you're going to be very sorry. You may be younger and stronger than I am, but I'm older and meaner than you, and I am going to hurt you."

Fortunately, sometimes I'm a better actress than teacher. Victor dropped his arms, kicked his desk over, and stalked out of the room. As he turned to slam the door, I said, "Don't come back to this classroom until you can be polite." He slammed the door so hard that its glass window shattered.

We didn't read any *Othello* that day, and I agonized for an hour after school, trying to decide whether to write a referral to the principal's office. I didn't want to write it, since I was the one who had initiated the incident, but if I didn't write one, other kids would think they could threaten me, stomp around the room, and destroy property. I wrote the referral, explaining that I would not allow Victor to return to my classroom unless he brought his parents to school, made a formal apology, and agreed to conduct himself with courtesy and self-respect for the rest of the school term. Then I went home and cried myself to sleep.

Victor knew me better than I knew myself. He showed up at school the following day with his father and mother. The Rodriguez family arrived at the disciplinary vice principal's office before Dr. Horner had a chance to open his mail to find my referral. Dr. Horner rang my office.

"I have Victor Rodriguez and his parents here in my office," Dr. Horner said. "He says he's willing to apologize, but he can't promise to be polite, although his father thinks he can. Should I send them over to see you?"

When they arrived, I shook Mr. and Mrs. Rodriguez's hands and thanked them for taking the time to escort Victor to school.

"If you have any problem with my son, please call me and I will take care of it," Mr. Rodriguez said. From the look on Victor's face, the tears in his mother's eyes, and the steel in Mr. Rodriguez's handshake, I knew that future problems were out of the question. After his father left, I asked Victor why he said he couldn't promise to be courteous. His refusal guaranteed a week of walking around campus with a black plastic trash bag, picking up trash and litter during his lunch hours.

"Wouldn't it have been easier just to agree and sign the referral?"

"It would've been easier," Victor agreed, "but I thought you didn't want us to lie to you. I might get mad at you again; you never know. Isn't that what you always tell us—don't lie, because you have to waste all that time trying to remember what you said, and don't make promises you can't keep?"

That had been our last real conversation. Victor continued to come to class every day for the rest of the semester, as usual, but he tore most of the pages out of his personal journal and was the first one out the door when the bell rang. It hurt my feelings, although I tried to be "awesome and ruthless" about it.

I liked Victor, and I thought he liked me. What had made him turn on me like that? I wondered, as I lay in bed one night, replaying the conversation in my mind over and over and over. Why, after three years would he suddenly ruin the rapport we had both enjoyed? Hadn't I always been straightforward and fair with him? And I did my best to remain nonjudgmental, no matter what he said or did. Surely he felt some sort of affection or respect for me. Otherwise, he wouldn't have felt comfortable writing such personal entries in his journal, asking for my advice about his girlfriend, for example. I smiled, remembering how surprised and amused I had been when I read his latest freewriting entry. Usually Victor wrote about things that happened at work or cruising with the guys. But this time he had spilled his heart directly onto the page.

Well, let me tell you what's on my mind right now, Miss J. Well, you know Leroy's girl just let go of her puppy. It's a girl and I'm happy for him. I'd prefer a boy, though. They are so much better than girls (ha! ha!). I hope my girl has a boy. She wants a boy, too. That's weird, huh? I kind of expected her to go for her own sex, but I guess she's smarter than I thought. Well, I've been thinking about this a lot. I was talking to Leroy about his girl and he said he witnessed the whole birth and we wound up on the topic of sex. You know, we were wondering after Leroy's girl squeezed something that big out of her, would she still want something way smaller, if you know what I mean. We started talking about how embarrassing that would be. She probably wouldn't feel anything. She would fake it. And I guess he would, too, to try and satisfy each other. So he said he would have to wait a while before they do have sex, about six weeks, to see if his girl got all loose or not. God, I hope they don't. But I think they probably do. Anyway, I think my girl is going to be in a lot of pain during birth. I mean, she can barely handle me, if you catch my drift and the image of her having something that big (that makes me look so small) go through her is amazing. What do you think, do their things get loose or not? I really want to know. I was talking to my girl about it last night and she wanted me to find out because she wants to know what she'll go through in about 7½ months. Leroy said that he was talking to somebody and they said that the girl's thing kind of tightens up a while after the birth. But that seems weird. I guess I will need to talk to someone who knows about it. I was hoping you knew. If you don't, I think I'll go to Planned Parenthood and find out. That's all for now.

My response was almost as long as Victor's entry. I told him that the human body is truly a miracle and that the vagina has remarkable recuperative powers, but that I wasn't sure tightness should be the primary concern of people who were about to be parents. I recommended that he visit Planned Parenthood and that he learn a lot more about sex and women before he fathered any more children. When I returned the journals, he eagerly opened his, read my remarks, closed the book, and gave me a thumbs-up and a grin. It was the closest I had ever felt to him in the three years he'd been in the Academy program.

That was it! It was so obvious that I wondered why it hadn't occurred to me sooner. I was too close for comfort. When parents called me and asked why their teenagers hated them, no matter what they did, I advised them to wait until puberty passed.

"It's natural for teenagers to want to develop their own, independent selves," I'd say. "But some kids don't know how to do it naturally, so they create arguments and declare war on you, even when you're on their side. Eventually, they'll get over it."

Victor was now facing an entirely new world, one in which he would be a full-time working man and father. He had been trying to leave before we had to say good-bye, so it wouldn't hurt as much when it actually happened.

Since the moment I first started teaching the Academy English class, people had been telling me that I needed to prepare myself for the day when "my kids" would graduate and move on. Since I had the same students for three consecutive years and became so involved in their personal lives, the separation would be especially painful, they said.

"You're setting yourself up for a bad bruising," Hal Gray warned me at least once a week, more frequently as graduation for the first Academy class drew near.

"Love 'em and leave 'em," Hal advised. "That's what you have to do. Wave good-bye. Cry in private. Then turn around and wave hello to the next group."

"Don't worry about me," I had assured Hal. "I can handle it."

I wasn't worried then, but now, as I stood waiting for the ceremony to start, I could feel my confidence begin to crack. If I got this upset over a break in communication with Victor, what would happen when all twenty-seven of my students kissed me good-bye and walked out of my life?

When Victor's name was called, he adjusted his sunglasses, stood up, and slowly strolled to the podium. He took his diploma, shook hands with the principal and superintendent, then walked directly toward me instead of back to his seat. He tucked his diploma under his arm, took both my hands in his, and brought them to his lips. He kissed each of my hands and then leaned forward and kissed me on the forehead.

"*Gracias, Maestra,*" he whispered.

That did it. Until then, I had managed to control myself. But when Victor hugged me, he squeezed the tears right out of me. And as he hugged me, I could see, over his shoulder, rows and rows of seats, with another empty chair in the Academy section—Raul Chacon was missing. That second empty chair was too much. I started crying in earnest and couldn't stop.

My first thought was that Raul's father had made him work instead of attending the graduation ceremony. Several times during each school year, Raul had disappeared for days at a time, each time returning a darker shade of brown, having spent twelve hours each day mowing lawns for his father's landscaping business. I could understand Mr. Chacon's position—with eleven children to feed, he needed the income from everybody who was old enough to work. But I also understood, and so did Raul, that the only way to break the cycle of poverty that trapped his family was to get an education that would allow him to earn enough to support his brothers and sisters so they could finish school and find decent jobs.

Up until that moment, I had been certain that Raul would show up. He had given me his word, with the official five-part posse handshake as insurance. In three years, Raul had never broken a promise to me, but when Dr. Norton reached the *C*'s on his graduation roster and Raul's chair was still empty, I finally faced it—he wasn't coming. When Dr. Norton called Raul's name, I started forward, planning to accept his diploma for him.

"Here I am," Raul called, running onto the stage from the

wrong side, his gown flapping in the breeze, wearing his old red baseball cap instead of his blue satin mortarboard.

"Sorry," he said, loud enough for the audience to hear, "I forgot my little flat hat with the tassel on it, but Miss J said we had to wear a hat to graduate, so I went home and got this one."

Raul accepted his diploma, shook hands, saluted the cheering crowd, and strolled across the stage toward the stairs that led down to the student seating area. When he saw me walking toward him, he leaped off the side of the stage and ran to meet me.

"Hey, Miss J," he said. "I did it. Just like we said." I couldn't say anything through my tears, so I just nodded and blubbered. Raul leaned closer.

"Do you need a tissue?" he asked, in a perfect imitation of my voice. I had to smile. Although I always kept a box of tissues on my desk, most of the boys were too macho to use them, preferring to sniff their way through class when they had colds. When the sniffles started interfering with the lesson, I'd pick up the box and offer the boy a tissue in a tone of voice that made it impossible to refuse.

"Thanks," I said, "I have a tissue."

"Too bad I don't have your hundred dollars."

"That's okay."

"No, it isn't," Raul insisted. "A deal's a deal. Just like you said. We shook and I gave my word of honor. Don't you remember?"

"Of course, I remember. But it's worth a million dollars to see you get that diploma."

"You mean you wouldn't be mad if I didn't pay you the money?" Raul asked.

"No."

"Too bad I didn't know that before I took this out of the bank." He handed me a crumpled envelope.

I pushed the envelope back toward Raul. "I meant it. You don't have to pay me back."

"Yes, I do. I owe you a lot more than a hundred dollars, but I can't pay back the rest of the stuff you gave me." He took my hand and folded my fingers around the envelope.

"Hey, Miss J!" Stacey Wilson grabbed my arm, and DaShaun Washington grabbed Raul. They pulled us to the back of the bleachers where the rest of the Academy students stood, posed for a group photo. Stacey joined the other girls in the center of the group, their gowns a spot of shining white in a sea of royal blue satin, with DaShaun's face hovering above the others, a beautiful black sun.

Before we took pictures, I blew my nose, dried my eyes, and hugged the students I had missed coming off the stage while I had been talking to Raul. As soon as the flashbulbs stopped popping, I ducked through the crowd and made a break for my office, tears once again streaming down my face. I couldn't stand another second of watching "my kids" preparing to leave Parkmont for the last time. I had expected to feel sad. I knew I would cry. But I had vastly underestimated how much it would hurt to let my darlings go. After three years of seeing them every day, I had grown to love them far more than I thought possible, more than I could stand. As the crowd surged around the graduates, pulling them away from me toward their futures, it felt as though twenty-seven of my own children were abandoning me en masse. My heart hurt.

I drove home, went straight to bed, and stayed there for three days. I would have stayed longer if I hadn't signed on as a summer school teacher. Even so, I might have broken my contract, but I needed the money to pay my rent so I could stay in bed. When I got up, I felt empty, emotionally and physically depleted. I swore I'd learned my lesson. Next year, I'd take Hal's advice and keep more distance, hold more back. I'd still love my students, of course, but I would do what my students, in their natural wisdom, had been urging me to do for the past three years.

I'd get a life.

Chapter 6

So, You Gonna Flunk Me?

Don't do it," Hal Gray had warned when he saw me in the staff mail room filling out the summer school teaching agreement. "Scientific studies show that teaching summer school for more than three consecutive years causes irreversible brain damage."

At the time, a week before the first Academy graduation, I had been feeling feisty, unaware of how much emotional energy that simple ceremony would exact.

"I'd like to take the summer off," I told Hal. "But I also like to sleep inside a building and eat food on a daily basis."

Hal slapped one hand to his forehead in mock dismay. "Of course, how silly of me to forget that you don't yet earn the astronomical salary of a full-time teacher that allows us to spend our summers frolicking about the European countryside."

On my budget, I could just about afford to skip to the corner and back. I asked Hal, "Can you believe that I make less money teaching full-time, five classes per day, with a master's degree in teaching and three years of experience, than I did as a first-year secretary at Xerox?"

"Yes," Hal said. He picked up his mail, glanced through the stack, and tossed the entire pile into the wastebasket. Then he poked me in the arm with his finger.

"At Xerox," he said, "your job was to support brilliant scientists who earn large sums of money for developing new computer technology. Your job here is to support brain-dead bureaucrats who earn large sums of money for developing new ways to bore children into submission. Computers present a constant challenge, but kids give up after ten or eleven years. Ergo, teachers don't get paid as much as computer scientists. It's simple."

Hal put his arm around my shoulder and guided me out of the mail room, down the hall, and into the vice principal's empty office, where he deposited me in a small wooden chair in front of Dr. Horner's desk. Hal sat in the worn leather armchair behind the desk and gave me a long look, long enough to show the genuine concern behind the sparkle in his blue eyes.

"Get a summer job," Hal said. "Anything except teaching."

"But I like teaching summer school," I insisted. "I enjoy the challenge of making learning fun for students who don't believe 'school' and 'fun' could possibly be in the same Funk and Wagnall's."

Hal picked up Dr. Horner's NO SMOKING placard and stuck it into one of the desk drawers, then pulled a cigarette out of his shirt pocket and broke it in half. He rolled the ragged edge of the filter half between his fingers to seal it and dropped it back into his pocket. He lit the unfiltered half and left it dangling from his lip, à la Bogart, as he placed both elbows on the desk and propped his chin on his hands. He squinted at me through a cloud of smoke.

"I thought you promised your wife you'd quit," I said.

"I did," Hal said out of the corner of his mouth. "I don't smoke at home anymore."

"If I see her, I'm going to tell on you."

Hal sat up suddenly and pointed at me. "Great idea. I could report you for kissing kids. That would keep you out of the classroom for a few months this summer while they investigate your degenerate behavior." He picked up the telephone and asked the switchboard operator to connect him with the district office. I cut the connection and took the phone away from Hal.

"I kissed one boy who was sleeping in class, on the cheek, three years ago," I reminded Hal, although he knew the story as well as I did. I didn't plan the kiss; it just happened. That single kiss had effectively stopped sleeping in my class for more than three years but had also caused more concern among the administration than the sorry statistics of our increasing dropout rate. So I changed my strategy to one that was nonphysical but equally effective. At the start of each class, I circle the room, shaking a small bottle of white typewriter correction fluid. When the lesson begins, I put the bottle in a pocket so it won't distract the students during the lesson. But if anybody goes to sleep, I sneak over and quietly paint one of the sleeper's fingernails. Five minutes later, I paint another nail, and so on. At the end of the period, I write on the chalkboard: YOU OWE ME 5 MINUTES AT LUNCHTIME FOR EACH WHITE FINGERNAIL! When the bell rings, I point to the board and smile.

If anybody argues, claiming "I wasn't sleeping," the other kids point to the telltale painted fingernails and yell "Busted!" It was a perfect solution—kids tried harder to stay awake but accepted the consequences in good humor when they were caught in the act.

"What an amusing little anecdote," Hal said when I finished telling him about my new antisleeping device. "Thanks for sharing your strategy with me." He took one last puff on his cigarette, which was so small that he had to hold it between his fingernails. He wet the thumb and index finger of his left hand and pinched the glowing tip, rubbing it between his fingers until it disappeared, a few crumbs of tobacco lost in the institutional brown carpet.

"It didn't work, you know," Hal said.

"What didn't?" I asked.

"I'm not changing the subject until you promise to slow down. You think you're doing fine, and you'll think that right up until the minute you slip over the edge. You're on the edge right now, even if you don't know it."

"I'm fine—" I started to argue, but Hal held up one hand. His expression was so solemn, so serious, that it chilled me into silence. Normally Hal's face was a network of laugh lines intercepted by a pair of smiling blue eyes.

"I won't be here next year to catch you," he said softly. "That's what I'm worried about."

Until then, Hal's retirement had seemed vague and distant, like mountains that loom on the horizon but seem to match your pace, maintaining their distance in spite of your progress, so you never draw close enough to see them clearly. Hal had been my touchstone since the first day I stepped into the classroom, and I would miss him dearly, but he had spent thirty-five years teaching high school and the last three teaching me, as well. It would be doubly hard without him, since Dr. Norton was also retiring, but I was determined not to rain a single drop on Hal's parade. So many times I had sat in the teachers' lounge, listening to him describe the carefree, nomadic life he and his wife planned to live, floating about the oceans, soaking up sun on the deck of their sailboat. Although he had never said as much, I knew he would delay his retirement to stay on another year as my master teacher if he thought I needed him.

"I'm a young idealist with boundless energy," I assured him. "Trust me. I can handle it. Summer school will be a piece of cake."

I started eating those words the first minute of the first day of the first session of summer school. As soon as I took the roll, I launched into my card trick, which usually breaks the tension and creates a good rapport between me and my students. I passed out index cards and asked the students to write their name, address, phone number, parent or guardian's name, and hours of employment, if applicable. I also asked them to list any personal information or comments on the back of the cards. As they filled out the cards, I walked around the room, checking the roll sheet, peeking at the index cards, secretly memorizing their names. I collected the cards personally, taking care to look at each student's face as I accepted the card.

"Thank you," I said, as I shuffled the cards. "Now it's time for our first test."

"Aw, man," one of the boys muttered under his breath. "That sucks." Clearly, everybody agreed with him.

"Remain calm," I said, when the hissing and booing finally subsided. "This test is for me. There are thirty-three names on our roll. I'm going to go around the room and say each person's name. If I get them all right, I win."

"What do you win?" asked a girl with a diamond stud in her nose and a ring on each finger.

"Everything," I replied. She nodded. It made sense to her. School is a terribly unfair place.

"But if I lose," I explained, "then you all get an A on your first test, automatically." When I said that, the grumbling stopped and the eye shifting began: Check this out, does anybody believe this woman? They weren't sure, but nobody wanted to mess up a possible good thing, so they waited. The girl with the rings held out one hand, palm up. Go ahead.

So far, I've managed to do it every time. The day will come, I expect, that I'll forget a name, and the kids will all get an A in the gradebook. It won't matter, because I won't include it in their final grades, but they won't know that. They'll be happy because they'll have scored a freebie off the teacher. For a while they'll believe in miracles; they'll have proof that teachers make mistakes. Not a bad lesson.

I remembered all the names that day. I still remember some of those names and quite a few faces. One I will never forget.

Of all the classrooms in all the schools in all the world, she had to walk into mine. Araceli Andrade. Four feet eight inches of attitude wearing thick black eyeliner, a slash of blood-red lipstick, and a permanent sneer. We had met once, at Parkmont, when I had invited Araceli to join the Academy program.

Araceli had never been assigned to any of my classes, but I had seen her quite often, waiting outside my room for one or another of her friends. One day I took a copy of the Academy brochure outside and handed it to Araceli—or rather, I tried to hand it to her. I held it out, but she made no move to accept it. She stood, staring over my shoulder at nothing, until I finally reached over and put the brochure on top of the black leather purse she held clasped against her chest. Araceli ignored the brochure, and me, until I finally turned and went back into my classroom. When the bell rang, she was still standing outside, her back against the wall, the brochure resting on top of her purse. It stayed there until a breeze blew it onto the sidewalk where it drifted away with the passing students, collecting footprints and soda stains.

Araceli stopped standing outside my classroom after that day, and I didn't see her again until she showed up in my summer school class. Arms crossed over her unauthorized tank top and legs crossed beneath her skin-tight leather miniskirt, she stared at me from the far corner of the room near the windows, unimpressed by my index card trick. She stopped staring for a split second to roll her eyes toward the ceiling as a smattering of applause greeted my correct identification of the last student on the roster.

"Not bad," a boy in the front row said.

"Yeah," the boy beside him agreed. "How'd you do that?"

I love it when they follow the script. I hesitated for a few seconds, to underscore the importance of what I was about to say.

"I know your names because you are important people to me," I said, as I looked around the classroom, making eye contact with each student. "When I look at you, I see you. I like you.

And I care about you. That's why I'm here."

From their expressions, I could tell that most of them believed me, and they liked the idea. A few holdouts chose to reserve judgment, but there were a few in every class. They'll come around, I thought, they always do.

"*Pfffft.*" Araceli exhaled in a long, loud huff. "You like me? Shit. You don't know nothing about me."

"That doesn't mean I can't like you," I said.

"Well, I don't like you," Araceli said. "So why you don't give up on this damn little baby games and teach us some English?"

It wouldn't be hard to humiliate such an easy target, especially if I started with her grammar. I was tempted, but it wouldn't be fair. I had learned that lesson the hard way, and I still regret that I learned it at a child's expense.

One day, during my first year at Parkmont, a boy interrupted my sophomore English class. He knocked on the door once, loudly, then walked in and handed me an add slip from the office. He looked like a young, Latin version of Elvis Presley— bold, blue, bedroom eyes, black hair slicked carefully back from his angular face, the top three buttons of his shirt open to reveal a remarkable amount of chest hair. He looked so mature that even after I had checked his records in the office, I still found it hard to believe he was only fifteen.

The man-child offered me his admission slip and a calculatedly charming smile. I checked the name on the slip. Adelberto Vega.

"Welcome to class, Mr. Vega," I said. "Please join us." I indicated the only empty seat in the class, front row center, near my desk.

"My friends call me Berto," Adelberto announced to the room, as though addressing an audience of adoring fans. He walked to his seat, rolling his hips like a rhumba dancer, and melted into his chair. Several girls sighed. I handed Adelberto my copy of *The Red Pony* and asked one of the other students to begin reading where we had stopped. Adelberto obediently located the passage and followed the text for a few minutes. Then, in the midst of a dramatic scene where Billy Buck has to cut the pony's windpipe to save its life, Adelberto suddenly slammed his book facedown on his desk, leaned back in his chair, and put his legs up on the desktop. He crossed his ankles, stretched his arms, thrust his chest forward, and locked his hands behind his neck.

Stunned into momentary silence, I stared at Adelberto. And he stared at me, starting with the top of my head and working his way slowly over every inch of my face and body, with such intensity that I felt as though his hands were doing the exploring. Adelberto's eyes reached my feet before I found my tongue. Raising his eyes to meet mine, he gave me a come-hither look and licked his lips.

"So, how old are *you*, Miss Johnson?" he drawled.

The knowing smile was too much. I looked him up and down, just as he had done to me, letting my eyes linger at strategic locations. Then I leaned down so that our noses were inches apart, close enough that he could feel my breath on his face. Mimicking his seductive tone, I purred, "I'm old enough to be your mama, honey bun. But when you're twenty-one, you call me, and I will *wear you out.*"

The students seated nearby must have overheard me, but nobody made a sound. Adelberto blanched and, after he regained his composure, stood up and stalked out of the classroom. He never came back. Perhaps his family moved, or his parents separated, or he got in some kind of trouble—there are any number of reasons why Adelberto might have left Parkmont. But I would always wonder whether my taunting made him feel that his dignity had been injured beyond repair. And I would never forget the look of pain and humiliation on Berto's face, which was a child's face in spite of his pseudosophistication.

Araceli was a child, too, somewhere behind all the cosmetics and cursing, and I didn't want her to walk out of school forever. So I held my temper and my tongue and reminded myself of my basic belief: Bad kids don't come to school. They don't care enough to come. Students who come to class—even those who spend all their time and energy sabotaging lessons—are asking for help in the only way they know. When they ask, it's my job to answer.

Araceli's call for help was a silent scream that deafened everybody in the room. Unfortunately, I was the only one who interpreted it as an SOS. The other students were convinced that Araceli was too cool for school. In the midst of an animated class discussion or a dynamic group exercise, Araceli could squelch the energy in the room with a single look or a sharp sigh. Immediately the class would remember that they were supposed to hate school. Then they'd retreat into their impenetrable adolescent shells.

Nearly every day, I would hold Araceli after class, because I didn't want to embarrass her in front of her classmates. Each time, Araceli would slump in her seat, expressionless, as I explained the particular behavior that needed to be changed. She never argued and always agreed not to repeat the behavior. She kept her word—each day, she devised a different strategy, some new, ingenious way to disrupt what precious little learning took place in my classroom. Once I asked her not to sneer and snicker when somebody made a mistake reading out loud. The next day, she covered her mouth and slammed her head down on her desk when the girl beside her mispronounced *depot* as "dee-pot." The next day, I informed her that if she couldn't be polite during group exercises, she should keep her mouth shut. She took me literally and refused to utter a single word to the four other students in her discussion group. Instead she sat staring at whoever spoke, until the entire group collapsed into self-conscious silence.

Each day, I'd pray that somehow I'd find the right words or do the right thing to break through the barrier and connect with Araceli. Usually I try to handle all problems in my classroom, making the students responsible for their behavior, instead of expecting somebody else to correct their mistakes. But when I found myself seriously considering whether it would be worth my job to throttle Araceli with my bare hands, I threatened to call her parents. For a split second, Araceli dropped her guard. Then just as quickly, she recovered.

"Go ahead," she said, trying too hard to sound nonchalant. As soon as she left the room, I called our school nurse and asked for information about Araceli's family. Several reports of suspected physical abuse had been filed by teachers, but Araceli had insisted that her black eyes and bruises and broken bones were due to accidents.

I had not suffered black eyes or broken bones as a child, but I recalled the suffocating feeling of choking on my own rage as my father whipped me across the back of my legs with a leather strap, my shame in the locker room at having to remove the heavy knee socks that hid the welts on my legs, my anger at a world that permitted such things to happen.

I couldn't call Araceli's home or refer her to the principal without taking a chance of causing another "accident," so I decided to continue trying to work with Araceli on my own. I wasn't used to failing this badly. My Academy students were much tougher than Araceli, but they always responded, sooner or later, and no one had ever held out for an entire month. Finally I gave up trying to change her attitude. It hurt, but I didn't see any other choice.

Immediately, Araceli settled down. She actually allowed me to teach without interruption for an entire day. The following Monday, four days before the end of summer school, Araceli voluntarily participated in a group discussion. Foolishly I concluded that she had grown tired of the struggle, that my unconditional acceptance had worked its way around her attitude and into her heart. Never one to pass up an opportunity to use positive reinforcement, I paused by her desk as I was distributing vocabulary review worksheets and told Araceli that I appreciated her contributions to the class.

"Is that right?" she asked, as I held out a worksheet.

"That's right," I said. Araceli looked at me, looked at the paper, and back at me. I placed Araceli's worksheet on her desk and moved on to the next student.

"I'm sick of doing this stupid shit," Araceli said, shoving the paper to the corner of her desk. "I ain't doing it."

Under other circumstances, I might have explained that I had designed this particular worksheet to help her practice specific critical-thinking skills, or pointed out that the exercises were good practice for the exam, or that I could have her expelled from summer school by making one simple phone call to the office. But I was tired of explaining and pointing out and threatening, tired of holding my tongue, worrying about her precious dignity, waiting until we were alone before I reprimanded her.

"Fine, Araceli," I said. "Don't do the stupid worksheet. In fact, why don't you just rip it up and throw it in the trash?" I pointed to the dented metal trash can sitting in the corner of the room near the door. "Go ahead. It's right over there. Throw it away."

Araceli stared at me, the first honest expression on her face since we'd met. Before she had a chance to recover, I walked toward her desk and reached for the worksheet. I felt like ripping Araceli's hair out of her head, but I would settle for shredding her worksheet.

"Give me that," I said, as I approached. "I'll tear it up for you." Araceli grabbed the paper and held it out of my reach.

"Maybe I don't want to tear it up," she said.

"Didn't you just tell me you didn't want to do this stupid shit?" I asked. She shrugged, but I could tell she was shocked at hearing me repeat her own words.

"Didn't you?" I demanded.

"Yeah."

"Well, then, if you don't want to do it, and you don't want to rip it up, then I want you to turn it over and write 'I'm not going to do this stupid shit' on the back. And I want you to sign your name. Then I'll just put it in my files and keep it, in case you or your parents come around later on and ask me about your grade."

Araceli wrinkled her nose and exhaled in a huff, then clicked her tongue. "*Tsk.* I ain't signing nothing."

"Okay," I said, ignoring the whispers from the other students, concentrating on Araceli. She had my full attention now—not in a private conversation, but in front of the entire class—something she'd been asking for since the start of summer school.

"Let me get this straight," I said, counting out the options on my fingers as I listed them. "You don't want to do the assignment. But you don't want to rip it up. And you don't want to sign it. So I guess you'll have to leave." It took a second for the last option to register.

"What?" Araceli said. "Are you kicking me out?"

"Oh, no," I said. "I really like you and I care about you and I want to help you be an effective student, and kicking you out of class wouldn't help you." I froze, as though a sudden thought had occurred to me. "You don't think it would help, do you? Kicking you out?"

Araceli shook her head slowly, eying me warily. "Naw. I been kicked out of a lot of classes."

"Well, I hate to boss people around anyway," I said. "If I wanted to give orders, I'd have stayed in the Marines. I prefer to give people choices. And you have four choices in this class: One, you can do the assignment. Two, you can rip it up and throw it away. Three, you can sign your name saying you refuse to do it. Four, you can leave." I walked to the door and opened it.

"You have the right to choose your own behavior. But you don't have the right to sit here and waste my time trying to suck me into a fight with you when there are other people in this classroom who would like to learn something. You don't have the right to waste their time. So take your pick."

I waited at the door.

Araceli took her time deciding what to do. She stared at me, her eyes narrowing to two black slits. I was tempted to close the door, to keep her in the room, but I knew it had to be her decision to go or stay. I prayed she wouldn't bolt the way Adelberto had.

"So, you gonna flunk me if I rip this up?" She held up her worksheet by one corner.

"No way. I never flunk anybody. Every once in a while, somebody decides not to pass my class, but they choose to fail. I don't flunk them. And I won't flunk you, either. You can fail this class, but you'll have to work harder than you would to pass—and it will be your own fault. You won't be able to blame it on me and go around ragging about how 'that stupid bitch teacher' flunked you." Araceli raised one eyebrow, which was fuzzy around the edges where several layers of thick black eyebrow pencil were smudged, softened by the summer heat.

"What if I tear up *all* the assignments?" Araceli asked.

I shook my head. "Sorry. Can't let you do that. It's my job to help you pass this class. One zero won't hurt you, but if your grade falls too low, I'll have to get serious about trying to help you get a better grade. Whatever it takes."

Araceli glanced at the boy sitting next to her, to see whether he was impressed by her bravado. Before he had a chance to react, I clapped my hands and moved to the other side of the room, away from Araceli.

"Okay, we've spent enough time on this discussion. Everybody get to work. You all heard the choices. Take your pick." I rolled my chair to the back of the room and pretended to be engrossed in my textbook, oblivious to my students.

I adjusted my chair so that I had a direct line of sight on Araceli in the background beyond my book, so I could watch her without looking at her. Although she sat facing the other direction, her back toward me, I knew she was watching me just as closely as I was her. She put the worksheet down and pulled her makeup kit from her purse. She spent fifteen minutes removing then applying an identical thick coat of black mascara and eyeliner. Once or twice I caught her checking me out in the mirror on her powder compact.

She spent the next quarter hour staring out the window, twirling a strand of long, dark hair around one index finger. When the final fifteen minutes of the hour began to tick by, I got up and strolled around the room. As I passed her desk, I caught her eye, glanced at my watch, and motioned for her to sign the back of her worksheet. She picked up her pencil, stuck the eraser end in her mouth, and stared at me, her cheeks puffed with air. She looked like a naughty chipmunk. I couldn't help it. I stuck my pencil in my mouth, puffed up my cheeks, and crossed my eyes. Then I quickly walked away, so that she couldn't be sure she hadn't imagined me making faces at her.

Araceli finished half her worksheet before the bell rang and dawdled behind the others until we were alone in the room.

"I didn't have time to finish the whole thing," she said. I looked at her but refused to say what she expected me to, that she had had plenty of time—if she had used it. I mimicked her habit of raising one eyebrow, to indicate that I was listening. She glanced around the room, intently, as though the industrial green walls and dingy, pocked ceiling tiles were incredibly interesting.

"Can I take it home and finish?" she asked, looking over my shoulder at the wall behind me.

"Would you let me take it, if you were the teacher and I was the student?" I asked her.

She looked at me briefly, to make sure I was serious, then cocked her head, closed one eye, and considered the question.

"Yeah," she said, after several seconds. "I'd give you a break. Once."

I laughed, not because Araceli's response was amusing, but because as she answered, I heard the echo of my own voice saying those same words, twenty years earlier, to my Marine Corps drill sergeant.

During the final weekend before graduation from Officer Candidate School, the women in my company received a long-awaited two days of liberty. The moment Sergeant Hawke released us, we dropped our duffel bags and raced out of the barracks to kick up our combat boots in the tiny town of Quantico, Virginia.

In my excitement, I forgot to lock my wall locker, which wouldn't have been such a serious mistake if I hadn't also neglected to lock my M-16 inside the locker. Because the combination on my cable lock was unpredictable and often required six or seven tries and a smack on the side before it would release the lock, I had stopped using it to secure my machine gun inside my wall locker. Instead, I looped the cable around my rifle so that it appeared to be locked and hung it on the coat hook inside my wall locker. That way, when Sergeant Hawke called inspection, I could open my wall locker, grab my M-16, and hit the line in ten seconds. My quickness earned me extra points and contributed to my status as honor woman for the company, because the award was based on grades during inspection as well as physical training, leadership, and classroom exercises.

I was the first woman to arrive back at the barracks on the Saturday of our pregraduation liberty, but I wasn't alone.

"Candidate Johnson." A familiar voice stopped me in the doorway. Sgt. Bertie Hawke was sitting at a table against the wall just inside the double doors of the bunk room, her back to me.

"Yes, ma'am?"

"Did you enjoy your afternoon?"

"Yes, ma'am." I started to sweat. Sergeant Hawke didn't engage in chitchat. She leaned forward, peering at something on the table, then turned around, but instead of looking at me, her gray eyes stared past me at my bunk in the far corner of the room. I followed her gaze. My locker door stood wide open, all my possessions strewn across my bunk and the floor surrounding it. My bedclothes sat in a crumpled lump on top of my bare mattress, and my clothes were draped over the railings of my bunk.

"I believe something is missing from your locker, Candidate," Sergeant Hawke said. "Maybe you'd better go see."

I hurried to my locker, although I knew it was pointless. No M-16 in sight.

"Oh, shit." I covered my face with my hands. I couldn't remember how many times Sergeant Hawke had reminded us that it was a court-martial offense to leave a weapon unsecured. I walked back to Sergeant Hawke's table. On the table were hundreds of jigsaw puzzle pieces and a cardboard box bearing a photograph of two fluffy white kittens peeking over the edge of a wicker basket. Hardly the sort of pastime one would expect for a woman whose idea of a good time was hiking fifteen miles in full combat gear.

"I . . . I don't know where my weapon is, Sergeant," I stuttered.

Sergeant Hawke didn't answer until she found the piece to complete the pink bow on the basket. "Check the shower."

As soon as she spoke the words, I realized that the sound of running water had been in the background all along, which meant that my M-16 had been lying in the shower, getting waterlogged, for longer than I cared to consider.

"Move," Sergeant Hawke muttered.

I retrieved my rifle from the shower and returned to the bunkroom, where I stopped in the doorway, holding my wet weapon at port arms, unsure of my next step.

"Candidate Johnson, I have a question for you." Sergeant Hawke stopped poking through the puzzle pieces and trained her unforgiving gaze on me. "What would you do if, in your career as an officer of marines, you had one young troop, sharp as they come, but he never quite got with the program, thought he was to slick too follow the rules. And one day you found that this particular marine had endangered the safety and lives of his entire platoon, perhaps his entire company, by failing to follow regulations about weapons security? How would you handle the discipline in this case?"

"I don't know." I couldn't think of a single suggestion. How could I, with Sergeant Hawke staring me down with those ice-cold eyes? The woman never blinked.

"Well, I suggest you go over to your bunk and think about it. When you come up with an answer, you let me know. I'll be waiting."

I went to my bunk, as directed, and sat on the edge of my lumpy mattress, wishing I'd stayed in bed that morning. Better yet, wishing I'd stayed in the Navy and continued my career as a journalist, even if I had to fight constantly for assignments more challenging than hand-delivering invitations for the annual Azalea Festival to civilian bigwigs in Norfolk who assured me that I looked "very cute in my little Navy suit." Oh, no, I had to volunteer for Marine Corps Officer Candidate School, so I could be one of the few, the proud, the Marines. I was so close, too. Nineteen weeks down, one to go. Nineteen of the hardest weeks I ever hope to live.

I knew what I was supposed to do—apologize profusely and promise to reform immediately and permanently. But I've always been too stubborn to tell a lie, especially after I joined the Marines and found out that they regard mule-headed people like me as folks who are instilled with large amounts of integrity. I stood up, locked my soggy M-16 in my locker, and marched back to Sergeant Hawke.

"Ma'am, I have an answer for you." She stopped working the puzzle but stayed as she was, her back to me. "I would scare the shit out of that sharp young troop, ma'am, like you just did to me. But I'd give her a break. Once."

Sergeant Hawke let me stand there for a long, long time before she finally, ever so slowly, turned around. For a moment, I thought she might smile, but I should have known better. She didn't raise her voice a single decibel, but she overenunciated, firing her words at me, slow-motion bullets.

"I don't care if you have the highest grades in this company. It's not over yet. I still own your soul for one more week. And if you make one mistake, if you so much as breathe out of your left nostril when I tell you to breathe out of the right, I'll make you sorry your mama was ever born. Is that perfectly clear, Candidate?"

"Yes, ma'am."

Satisfied that I was scared enough to wet my khakis, Sergeant Hawke turned back to her puzzle, without dismissing me. After another interminable wait, she glanced over her shoulder and pretended to be surprised to see me still standing there, waiting for my punishment to be pronounced. I hadn't realized that my sentence had already been served.

"Get out of here," Sergeant Hawke said, and immediately turned away. I like to believe she turned away so I couldn't see her smile.

I made sure Araceli could see my smile, because when she said she'd "give me a break, once," I realized why I cared so much about her in spite of herself: I saw my teenaged self in her.

"Get out of here," I told Araceli. I didn't need to scare her, the way Sergeant Hawke had scared me. Araceli was already scared.

When regular classes resumed that fall, I remembered the lesson Araceli had taught me. When one of my Academy kids refused to do a particular assignment, I spared myself and everybody else the long, useless lecture. Instead, I listed the four options and insisted that they make their own choices. I stopped making myself responsible for their success or failure.

Letting go was a hard lesson for me to learn. It wasn't a new lesson; it was one I had faced, in various forms, since my first day in front of a class. For years I managed to avoid doing my homework for that important assignment, until Araceli Andrade got my attention and made me learn the lesson. I couldn't have asked for a better teacher.

Chapter 7

Howdy, Ma'am

My divorce papers had arrived in the same mail with my teaching credential three years ago, and since I strongly suspect that my ex-husband didn't notice I was gone until he ran out of toilet paper, I was not in a hurry to bite the matrimonial bullet again. Instead, I channeled all of my energy—physical and emotional—into teaching. I don't think I used my students as a substitute for love or marriage; I simply didn't have the time or the inclination to worry about dating. Eventually, I believed, somebody would come along and grab my attention.

Nobody grabbed.

When Raul and Richie and Victor and Shamica and Emilio and the rest of my beloved seniors graduated and waved goodbye to Parkmont and me, I nearly disappeared into the void their leaving created. That's when I realized it was time to rejoin the social scene and establish some sort of balance between work and play in my life, but because I'd been so involved in my work, I had nobody to play with.

So I called Susie McKenzie, one of the secretaries at the Xerox Research Center, where I had worked while attending college to earn my teaching credential. Susie was a tall, elegant brunette with a bewitching personality and a full social schedule. I wasn't sure she'd be interested in introducing me to anybody because she had called several times in during the first weeks after I had left Xerox to ask if I'd like to meet some "perfectly acceptable man" who simply couldn't be squeezed into her social calendar, and I had declined each offer.

"It's about time," Susie said when I explained that I wanted to ease back into the singles setting. "In fact, your timing is perfect. I have an extra man tonight."

"You're dating two men on the same night?" Apparently Susie stood more than a few rungs above me on the ladder to love and happily ever after. I started thinking of excuses for why I couldn't go.

"I have only one date," Susie assured me, "but his brother's in the dumps over some girl he just broke up with and we promised to take the brother out dancing. We're going to the West 40."

"The West 40 . . . " I repeated, stalling.

"It's a country-western nightclub. You'll love it," Susie said. "The place is full of long, lean cowboys who wear big black hats and high-heeled pointy-toed boots made out of snakes and bulls and lizards and all kinds of wild animals. And these boys are capital-P polite. They say things like, 'Howdy, ma'am. Would you kindly do me the honor of dancing with me?' "

I told Susie I wasn't sure I wanted to dance with anybody who actually said howdy, and I hate to be called ma'am. I still remember the first time it happened. I was still in my early thirties, a mere child, and I was standing at the checkout counter at Safeway daydreaming when the bag boy said, "Do you want some help out to your car, ma'am?" I assumed he was addressing an older woman, someone my mother's age. He repeated his question, and when I glanced up to see why the woman didn't answer, the boy was looking at me. I was devastated. There I had been, walking around thinking of myself as a Miss, or at least a Ms., while young, attractive people had been regarding me as a ma'am for who knows how long.

Susie interrupted my whining. "You'll have fun, I promise.

There's a free dance lesson tonight. You can learn the Tush Push."

"No, thanks," I said. "I may be out of practice, but I do remember how to perform that particular maneuver, and I have no intention of performing it in public, especially with some hayseed who thinks *howdy* is a real word."

Susie explained that the Tush Push was a line dance. "And don't be such a snob," she said. "I promise you won't see anybody wearing bib overalls or meet anybody named Jethro."

I agreed to go. After all, I hadn't liked rap, heavy metal, or ranchero music until my students introduced me to it. And if I could learn to do Roger Rabbit, Running Man, and the Electric Slide, I could probably handle the Tush Push.

We arrived at the West 40 early, before the band started, and took a table near the jukebox. Susie and her date, Tyler, claimed a spot on the dance floor and stayed there, practicing elaborate spins and turns, stopping only to slurp their drinks or slide more quarters into the jukebox. The song selection was limited, and after thirty minutes of listening to one of those cowboy singers with three first names, Billy Joe Bob Cyprus or some such thing, I found myself actually longing for a little Queen Latifah or Los Lobos. But I would have sat there all night listening to Donny Osmond sing Barry Manilow's greatest hits if it meant I could stare at the brokenhearted brother, Cody.

Except for his shirt, which was brilliant and white, and his jeans, which were blue and tight, the man was decked out like a gunslinger in dangerous, delicious black: black leather vest, black silk string tie, black leather belt, black felt hat, black black hair cut short in the front and longer in the back so that a handful of dark curls—just enough for a woman to grab on to if she needed—teased their way into the collar of his shirt.

What really impressed me, though, was that, unlike most of the men at the West 40, Cody's vocabulary was bigger than his belt buckle. And he seemed to be the only man who didn't have a flat, round bulge in his hip pocket, which puzzled me until I saw a man who had been attractive until that moment whip out a can of snuff and poke what looked like a clump of wet dirt into his mouth.

I nearly fell off my chair the first time one of the good old boys at the table beside us cleared his sinus cavities with a long, loud sniff and spit a stream of thick brown slime into an empty beer bottle. When Mr. Spitter saw me staring at him, he lifted the bottle in a mock toast and winked at me as he pretended to drink the spittle. I gagged. Cody leaned forward, intercepting the exchange.

"Would you like to move to another table, darlin', so's you won't have to listen to these barnyard critters expectoratin' their ignorance all night?"

I glanced around the room, which was filled to its capacity with both smoke and people. "I think all the tables are taken."

"That's all right. If you see a table that appeals to you, you just let me know, and I'll go on over and clear it for you." Cody sat back in his chair, tilting his head down so that all I could see beneath the brim of his hat was a flash of white teeth. "You just say the word, darlin'."

I didn't say the word, but darlin' is a definite improvement over ma'am, and later that night, on our way home, when Cody asked me if I'd like to go out with him the following weekend, I said yes. He smiled, nodded his head, and sat there beside me in the backseat of Susie's car, silent and gorgeous. When we stopped in front of my apartment, Cody climbed out of the car and offered me his arm. As we walked to my door, I fished around in the pockets of my jacket, hoping to find a tissue to wipe off some of my lipstick, so I wouldn't smear any on Cody's clean white shirt when he hugged me good-bye. I couldn't find a tissue, but I didn't need one. When we reached the front door, Cody tipped his hat, turned around, and headed straight back to the car. He opened the door and climbed into the backseat without even turning around to look at me. I thought he must have changed his mind about asking me out, but at the last second, as the car started to pull away, he rolled down his window and grinned.

"You busy Friday night, good-lookin'?" he called. I shook my head. "Then I'll be here to fetch you. Eight o'clock sharp."

The following Friday, Cody came to fetch me in a black four-wheel-drive Chevy pickup that was almost as shiny as his lizard-skin boots. In fewer than three hours, Cody the Cowboy single-handedly made up for my three years of downtime in the dating department.

During dinner, Cody repeated his cool, quiet performance of the previous week. His manners were impeccable, and he turned out to be adept at conversation, although he did more listening than talking. He asked a lot of questions about my job and seemed to find the thought of teaching high school English as difficult and dangerous as I considered his job of training bucking and roping horses for rodeo riders.

After dinner, we went to a different dance spot, the Palomino Club, a giant barn-shaped building with an anatomically correct plastic bucking bronco perched on the roof above the entrance. As we crossed the parking lot toward the club, Cody put his hand lightly on the nape of my neck, the first time he had touched me other than to take my elbow to escort me across the street or through a door. His touch was so unexpected and so tender that it sent a shiver dancing down my spine. Immediately, he dropped his hand. He seemed embarrassed, and I wanted to reassure him, but I didn't know how to tell him. If I said, "That felt good," he might get the wrong idea, which actually would have been the right idea, but not one that I intended to entertain at that moment or any moment in the foreseeable future. So I said nothing, and Cody kept his hands to himself for the next two hours, except to lead me to and from the dance floor.

Just before midnight, the band played a slow ballad called "The Dance," which seemed to speak to me personally. The singer claimed that his new love made all his past heartaches worthwhile. "I might have missed the pain," Cody sang softly with the band, his lips brushing against my hair, "but I'd have had to miss . . . the . . . dance." As the song ended, Cody turned to his left and pulled me across his body, dropped me into a graceful dip, and kissed me. Everything between my neck and my knees melted, and my brain took a temporary vacation.

During the drive back to my apartment, I struggled to collect my thoughts and control my feelings. You're acting like a silly little girl, I silently scolded myself. You're just overreacting because it's been so long since you even held hands with a man.

Fortunately it was a long drive, since I lived on the west side of San Francisco Bay and the Palomino Club was on the East Bay, just north of San Jose. I rolled down the window as we crossed the Dumbarton Bridge and stuck my head out into the night. I wished on a star that the wind would blow some sense back into my brain. It must have been my lucky star.

When I thanked Cody and gave him a quick good-bye kiss and hug, he said, "If you'll excuse me for asking, I'd like to come upstairs with you, darlin'. We could have us one hell of a night."

"Oh, I don't think that's a good idea," I said. "After all, this was our first date, and we don't know each other that well." What I was really thinking was, if I get alone in a dark room with this man, I'm history.

Cody considered my words for a second, then shook his head. "I'm afraid I disagree with that. The best way for two people to get to know each other is to spend a lot of time together. My daddy gave me some good advice. He said, 'Son, don't never buy a pair of boots until you've tried 'em on.'"

"Well, ain't that special," I said. "My mama told me ain't no man gonna buy a cow who gets the milk for free."

"Hooo-ee!" Cody took off his hat, slapped it against his thigh, and laughed out loud. "I believe I've met my match." He swooped me into a hug, held that big black hat against my back, and laid a kiss on me that still makes the back of my knees tickle when I think about it. When he finally let go, I couldn't catch my breath, so when Cody said, "You sure you don't want to ask me in?" I shook my head, a silent no.

Cody sighed and opened the door of his truck. Instead of climbing up into the driver's seat, as I expected him to, he nodded his head toward the cab and said, "All right, have it your way." Dumbly, I stared at him. He put his hat back on, grabbed the door with his left hand, and pulled me toward him with his right hand. He slapped me on the butt and said, "Get in, woman."

"I beg your pardon?"

"Get in the truck," Cody repeated.

He pushed me back into the truck and pressed himself against me. He clamped my arms behind me and forced a knee between my legs. I opened my mouth to yell, but he swallowed my shout with a kiss so hard and furious that my bottom lip started bleeding where my teeth bit into it. I jabbed two fingers into his neck, on either side of his Adam's apple, hooked one leg behind his ankle, and shoved him backward. He was so surprised that before he had a chance to get up off the ground, I had my can of pepper mace out of my purse, aimed at his face. Cody didn't look nearly as handsome sprawled on his butt, with his pretty hat rolling around in the dirt. He stood up, holding both hands in the air above his head.

"Whoa," he said. "Take it easy. Don't shoot. You're all right. I never force my attentions on a lady."

"Oh, spare me." I stepped away from the truck, still holding the mace, as he picked up his hat and tenderly brushed away every last speck of dirt from it. He put it back on and carefully adjusted it, using the side mirror on his truck, so that it dipped just a hair to the left. Satisfied, he smiled at himself, then turned to me.

"I know you want me," Cody said. "I can feel it."

"I don't want anything right now except to go inside my apartment and go to sleep—by myself."

"Fine. Like I said, I never force my attentions on a lady. But if you reconsider, you just holler. I'm ready and willing."

I stood in the driveway and watched until the taillights of that shiny black pickup truck became tiny red stars in the darkness.

After that memorable evening, I seriously considered giving up on men and going back to my safe, secure workaholic world, but I knew I wouldn't survive another graduation if I didn't develop a life of my own. When I told Susie what happened, she offered to set me up with a professional bull roper, but I passed. I thought it might be a good idea to start out slowly and work my way up the testosterone scale, beginning with a computer programmer or an accountant, then a financial adviser or a musician, maybe a couple of heavy-equipment operators or truck drivers, before I tried two-stepping with a man whose idea of a good time involves wrestling around in the dirt with extremely large, potentially lethal animals.

Susie promised to call as soon as she found a likely prospect. In the meantime, I decided to change my personal policy about dating co-workers. One of Parkmont's math teachers, Justin Bernard, had asked me out several times, and each time I had explained that I never dated people from work. Justin seemed to understand, and since he had asked me out more than once, I believed he accepted my explanation and didn't attribute my refusal to the difference in our skin color. Because I had turned down all of his offers, I invited Justin out for dinner and a night at the theater as my guest. He agreed, but insisted that he had to drive because he was too old-fashioned to let a woman provide his dinner, his entertainment, and his transportation, too.

A few minutes before Justin was scheduled to pick me up, I was in the bathroom, bending over the bathtub, brushing my hair upside down to give it that "full, natural look," when I happened to glance under my arm at the photo taped to the mirror over the sink—my smiling seniors at their graduation ceremony. For the first time, perhaps because of the unusual perspective, it struck me that the boys' blue gowns greatly outnumbered the girls' white ones. I couldn't believe I hadn't noticed sooner how few girls were in the graduating class. I was still staring at the photo when the doorbell rang. Instead of inviting Justin to make himself comfortable in my living room, I ushered him into my tiny bathroom.

"Look at this," I said, pointing at the photo. "Do you notice anything unusual about this picture?" Justin bent down and inspected the photo carefully. As track coach, he had worked with several of the boys and one of the girls in the photo.

"I see a lot of faces I never expected to make it out of high school," he said. He stood up straight and patted me playfully on the head. "You done good."

"But there are only five girls in this picture, and three of them are white. We had twenty girls three years ago, and most of them were black or Hispanic or Pacific Islander. Where did they go? They didn't just disappear."

My stomach tightened with the same sickening sensation that I had felt in my classroom when so many kids skipped my final exam: I was a fraud. Certainly I was not the teacher I had thought I was. Otherwise I would have noticed what was happening to the Academy girls. I felt like flopping down on my couch and crying the night away, but dinner at Maxwell Plum's and two front-row seats to August Wilson's *Fences* were waiting.

En route to the city, Justin spent the first half hour brainstorming with me, trying to remember the names of my departed female students, and the rest of the time considerately creating excuses for my having forgotten their names. The Academy had a full house now, two classes each of sophomores and juniors, one class of seniors—too many for anybody to keep track of them all every single minute. I had five full classes last year, plus department head duties. Kids moved away or transferred to other schools. Some were suspended from the Academy for a year in a last, desperate attempt to catch their attention and convince them to change their behavior. . . .

By the time we finished dinner, Justin had nearly convinced me that my lack of awareness was forgivable and had completely convinced me that he was far too interesting and charming to be bored to death with my selfish obsession. I apologized for monopolizing the conversation and made up my mind to focus my attention on Justin and the play, but by the final curtain, I was thoroughly ashamed of myself again.

While we had waited for the play to begin and during intermissions, instead of talking to Justin, I had spent the time trying to create a mental roster of all the sophomore girls who had volunteered for the first Academy class. Although I knew there were twenty, I could list only fourteen names. And I couldn't concentrate on anything else, not even on an intelligent, articulate, attractive man like Justin.

When we returned to my apartment after the play, I invited Justin in, offering a cup of cocoa and some serious attention as an inadequate apology for my rude behavior.

"I would like to come in for a while," Justin said. "There's something I'd like to discuss with you. And believe it or not, I wasn't a bit insulted this evening. I enjoyed spending time with a woman who takes her work to heart, somebody who is as beautiful inside as outside." Aw, shucks. I escaped to the kitchen.

As our hot chocolate heated up in the microwave, I popped into my office/gym/bedroom to check my file cabinet and see if I could find the original Academy roster. The original wasn't there, but the second-year roster listed eighteen girls. I quickly scanned the list, making a short note after each girl's name.

Tiffany Sweet—went to live with her grandmother in Sacramento after her father died from AIDS. Silvia Garcia—ran off to Mexico to escape from her violent father. Nicole Bennet—dropped out of school to become a full-time Jehovah's Witness. LaShanda Cole—transferred to an alternative school for teenage mothers. Jeannie Wilson—quit the Academy because the boys teased her mercilessly about her weight. Shonte Haqq—

A dull thump from the living room, the sound of my front door shutting, startled me back to the present. I glanced at the alarm clock on my dresser. 2:06 A.M. I'd been sitting on my bedroom floor scribbling on a legal pad for nearly an hour while my date sat in my living room! I raced to the living room and opened the door, just in time to see Justin's red 280Z turn the corner at the end of my street.

On the coffee table was a note: "L.A.J. The hot chocolate was delicious. So was your company. Thanks. Don't worry about tonight. I'll see you at school Monday. J.B. P.S. I still need to talk to you."

I called Justin's house immediately, planning to leave a message on his answering machine, but at the sound of the tone, I couldn't come up with a single coherent thought. I hoped his machine was one of those intelligent ones that erase nonverbal messages such as the sound of a frustrated woman sighing into the receiver. I'd send him flowers in the morning, I decided. It was the least I could do. For another hour I lay in bed, beating myself up mentally. As I began to float into serious sleep, the phone rang.

"Lupe Ramirez," said a man's voice.

"Sorry, wrong numb—" I started to mumble.

"She was one of your students. I just remembered." Awake, I immediately recognized Justin's voice.

"You're right," I said. "How could I forget Lupe?" A meaner man might have asked how I could forget *him,* but Justin passed up the opportunity.

"Lupe tried to disappear," Justin said. "The only reason I knew her was because she came to every practice and every track meet with DaShaun Washington."

I remembered seeing Lupe and DaShaun walking around campus, her arm around his waist, his draped over her shoulder. Her head barely reached his chest, and Lupe took three or four small steps to each one of DaShaun's size-fifteen strides.

"I always wondered what happened to Lupe," I told Justin. "She was doing so well. Then, boom, one day she just vanished. Her whole family disappeared. No forwarding address, no phone. Nothing."

"Her parents moved the whole family back to Mexico," Justin said. He added something else, but said it so softly that I had to ask him to repeat it.

"They moved the same day they found out Lupe's boyfriend was black."

For the second time that night I found myself without words. The faint hum of the telephone line wasn't enough to fill the silence between me and Justin Bernard.

Chapter 8

There's Some Things
You Can't Fix

If I hadn't forgotten my briefcase on the day of my second date with Justin Bernard, I would never have known that Rico Perez had planned to murder a man that night. I was supposed to meet Justin at the Guild Theatre in Menlo Park, where we would watch *Entre Nous* and then, finally, have our long-delayed "discussion." But that Friday afternoon I was in my car, driving out of the campus's main gate, when I realized I had left my briefcase with the papers I needed to grade for the following day in my office. When I went back to retrieve my briefcase, Rico was sitting on the sidewalk outside my classroom, his eyes closed, his back against the green stucco wall.

"Are you lost, little boy?" I teased, as I unlocked the door and went inside without really looking at Rico. He didn't respond, so I assumed he hadn't heard me or had chosen to ignore my silliness, but when I turned to leave my office, briefcase in hand, Rico was standing in the doorway, his mouth half open, as though he had forgotten what he wanted to say. He closed his mouth, opened it, closed it, and burst into tears.

I was too surprised to respond for a moment. Rico collapsed into the chair beside my desk and hunched over, his shoulders shaking with sobs. Seeing him cry unnerved me. I knew that only something truly serious could make him break down, especially in front of a woman. After my initial shock subsided, I knelt beside Rico and tried to put my arms around him, but he shook himself free and sat up straight.

"This is so stupid." He slapped at the tears on his cheeks with the back of his hand, angry swipes at his body's betrayal. I pulled the chair from my desk over beside Rico and sat down to wait. He breathed in and out several times, slowly, with concentration, like a weight lifter intent on forcing his body to obey his mind. In and out, in and out, three four five times, each breath a little stronger. After a few minutes, eyes dry, breathing normal, Rico cleared his throat.

"A guy tried to shoot me yesterday. He fired twice, and I didn't even flinch. I just walked away, cool as a cucumber. I didn't feel a thing." He had been looking at the floor as he talked, ashamed of his emotions, but at that point, he raised his head and looked at me. "I was real cool then, like I didn't feel a thing, but now I can't stop feeling stuff. I keep thinking that my girlfriend was standing right there, right beside me, and he could have killed her. He could have killed us both." Rico's eyes filled again, and he pressed his fingers against his eyelids to stop the tears. I put my arms around him, and he leaned into them for the briefest second before stiffening, back in control.

"Do you know this guy?" I asked.

Rico nodded. "Omar Corona. Everybody knows him. He's a crackhead loser. He's always talking shit. He told me a lot of times he was gonna shoot me. But he never had a gun with him before. This time, he put it right in my face." Rico reached out and aimed his index finger at my temple. "He cocked it and everything, and then he said, 'I'm gonna kill you,' and I said, 'Go ahead and shoot, muthafucka.' But I didn't think he'd really do it." Rico's voice cracked on the last sentence, and his hand started to tremble. I took his hand and held it between both of mine. He looked at the ceiling and sucked in a hard breath, cutting off the tears before they could start again.

"Oh, Rico." I wanted to hug him. I wanted to swoop him up and carry him away someplace where I could protect him from his life. "Did you call the police?" It was a stupid question, but I had to ask.

"Oh, yeah, like they would believe me."

"They might," I said, although we both knew Rico was right. "Omar was probably just playing with you, don't you think? I mean, if he was that close, he would have hit you, wouldn't he?"

"Maybe he missed. Or he was using blanks or something. I don't know. But I'm not gonna wait around and find out. I'm gonna waste the dude next time I see him. I'm gonna get him first."

"Oh, Rico, no. Not you."

"I have to," Rico insisted, "or he'll waste me."

"Where does it stop? You shoot him. He shoots your brother. Your cousin shoots him. Maybe somebody shoots your mother, or your little sister, or your girlfriend."

Rico sighed. I knew he was expecting another of my antiviolence lectures, and I was tempted, but I knew it wouldn't help. I tried to think of something that might.

"What about your mother?" I said. "And your father? Your little brothers and sisters. Think how they would feel if something happened to you. Or if you went to jail for killing some stupid jerk."

Rico nodded. "I *have* been thinking about them. That's the only reason I didn't kill Omar already. But now I got no choice. He's trying to make me go down, and if I do, I'll be a target for every punk on the street. I gotta take him down first."

"No, you don't."

"Yes, I do."

"You don't have a gun, do you?" I hoped he didn't, that it would take him a while to find one, long enough to cool down.

"Yeah. I got a three-eighty Colt Mustang," Rico said.

"Oh, my God." I felt that peculiar dry-mouth, heart-pounding, stomach-sickening sensation of impending and unavoidable disaster. Until then, our conversation had seemed unreal, as though Rico were describing a scene from a movie or summarizing the plot of a short story. But the second he said ".380 Colt Mustang," I knew we were talking about real life. And real death.

Rico had a gun, all right, and I knew exactly where he got it—Sean Collins. And it was as much my fault as if I had handed it to him myself. Surely Rico could have gotten a gun anytime he wanted to, but if one of his own classmates hadn't happened to have one on hand—and if his pigheaded, arrogant teacher had followed the rules instead of making up her own—it surely would have taken more time for Rico to get his hands on a gun, perhaps enough time for him to reconsider killing Omar Corona.

Sean Collins was an experienced shoplifter. I knew that. But he was also addicted to telling wild stories, creating incredible adventures that took place within his round, blond head with its pale, myopic eyes and milk-pitcher ears. When Sean had joined the Academy as a sophomore, he was one of the smallest boys in class, a sapling of a boy with arms like skinny twigs, his elbows a pair of oversize knots. In his first personal journal entry, Sean had confessed his shoplifting habit. He had started stealing when he was five years old, candy bars and Matchbox cars, but he had gradually moved into the big time—stereos, computer components, expensive jewelry. He concluded that first essay with a description of his most recent misadventure.

The last thing I took was a two-thousand-dollar diamond ring that I hid under my mattress. I know it's wrong to steal, but I keep doing it anyway. I never told anybody about this in my whole life. It would kill my mom if she found out. She's already flaky since her and my dad got divorced. But I can't stop stealing. I thought maybe you could help me or give me some advice, but don't tell anybody, especially my mother, or I'll steal a car and run away and crash it on the freeway and you'll never see me again.

At the time, I couldn't envision Sean Collins stealing a diamond ring, much less committing suicide on the interstate. Aside from the fact that the boy was too short to see over the steering wheel of a car, he was a straight-A student with Sunday school manners and perfect attendance, so shy that he blushed every time I called on him in class. Most likely, I thought, he had invented the whole story, testing me to see whether I would keep my promise not to reveal the contents of their private journals, no matter what. I had written a note on Sean's journal and asked him to come see me after school that day. Sean appeared promptly, five minutes after the final bell. He assured me that he had been telling the truth but refused to talk to a counselor, for fear that his mother would find out. I checked with the school psychiatrist and found a clinic that provided free confidential counseling to teens. Sean swore that he had returned the ring. He reported faithfully for counseling for several months, stopped writing about stealing, and started creating elaborate tales of espionage agents and science fiction creatures.

When he returned to school for his junior year, Sean was transformed. He had shot up nearly a foot and had traded in his thick glasses for contact lenses. Although he was still thin, he no longer looked frail, and I wrongly assumed that, along with outgrowing all of his clothes and shoes, he had outgrown his shoplifting habit. Then, just a week before Rico told me about Omar Corona, Sean had switched from spy stories back to shoplifting.

I stole something really big this time. It's a .380 Colt Mustang, semi-automatic, hammerless, pistol-grip nine-shooter. This gun makes me feel powerful and I like it. The first time I saw it, I knew I was going to steal it. I tried not to, but I couldn't help it. I'm not going to tell you where I stole it from because it belongs to this kid's father and you know the kid.

I considered calling the police at that point, but I wasn't at all convinced that Sean was telling the truth. Many of his stories involved James Bond characters with high-tech weapons. I read on.

I almost passed out when I was walking home with the gun wrapped inside my gym shorts in my backpack. I could even hear my heart, right in my ears, like a drum, whenever I took a step. I ran most of the way, even though my mother was working and I knew she wouldn't be home for two or three hours because I wanted to just sit in my room and hold the gun. It's a great gun. I don't like how I got it, but I like having it. I get an adrenaline rush just holding it in my hand. Now I'm the one with the power.

Instead of calling the police when I finished reading, I drove directly to Sean's apartment and pounded on the door. His mother worked at night, so I knew he would be alone. Sean didn't seem at all surprised to see me standing on his doorstep at 11:30 P.M. He invited me in, but I declined. What I had to say didn't take long.

"I don't know if you were telling the truth about the pistol and I don't want to know," I said. If I knew he had a weapon, even if he didn't bring it to school, I was ethically and legally obligated to make an official report to the principal, who would contact the police. At best, Sean would be expelled from school permanently; at worst, he'd end up in juvenile detention for a very long time.

"If you do really have that gun, and it isn't just one of your stories, I want your word of honor that you'll get rid of that thing first thing tomorrow morning."

"Okay," Sean said, his voice small and shaky.

When he walked into my classroom the following day, Sean looked at me and nodded. I said a mental prayer of thanks, as though I had helped do something good. What I should have done was pray for guidance and forgiveness for my stupidity.

When Rico told me about the Colt, I felt as guilty as if I had handed him the gun myself. If I had followed the rules and done the responsible thing, reported that pistol the second I learned about it from Sean's journal, Rico wouldn't be walking around with that same pistol, planning to shoot some small-time thug with it.

"Where did you get the pistol?" I asked Rico.

"From Sean," he answered with his usual blunt honesty.

"You know it was probably stolen, don't you?"

Rico shrugged. "So? Everybody steals guns. They really rip you off if you buy them from a store, and besides, how could I? I'm only seventeen."

Only seventeen, I thought, and already so much older than I'll ever be. Rico noticed my expression and must have assumed I was upset because I thought he had stolen the pistol from Sean.

"Hey, I didn't steal it. You know I'm not no thief. I paid for it."

"You paid for it?" It hadn't occurred to me that Sean might sell it. One more thing to add to the long list of important things I had forgotten to think about.

"I didn't pay Sean the three-hundred-fifty like he wanted. Because he was so stupid, he gave me the gun before I gave him the money. He couldn't do nothing because he stoled it in the first place, so I gave him twenty-five dollars and said thanks. Pretty stupid for such a smart kid, huh? He thinks he's bad, but he isn't. Lucky he had me to teach him instead of somebody with no self-respect." Rico laughed, but there was no joy in his laughter, and I found myself wondering not about the pistol, but whether life had destroyed any chance Rico might have for simple joy.

"Please get rid of the gun," I whispered. "I don't want to see you hurt."

"I'm sorry, Miss J, but there's some things you just can't fix, even if you do love me."

As soon as Rico left my office, I went looking for his best friend, Cesar Caldera, a short, stocky boy with a round, pleasant face. Cesar was the only person I could think of who might be able to convince Rico not to shoot Omar.

"Please stop him," I pleaded with Cesar.

He crossed his arms and shook his head. "I can't. He has to take Omar out."

"He does not!"

"If Rico goes out without fighting this punk, it's over. He doesn't have no choice. There are things you just gotta do. I can't explain it. That's the way it is in our neighborhood, and nobody can't change it."

I stayed at work late that night, hoping that Rico might have second thoughts and come by my room for some moral support or to discuss alternative ideas for dealing with Omar Corona. I graded papers, made lesson plans, redecorated the bulletin boards, drew new spelling charts. At ten o'clock I finally ran out of tasks and energy. I went home and fell into bed. But I didn't sleep. Every night sound jangled my jittery nerves and echoed in my ears like distant gunfire.

"Me and Cesar planned out the whole thing how to take Omar out," Rico said in a voice as smooth and hard as I imagined the barrel of a .380 Colt Mustang must look and feel. Perhaps Rico's face revealed some speck of emotion, but I couldn't see his face. When he had strolled into my classroom during lunch hour on

Monday, my first inclination was to jump up from my desk and strangle him. My second response was to grab him and hug him forever. Instead, I sat and watched as he paced the room, reading the posters, scanning the bookshelves, walking between the rows of desks, his fingers trailing along the wooden tops, as though grounding himself in the familiar terrain of my classroom after a long absence.

Undoubtedly the weekend had seemed much longer than two days to Rico, but for me it had been an eternity. On Saturday, unable to stand the suspense any longer, I had called Rico's house, but there was no answer, so I drove to East Palo Alto and circled the block on Cooley Avenue where Rico lived. There were no children playing in the yard in front of the Perez house and no car in the driveway. Probably went shopping, I told myself, although in the back of my mind, I envisioned the entire Perez family—mother, father, *abuela,* sisters, brothers, cousins—at the hospital, holding hands, forming a circle around Rico's deathbed.

Back at my apartment, I had stayed near the phone all weekend, one minute willing it to ring, the next dreading that it might. Monday morning sent me to school exhausted and prepared for the principal to call me out of my classroom to hear the bad news. But Dr. Delgado didn't call, and second period came and went without any sign or word of Rico. So when he suddenly appeared and then pretended not to notice the dark circles under my eyes or the need in them, and answered simply "around" when I asked where he had been, I dropped my head on my desk and kept it there, shutting Rico out of my sight, as though that would somehow make me invisible to him and invincible against his ability to hurt me. Did you kill Omar? my voice shouted inside my head. Are you going to prison? Did you decide to become a living stereotype? As I put my head down on my arms and closed my eyes, for the first time in days I didn't see Rico's face staring back from behind my eyelids.

His voice was suddenly very soft and very near my desk. I kept my head down, my eyes closed, just in case. "My parents got a new office building on their cleaning route, so they don't get home until real late, and I put my brothers and sisters in bed and told them to stay there and shut up. They do what I say because I'm the oldest."

As he told his story, I watched it taking place on the miniature movie screen inside my head. Rico had sat in his house Friday night, with all the lights out, waiting for Cesar to pick him up. Their plan was to drive around in Cesar's car, cruising East Palo Alto until they spotted Omar, who claimed several streets in the neighborhood and usually stayed out all night patrolling them.

"Cesar said it would be better if I just stayed in the car," Rico said. "He said he'd drive, and when we saw Omar I could take care of him, *bam!* and we'd get out of there. But I said, 'I ain't doing no drive-by. That's for cowards. I'm going to do this face to face, so there won't be no doubt who did it. If I get caught, I get caught, but at least Omar will know it was me who did it.' And I told Cesar, 'You won't get busted because I won't be in your car when I waste him.' "

Honor among murderers, I thought, my head still buried in my arms, as though refusing to look could prevent me from loving this boy who seemed so determined to self-destruct.

"Cesar appreciated that, you know," Rico continued. "He appreciated that I was keeping him out of it. I think he might've been a little scared, too, because he never saw anybody get shot before."

Rico had. I knew that. Once, when the class was discussing the final scene in *Of Mice and Men,* where George shoots his best friend, Lennie, in the back of the head to save him from being lynched by a mob, the conversation took a wide turn and a detour and ended up in East Palo Alto. Kids jumped out of their seats, eager to share their stories of murder and mayhem. One girl described, in great detail, a dead body with both hands cut off that she and a friend had found lying in a heap behind a Dumpster outside the laundromat. A boy told of his neighbor, a fifteen-year-old boy, an innocent bystander, who was shot in the back of the head during a drug bust.

"Did you see him get shot?" Rico asked.

"No," the boy said. "Did you?" he challenged.

"No." Rico shook his head. "But I seen my own uncle get his head blown off right in our backyard when we were having a barbecue. He was playing poker and drinking with some friends and this one punk got mad and said my uncle was cheating and ran over to his house and came back with a gun. I was in the house and I saw him out of the window and I ran outside to warn my uncle, but the punk beat me to him and just shot my uncle right in the face. There was blood all over the place and some little bits of my uncle's brains got on me but I didn't even puke and I was only ten years old."

Seven years later, Rico was the punk with the gun, but the irony escaped him.

"I looked at my reflection in the window while I was waiting for Cesar to come by and pick me up," Rico said, "and I crossed myself for good luck. Then I started loading the Colt, and right then I heard something outside the house. I hurried up and finished loading in case it was somebody coming to get me."

With the pistol loaded, Rico had tiptoed to the door and slowly turned the knob, silently opening the lock. After a few seconds, hearing another footstep, he flung the door open, crouched low, and aimed the pistol into the darkness.

"I almost shot Tio," Rico said.

I didn't recognize the name. He wasn't a student. "Who's Tio?" I mumbled into my arms.

"Tio's an O.G. Original Gangsters. He just got out of prison a few weeks ago. You should see the pictures he drew in there. Man, is he good. Just like a professional artist."

Rico's voice hovered near my head, then moved away as he

got up and started pacing, as he usually did when things got too exciting for him to sit still.

"I told Tio, 'I almost blew you away, man. You shouldn't sneak up on people in the middle of the night like that. I almost shot you.' Then Tio saw the Colt and he asked me where did I get it."

From Sean Collins, your friendly neighborhood kleptomaniac, I thought, courtesy of your stupid teacher who used to think she was so smart.

"Tio lost it." Rico's voice grew louder, but less harsh. "He asked me what was I doing with the Colt and I told him I had some business to take care of and he went off on me. Next thing I knew, I was on the floor and Tio had the gun."

I had never met Tio, but I loved him. I wasn't aware of sitting up or opening my eyes, but I must have because I remember seeing Rico standing directly in front of my desk, both hands pressed against the front edge of the worn wood top.

"Tio unloaded the gun and put the bullets in his back pocket," Rico said. "Then he said, 'You ain't going nowhere, rogue, until you tell me what's up.' And he grabbed my shirt and yanked me up and threw me down on the couch."

"The more I hear about this Tio person, the better I like him," I told Rico.

"Yeah, he's cool," Rico agreed. "But he wasn't too cool about me taking Omar out. When I told him about Omar messing with me, sticking a gun in my face, talking me down, shooting at me and shit, I thought Tio would give me back the Colt, maybe even go with me and Cesar. But he didn't. He stuck the pistol in my face and grabbed my shirt again and hollered, 'That what you're gonna do with this? You gonna shoot a homeboy?' "

Bravo, Tio.

"I told him Omar ain't my homeboy," Rico said. "He's a *chopa*."

Tio let go of Rico's shirt and stepped back, as Rico had expected, but his next move took Rico by surprise. Tio shoved the pistol into his back pocket, planted his feet, and rolled up his sleeves.

"You ain't shooting nobody, rogue," Tio told Rico. "I ain't letting you mess up your life like I did."

"Tio, you know how it is," Rico said. "If I don't take him out, it's over."

"So you take him out," Tio said. "You think you won the fight? What did you win? Nothing. You win nothing. You go to jail, that's what you win. I been there. It's not winning. If you want to win, you stay in school and you graduate and get a decent job."

"I'm going to school," Rico said. "And I'm going to kill Corona. You can't stop me."

"Yes, I can!" Tio yelled. "Look at me." He pounded his fist against his chest. "I'm twenty-six years old. I should have my own house, my own car, be taking care of my wife and my little girl like a man. But instead I gotta ride the bus with all the other losers. Winos and perverts and crackheads. I still live with my father and mother and work at some stupid nothing job and I got no future. I'm not gonna let you make the same mistakes I did. If you want to walk out that door, you'll have to take me out first."

Rico stopped talking for a minute and glanced up at the ceiling, waiting for the tears in his eyes to subside. When they did, Rico finished his story, but his voice was softer than I'd ever heard it. He sounded awestruck, as though he still couldn't believe what had happened.

"I told Tio I couldn't fight him. So he handed me back the pistol and told me if I want to shoot somebody, I should shoot him," Rico said. "He said it would be doing him a favor."

It was my turn to stare at the ceiling to hold back the tears.

"Tio said, 'Vaya con Dios,'" Rico whispered, "and then he walked out the front door. I knew Cesar was out there waiting for me, but I just sat there in the dark, thinking, for a long time after Tio left. If he was willing to fight me, I know he really loved me."

"I would have been glad to beat you up," I said. "It just didn't occur to me at the time. Next time, I'll be sure to offer. Then maybe I won't have to cry myself to sleep worrying about you for days and days."

Rico shook his head, then squared his shoulders. I could sense him drawing back inside the hard shell that protected his softness. He walked to the windows and stared out at the parking lot.

"That car got anything?" he asked, jutting out his chin to indicate my old Spyder.

"It can move. Why?"

"I thought maybe you could give me a ride after school," Rico said. "I got some business to take care of."

After the last bell, I waited almost half an hour, but Rico didn't show up, so I wrote him a note, taped it to the door, and left. I put down my car's canvas top so I could enjoy the warm sunshine during the drive. As I pulled out of the parking lot and rounded the corner past the phys ed complex, Rico appeared from the shadows behind the gymnasium. He climbed over the door and plopped into the passenger seat.

"What do you say let's drive over the San Mateo Bridge," he said. I said I didn't mind taking a drive on such a pretty day. Rico nodded and settled back in the seat. I fished a spare pair of sunglasses from the side pocket on my door and handed them to Rico. With another nod, which I interpreted as a thank-you, Rico put on the glasses and leaned slightly to his right so he could admire himself in the side mirror.

Whatever business Rico had, it wasn't conversation with me. He didn't say a word as we wound our way down Alameda de las Pulgas and onto the freeway toward San Mateo. He glanced at me once, to make sure I saw the exit sign for the bridge, but didn't speak.

As we approached the crest of the bridge, Rico suddenly sat up and leaned out the window. I glanced over and saw the Colt pistol in his right hand. At first I thought he was going to see if he could hit one of the squawking flock of seagulls hang gliding just above the surface of the water. Instead, Rico drew back his arm and flung the pistol out into the air, where it seemed to hang suspended amid the circling birds for a long moment before it shot straight down into the murky waters of San Francisco Bay.

When I dropped him off in front of his house, Rico finally broke the silence. He put his left hand on my arm and whispered, *"Sueños con los angelitos, Maestra."* Dream with the little angels, Teacher.

Chapter 9

It Don't Mean Nothing

I headed back across I-101, past Stanford Shopping Center, up Sand Hill Road to my apartment in Woodside. I drove the long route—University Avenue across Palo Alto and down El Camino through Menlo Park and cut across the shopping center. After lying awake for three nights worrying about Rico and hearing about his aborted homicide scheme, I wasn't up to the roller-derby dodge of the freeway. On my way through Menlo Park, I passed the Guild Theatre and, for the first time, remembered the date with Justin that I had forgotten in all the excitement.

"Don't worry about it," Justin said, when I called to apologize.

"But I am worried," I said. "First, I take you out to dinner and talk your ears off, ignore you at the theater, abandon you in my living room, and then when you're good enough to give me a second chance, I don't even show up. And I didn't even call to explain what happened. Why didn't you call me up and tell me I'm an ungrateful jerk?"

"I knew something important must have happened," Justin said. "You don't give me enough credit."

"I give you a lot of credit."

"More than I deserve, probably." Justin must have tried to move the phone away so I wouldn't hear him sigh, but it was a big one. I could have heard it without the telephone.

"I'm really sorry," I said. "I don't expect you to forgive me."

"There's nothing to forgive," Justin said. For a moment, neither of us said anything.

"I won't blame you if you've decided to give up on me," I said. Another sigh.

"I didn't give up. But remember I said I wanted to talk to you about something important? Well, my ex wants us to give it another try. I wanted to talk it over with you, but—"

"But you couldn't talk to me because I wasn't there," I chimed in.

"No. I realized I had to call this play myself."

"And?"

"I said yes."

Part of me was disappointed, but another part, the honest part, knew that Justin had made the right choice. If he hadn't backed out, I would have, sooner or later. And I would have felt even more guilty than I already did.

"Good luck," I said, and I meant it. "I hope you make it. And I hope we can still be friends."

"Do you mean that?"

"Of course, I do. Why wouldn't I?"

"No reason," Justin said, but I didn't believe him.

"Come on. Why wouldn't I want to be your friend? You're good-looking, smart, a snappy dresser."

"I thought you might think I was rejecting you because you're white," Justin finally admitted.

I started laughing, not because it was funny, but because I had been very stupid, so blind. All the while I had worried about Justin thinking I turned down his offer of a date because I was prejudiced, it had never occurred to me to consider the reverse situation. I had been blinded by my whiteness.

That conversation sprang to mind several days later, when Cornelius Baker and Toshomba Grant got into a name-calling contest during a class discussion. Since neither of them seemed to take the insults to heart, I let them go until Cornelius called Toshomba a "nappy-headed, fat-lipped nigger."

"Time out!" I hollered. "You know the rule. No racial slurs in this classroom. Period."

"Black folks call each other nigger all the time," Cornelius insisted. "It ain't a insult."

"Yes, it is. And it won't be tolerated in this room."

Cornelius and Toshomba, united in their disgust at my ignorance, exchanged knowing looks and shook their heads sadly. I knew they didn't understand. I had tried to explain to them, and to other classes, that I didn't allow black students to call each other nigger because, in a culturally mixed group, it diminished their stature. And I didn't think it was good for their self-esteem, because, unlike stand-up comics like Richard Pryor, who seem to be able to turn the word *nigger* inside out, defuse it, and use it as a tool, I didn't think these kids, with their fragile egos, had the maturity to do that.

Until my discussion with Justin, I hadn't been able to articulate my argument. But after our talk, I had a better understanding of the psychological dynamics involved.

"How many of you kids are black?" I asked the class. Everybody snickered. They rolled their eyes and gave each other the look that said, "Teachers—they're so weird."

"Come on, I'm serious. You know you can't always tell people's ethnic background just by looking at them. And some people are lucky enough to have the best of two or three or four races all in one person. Now, please raise your hand if you consider yourself black or African-American." A few black kids raised their hands; some sat staring at me from beneath half-lowered eyelids, wary of any conversation concerning skin color.

"Thank you. Now. How many of you get mad if somebody nonblack calls you a nigger?" All the hands stayed up, and more than a few faces flinched.

"Thank you. You can put your hands down." They put their hands down, and several put their heads down on their desks, too. I was tempted to stop because I hated to pick at their tender wounds, but I believed I might help them heal, if they'd listen.

"Okay, how many people here are white?" The entire class laughed that time. Nobody raised a hand.

"I'm serious," I insisted. "If you consider yourself white or Caucasian, please raise your hand." About one-third of the students put one hand in the air. Their vanilla hands waved like clots of cream amid a sea of caramel, mocha, coffee, and chocolate faces.

"Now, how many of you get mad if somebody nonwhite calls you a honky?" All of the white hands dropped immediately. Smiles and snickers all around the room this time.

"Why is that? Why don't you get mad if somebody calls you a honky?" The kids shrugged and rolled their eyes, looked at each other sideways, suddenly shy, self-consciously aware of their different skin colors. I folded my arms across my chest and stared at them. "Why?"

"You tell us, Miss J," somebody called out from the back of the room.

I shook my head. "You figure it out," I insisted. "Think about it. Why don't these white people care if somebody calls them a honky?" They thought hard, I could see it, even the ones who didn't want to think about it, but none of them could come up with an answer.

"Come on, Joanie." Joanie Fisher grew up two blocks from Parkmont High. A tall, round, blond girl with green eyes and a contagious smile, Joanie looked like one of the lucky ones, a Brady Bunch girl. At one time, that description might have fit, but Joanie's parents separated during her freshman year and she took advantage of the distraction to sneak out of school and spend her afternoons watching TV talk shows and drinking the contents of the liquor cabinet. After a summer at a rehab camp,

Joanie joined the Academy, where she received rave reviews in the boys' journals. The other girls, black- and brown-skinned brunettes, weren't quite as thrilled with Joanie, but when they found out where she'd spent her summer, they accepted her, happy to hear that she was "damaged goods."

"Wouldn't you feel a little bit bad if one of the girls in class called you a honky?" I asked Joanie.

She shook her head.

"Wouldn't you be a little bit mad?"

No, she wouldn't, she insisted.

"But why not?" I pressed for an answer.

"Because it doesn't mean anything," Joanie blurted.

"Oh, yes, it does. It's an insult to your ethnic heritage."

"But it doesn't really mean nothing," said skinny Sean Collins, who always sat near Joanie in the vain hope that she might notice him.

"Why not?" I demanded.

"Because who cares what they say anyway?" Sean said, shrugging off my question as pointless. The palest boy in class, Sean tried hard to sound like his darker classmates. He imitated their walk, their talk, their syntax. "It just don't mean nothing, that's all," Sean said. "Who cares?"

A few mental lightbulbs lit around the classroom, but more than a few frowns grew deeper as the kids considered Sean's response. Cornelius Baker snorted and turned toward the wall, his back to the rest of the class.

"So, you're saying that people can't insult you unless you care about what they think of you?"

Sean shrugged again. "Something like that."

"If people aren't white, you don't care what they think? Is that right?" I looked at Sean, at Joanie, at the other white kids. They stared straight ahead, frozen in place, willing me to shut up or change the subject.

"Is that right, Sean? You don't care what nonwhite people

think about you?" Sean nodded and sneaked a guilty glance at the black girl sitting on his right. She was staring at him hard, as though she'd never seen him before.

"See that quote up there?" I pointed to one of the several hand-printed posters I had tacked on the walls of my classroom to encourage reflection among daydreamers. The poster said:

NOBODY CAN MAKE YOU FEEL
INFERIOR WITHOUT YOUR CONSENT.
—ELEANOR ROOSEVELT

"That's exactly what Eleanor Roosevelt meant. If you are black and somebody calls you a nigger, or you're Hispanic and somebody calls you a wetback or some other derogatory name, or if you're a girl and some boy calls you a stupid bitch, or you're gay and somebody calls you a fag—it hurts you or makes you mad because *you believe* that person has the right or the ability to look down at you. But people can't look down at you unless you look *up* at them, unless you respect them. I'm not saying that you should try to change places and put the other person down. I'm saying that you should choose the people you respect. I'm saying that each of us should make sure that we look everybody, every human being of every color, directly in the eye, because we are all people, and we all have a right to our dignity and self-respect. If you do that, and somebody calls you a name, it won't hurt you because it won't mean nothing."

Then I climbed down off my soapbox and taught them how to avoid using double negatives.

Chapter 10

Ain't Going Nowhere

At age fifteen, Cornelius Baker—six foot two, two hundred and twenty pounds and still growing—had been the only sophomore running back on the varsity team. Proud of the athletic honor, Cornelius carried a giant black leather gym bag with him to classes, unlike most students who carried their books in backpacks. Cornelius also carried a gigantic chip on his shoulder. I thought he might lose it as he matured, but the chip seemed to grow right along with him. By the time he reached his senior year, Cornelius stood six foot four, two hundred and sixty pounds, with a boulder on his shoulder that blocked his peripheral vision, leaving him blind to any perspective but his own.

A few days after Rico returned to school, just as I foolishly began to hope that the relative calm indicated a permanent improvement in the attitude and behavior of the Academy students, Cornelius crashed into the classroom and slammed his gym bag into his desk so hard that the desk tipped over.

"Do you have a problem you need to discuss?" I asked Cornelius.

Without looking at me, he shook his head and stalked to the back corner of the room where his friends were huddled in a circle, kneeling on the floor around a pair of playing dice that they believed I couldn't see because of my advanced age and failing eyesight. They weren't gambling, they weren't smoking, they weren't selling or buying drugs, and they weren't hanging around looking for a fight, so I let them think they were getting away with something. It made them happy, and for them happiness was a rare and precious commodity.

Cornelius must have confided in his friends, because I heard several loud comments.

"That's how it always goes. Shit just keeps on happening."

"Same thing happened to Leroy last week."

"Shit, man! I would of killed the bitch."

After the last remark, I called the class to order. The boys in the back sat down, but I could tell their attention was still on Cornelius.

"Are you sure you don't want to share what's bothering you?" I asked Cornelius. "Maybe we can help you."

"*Tsk*," Cornelius clicked his tongue in disgust. "Shee. I don't need nobody to help me."

"Well, maybe it would help somebody else who has the same problem."

"We all got the same problem, Miss J," Toshomba Grant said, "but it ain't gonna go away. It's just like that."

"Like what?"

Toshomba started telling Cornelius's story, but he didn't do the job well enough to suit Cornelius, who soon took over. It seems that the night before, Cornelius and a friend had stopped at the automatic teller machine at the bank in East Palo Alto to get some cash to go to the movies. Cornelius works part-time in an attorney's office in Palo Alto through the Academy work-study program and diligently deposits his paycheck into his college account. Once a week, he allows himself a small withdrawal for entertainment.

"I was standing at the teller, waiting for my cash, when I seen this black-and-white come rolling up the street," Cornelius said.

"I knew they was looking at me because I'm a black man and I'm outside a bank at night, so they think I'm getting ready to rob the place."

The police car sat at the curb while Cornelius withdrew his card, put his cash in his wallet, and returned to his car on the other side of the street. As he opened the door, a female police officer stepped out of the squad car and approached him.

"She axed me what was I doing?" Cornelius said, "and I told her what was she axing me for when she just sat there and watched me getting my money out of the bank. Then she got all hot and said watch how I talk to her, and I told her watch how she talk to me."

So far, I was on his side, but I didn't comment. I wanted to let Cornelius spit out the whole story instead of walking around chewing on it and getting indigestion.

"Then I told her she didn't have no business stopping me because I didn't do nothing, and I started to get in the car so me and my friend could leave, but she said wait a minute, she was going to write me a ticket. I said, 'What for?' and she said, 'Your tires are bald.'"

"That's some shit!" one of the boys hollered. "How could she see your tires in the dark?"

"That's exactly what I told her," Cornelius said, "and she told me to stop arguing and disrespecting her and give her my license, and I told her to go fuck herself."

From there, the situation went decidedly downhill, but after it hit bottom, it took a surprising upturn. The woman cited Cornelius for cursing at her, for refusing to hand over his license, and for having bald tires. When she handed him the citation, he ripped it up. She reached for her nightstick, but Cornelius beat her to it. During the shouting match, she had called for reinforcements, and the police captain happened to be in the neighborhood and answered the call to find Cornelius and the woman wrestling over her baton.

"I explained what happened, and the man told me she was wrong and I didn't have to pay no tickets or go to jail or nothing," Cornelius said. The class broke out in cheers. When they settled down, Cornelius added, "He gave me a form to fill out to make a complaint, too."

"Did you fill it out?" I asked. Cornelius shook his head. "Why not? The man is trying to help you."

"No, he wasn't," Cornelius said. "He just didn't want me to kill that stupid bitch pig."

"Watch it," I warned. "I know you're very angry, but you know the rule." Racial, religious, or sexual put-downs were never tolerated in my classroom.

"Sorry," Cornelius said. "He didn't want me to kill that stupid cop."

"Why is it so hard for you to believe that somebody could want to help you?" I asked. "The man didn't have to give you that form. Isn't it possible that he might be a good person even if he is white?"

Cornelius shrugged and had the good grace to blush, although it was hard to tell because his skin is such a deep brown that it looks purple in the fluorescent lights of the schoolroom. I knew he was remembering the day I had gone looking for him, the day he had stood up the personnel director of Kaiser Hospital who was waiting to interview Cornelius for a ten-dollar-an-hour job after school.

When Jim Bergie, the Academy computer teacher who was in charge of our work-study program, informed Don Woodford, Jean Warner, and me that several students had stood up their interviewers, Don, who was normally the most even-tempered one in the group, slammed his gradebook down on the top of the student desk where he was sitting.

"Gosh darn it!" Don said. "We already went through this with Raul and Gusmaro and that whole bunch. I thought we filled in all the cracks in our plan this year."

✿

Raul had been the star candidate from the first class to participate in the mock interviews conducted by the Academy teachers, but the day after we finished our unit on preparing for
interviews, Raul was absent. Three days later, on the date of the
"real" interviews with personnel managers from various local
businesses, Raul was still missing. Since he rarely missed school
and always called me to let me know why—he had to go to the
DMV with his mother and translate, his dad had a big landscaping job and insisted on Raul's help—I was concerned. I called
Raul, but he assured me that he was fine and would be back
soon.

"He'd be real pissed if he knew I told you," Gusmaro said
when I insisted that he tell me why Raul was skipping. I assured
him that nobody would ever know what he told me.

"Well, you know how you told us about getting ready for those
job interviews and stuff? And how we gotta have good hygiene
and wear clean clothes every day so we don't stink up the room."
I nodded, although I was certain that I had phrased it a little
differently.

"Well, Raul only gots a couple shirts and two pairs of jeans,
and a lot of people live at his house, uncles and aunts and stuff."

"How many people?"

"Seventeen," Gusmaro said. "And they only got one bathroom. So sometimes Raul don't get to use the shower before
school. That's why he been absent lately. If he don't get to take a
shower, he stays home so people won't think he stinks and call
him a dirty Mexican and all that."

If Gusmaro hadn't been standing in front of me, waiting for
my response, I would have burst into tears. How stupid and insensitive of me to have assumed that every child has access to a
bathroom. During the next week, I made a point of discussing
alternative strategies with all of my classes. If they didn't have

time to bathe at home, I suggested that they report for their interview early and ask the receptionist to direct them to the restroom where they could wash up. At school, they could use the showers at the gym or the private bathroom near the nurse's office. I vowed that I would take special care not to assume anything in the future.

A few months later, I forgot my vow and assumed that Raul and Gusmaro were ready for real job interviews. As part of our community interaction program, local businesses agree to hire Academy students at the end of their junior year. By then, all of the students have had two full years of computer applications such as word processing and spreadsheets, in addition to the standard high school curriculum.

Most of the kids jumped at the chance to work at law firms and computer companies instead of fast-food restaurants, but Raul and his posse held out. They all worked together in one of the dining halls at Stanford University, busing tables and washing dishes. The hours were long, and toting dish-laden trays was exhausting, but they were willing to do any amount of dirty work as long as they could work together. I didn't realize just how important their togetherness was until I tried to talk Gusmaro and Raul into taking an interview with Sun Microsystems. Sun was the first company to offer a summer job opportunity, and when the personnel manager called to invite two of our students to interview, I was ecstatic. I assured her that two ace students would report to her the following day and hurried to intercept Raul and Gusmaro who were standing by the door, ready to bolt at the sound of the bell.

"*Señores,*" I said, placing one hand on each of their shoulders. "Please step into my office. I have good news."

"Is it short news?" Raul asked, as they followed me into my office. "I gotta get some lunch so my stomach don't make noise all day and everybody thinks I'm farting or something."

"Short and sweet," I promised. "You both have interviews at

Sun Microsystems tomorrow afternoon, three P.M. sharp." Neither boy moved, except to shift his eyes sideways to check the other's reaction.

"What's the problem?" I asked. "Need a ride? No problem. I'll drive you."

Raul stuck the tip of his tongue between his front teeth and inhaled slowly. Gusmaro rubbed his chin, a habit he had recently acquired, along with a feathery mustache and a few tentative whiskers. Gusmaro shrugged. "How much does that job pay?"

"Five fifty an hour to start," I said.

"We make five seventy-five now," Gusmaro said and turned to leave.

"But you'll get a raise, I'm sure."

"Yeah. but we woulda probably had a bigger raise at Wilbur Hall before then," Gusmaro argued. Raul nodded.

"But you'll still be washing dishes." I forced myself to project a calmness I did not feel. "This other job is a chance for you guys to get into a really big company, with good benefits and a chance to move up into better jobs later on. Maybe even work full-time after graduation. It's a real opportunity."

"Maybe," Raul said, "but we're making more money now."

"If you get the job, I'll pay you the difference. I'll pay both of you." I could feel the color burning up the back of my neck. "You give me your pay slips and I'll pay you fifty cents for every hour you work to make up the difference until you get a raise."

Gusmaro laughed. "You're crazy, Miss J. Besides, we know teachers be poor."

"Yeah." Raul pointed out the window. "Look at that old junky car you gotta drive." I never could convince them that a twenty-year-old Fiat was a valuable collector's item. "And I seen them little bitty lunches you be eating every day. Carrots and apples and shit like that."

Gusmaro moved sideways, closer to Raul, and shook his head.

"We can't take your money." He stuck his hands into the back pockets of his jeans. Raul mimicked the move.

"Come on, guys," I said.

"Can we think about it for a couple days?" Raul asked.

"Sorry. They're interviewing tomorrow."

Both boys moved back, a step closer to the door.

"Well," Gusmaro said, "maybe you could send some other guys who don't already got jobs." He turned away, then turned back. "Thanks anyway, though."

"Yeah," Raul said, clearly relieved that the issue was settled and lunch was imminent. "Check you later, Miss J."

They turned to leave, but I sidestepped them and stood in the doorway, one hand on each side of the door frame, blocking their exit.

"What if I get them to raise to salary?" I asked. The accountants at Sun would think I was crazy, but I thought they might agree to let me pay the additional fifty cents per hour.

"Aw, I don't know, Miss J. Let us think about it."

"Think about it now. I need to send two kids for interviews tomorrow."

Gusmaro traced a pattern on the tile floor with the toe of his sneaker. Raul stared straight ahead, his eyes glazed, looking at nothing, waiting for this torture to end. I wanted to scream: THIS IS YOUR CHANCE TO MOVE OUT OF YOUR POVERTY-STRICKEN NEIGHBORHOOD, TO LEAVE THE VIOLENCE AND DRUGS AND GANGS BEHIND, TO MAKE A DECENT LIFE. DON'T BE SUCH FOOLS!!!

But I didn't scream. I couldn't insult their families who worked hard to buy their ramshackle houses in the only neighborhood they could afford to live in. I thought about threatening to flunk them if they didn't take the interviews, but Gusmaro was just stubborn enough to take the F, and Raul had so many F's already on his transcript from his freshman year that one more wouldn't make much difference.

Finally it dawned on me that it might not be simple stubborn-ness. I moved one foot forward and bumped the toe of Gus-maro's sneaker. "What's the real problem?" I asked softly.

Gusmaro looked up, only for a split second, but I saw the fear in his eyes before he forced it down. He shrugged. "I kinda like working with my homies. You know we hang together, look out for each other's back. And everybody at Wilbur is Mexican, ex-cept Emilio, but he's cool."

"It's probably fun to work with your friends," I said.

"Yeah," Gusmaro said, warming up. "Nobody gets on us for speaking Spanish, and we don't gotta wear all them fancy clothes and stuff."

"But you aren't going to marry your friends, are you?" I asked. "Shouldn't you start thinking about making your own life for your own family someday? What kind of future do you have at Wilbur?"

Gusmaro stepped back, out of my reach, and gave me a look. "My friends will always be my friends. We hang together. Be-sides, we get raises all the time."

"There are other factors to consider besides money," I said. "Do you want to wash dishes all your life? And where do you go from there? There isn't anyplace to move up. You could be the head dishwasher. But I don't care how well you wash dishes, you're going to hit the pay ceiling soon. They are never going to pay you fifteen dollars an hour to wash dishes."

I dropped my hands and moved out of their way. Relieved, they started past me.

"Every other day you decide you don't want to go to college, so I'm trying to give you a chance for a job and a future you can be proud of. Something you might like to do for twenty or thirty years. So I won't have to worry about you being able to take care of your wives and children."

Raul kept walking, but Gusmaro stopped dead. I knew he had cut my class one day the previous week to take his girlfriend to the clinic for a pregnancy test. It was a false alarm, but it had made him much more conscious of the future looming in his face.

"Come on," I urged him. "I'll drive you there. I'll go in with you. I'll hold your hand and give you moral support. Do it for me, please. I'm an old woman. This may be my last wish."

Gusmaro rolled his eyes to the ceiling and sighed. From outside the doorway, Raul shook his head, but he was smiling.

"You don't play fair, Miss J," Raul said.

"I'm old," I said. "This is killing me."

"All right," Gusmaro said, "we'll go."

They turned down my offer to drive them to the interview but promised to let me know every detail. The following day, when I asked them about it, both pleaded previous engagements and raced from the room. A few minutes later, I found out why. The personnel manager called to ask me whether I had accidentally written down the wrong time and date for the interviews. Raul and Gusmaro had never arrived.

"We did so go," Raul insisted, when I tracked them down and cornered them outside the boys' locker room.

"Then why did that woman tell me you didn't go? Do you think she's lying?"

"Well, we went in the building, but then we left."

"Why?"

"They had all these fancy leather furnitures and expensive-looking paintings hanging all over the place," Raul explained.

"Yeah," Gusmaro said, "and the floor was real shiny and it was real, real quiet like a church or something. And everybody was wearing them three-pieced suits that cost a million dollars or something. There wasn't no Mexicans in there. Even the janitors was white guys. We figured Mexicans probably aren't even allowed to go in there or something. And we was just standing there looking around and the receptionist looked at us hard and asked could she help us, so we just left and went home."

✿

Raul and Gusmaro weren't the only ones who were too scared to venture past the receptionists at their interview sites. So we altered our program and addressed all their concerns to ensure that our next class, Cornelius Baker's class, wouldn't have the same problems. Confident that we had covered every possible problem, I was furious when I found out that Cornelius had stood up his interviewer. I couldn't imagine that he'd have a reasonable explanation, but I was determined to hear his unreasonable one.

Cornelius played quarterback for the Parkmont Panthers, so there was no escape for him. I waited until the end of football practice and cornered him behind the bleachers. Jogging across the field, he had pulled off his helmet and had his jersey halfway over his head when I grabbed the sleeves and hung on while he struggled to get his head free. He looked angry, until he saw who it was, then his expression turned sheepish.

"Hey, Miss J," he said, trying to sound casual. "What's up?"

"Why don't you tell me?"

"Nothin' special," he said, with a too-elaborate shrug.

"I think an interview with the regional manager of Kaiser is something special." Cornelius flopped down onto the cinder track and sat staring across the field. "What is *wrong* with you?" I asked. "Do you know how many people would kill for an interview like that?"

"Yeah," Cornelius whispered. He cleared his throat and raised his voice. "Look, I'm sorry. I just couldn't make it. Something came up." He stood up and started to walk away, his shoulders sagging, his cocky swagger gone.

"I'm sorry, too," I said, as I caught up with him and tried to match his giant's stride. "I'm not mad at you, but you make the whole program look bad when you do something like that. It could hurt somebody else's chance to get a job."

"I said I'm sorry, real sorry."

"What happened? Did you forget? Couldn't you find a ride? What? At least tell me that." Cornelius shrugged and kept walking. I followed him to the locker room door. He glanced at me one more time and started inside.

I stomped my feet and shouted. "Dammit! I am so sick of begging people to give you guys a chance just to have you blow off the whole thing. The least you could do is stand up and take your lumps like a man."

Cornelius turned around very slowly. "I went," he said, so softly that I barely heard him. "I just didn't go in."

"What happened?" He shrugged again.

I sighed and turned away. I was exhausted. It was just too difficult. "I give up. We bust our butts to give you kids interviews, and you don't even have the decency to go or the common courtesy to call and apologize."

"I said I went," Cornelius repeated. "But I didn't go in. I just kind of walked past the office and checked out the dude I was supposed to talk to."

"You were there and you didn't take the interview?" It made no sense to me at all.

"He was just sitting there at this big desk in his suit and his fancy tie. And he was wh—" He cut himself off.

"He was what?" I asked.

Cornelius shrugged.

"Say it. I won't laugh. Word of honor."

"He was this old white guy. I've seen a million guys like him. They look at me, and I know what they're thinking. He wouldn't hire me in a million years."

"Because you're black?" I asked. "Is that what you mean?"

"Yeah, that's exactly what I mean. And it's true."

"Well, you're wrong this time, Mr. Baker," I said. "That old white man specifically requested students from East Palo Alto for this job. He expected you to be African-American or Hispanic or Tongan—somebody with beautiful brown skin."

Cornelius tried, but he couldn't hold back the tiniest of smiles.

"You realize what you did?" I asked.

"Yeah. I messed up big time."

"You were prejudiced."

Cornelius stared at me, eyes wide, mouth open.

"You didn't even give that man a chance—just because he was white. And I know I've heard you ragging on other people about being prejudiced. Now you know how the other side feels."

Cornelius's eyebrows shot up. This was a novel idea for him.

"You call that man. Make up some excuse. Tell him you had to eat dinner at the White House or sign up for the Super Bowl or something. Tell him anything. Then tell him you're sorry and ask for another interview. Give him a chance. There are two or three nice white people in this world." I glared at him. "But I'm not one of them. I'd just as soon kick your butt as look at you."

Cornelius actually smiled at me then, the first real smile I'd ever earned from him in two years. He went to my office with me and called, but the man had already hired another student. He thanked Cornelius for his consideration and referred him to the office of some local attorneys who were looking for an office clerk. Cornelius got that job.

"It's your dream come true," I teased him when he told me. "Now you can work in an entire office full of white boys in three-piece suits."

"Yeah, well, I figure if they gave me a chance," Cornelius said, "the least I could do is give them one. But they're only getting one. If they mess up, I'm out of there."

The attorneys passed muster, and Cornelius impressed them so much that they rehired him during his senior year and helped him set up an investment fund for college. That's the reason he had such a healthy bank account, and had an automatic teller card, and had been at the bank on the night of the incident with the female police officer.

The other kids might not have missed the irony of the situation, but I knew that Cornelius was thinking about it. If it wasn't for the white men who had hired him and helped him, he wouldn't have been there for the white police officer to harass. He knew it was a cop-out to chalk it up to prejudice alone. Stupidity is an equal opportunity attribute, and nobody knows that better than Cornelius Baker.

"You guys are right to complain," I told Cornelius, "but whining and moaning won't change anything. You have to take legal action. You have to file a complaint every time somebody discriminates against you because of your skin color. It's the only way you'll make it stop."

"But it won't stop, Miss J," Toshomba said. He was perched on the back of his chair, feet on the seat, elbows on his knees, chin in his hands. His posture portrayed his hopelessness better than any words could.

"It's always been this way for black men," Toshomba said. "Always gonna be this way."

Justin Bernard had said the same thing one day when we were talking in the teachers' lounge after school and the conversational ball happened to bounce onto the color court. A native of Georgia, Justin had left the South after high school graduation and never returned.

"I thought I could get away from the whole thing if I came out to California," Justin had told me. "And I did, for the most part. But every now and then something happens to remind me that race prejudice is still there, alive and kicking butt. You can fight it, but you'll never get rid of it. It ain't going nowhere."

Justin then told me about the time he and a lady friend had been enjoying a walk along the bay after eating brunch at an upscale restaurant in Tiburon, a ritzy little village north of San

Francisco that caters to the cappuccino crowd.

"We were walking down the street, talking, when all of a sudden these two white cops jump in front of us and say to my date, 'Is this person harassing you?' I was speechless, but they weren't interested in what I had to say, anyway. My date told them politely that she was fine, that we were on a date, but they still stood there, one on each side of me, hands on their pistol grips, like they might have to rescue this white woman at gunpoint. And I knew if they did shoot me, even if she told the truth, people would think I somehow deserved to be shot. For having the audacity to eat an omelet for breakfast instead of chitlins and grits."

At that moment, listening to Justin's story, I was so thoroughly ashamed of being white that I couldn't think of a single thing to say. I just took Justin's hand and held it. I would have liked to hold Cornelius's hand, but I knew he wouldn't let me. He had never said anything outright, but his message was clear: Stand back, white woman.

"I know there will always be stupid, mean people in the world," I told Cornelius's class, "but there are a few good people out there. And you have to let them know what's going on. If Cornelius files a complaint today, and Toshomba files one tomorrow, and Leroy files one the next day, then somebody will notice."

"Yeah," Leroy said. "They'll notice, and they'll pay us back for telling on them."

"Then you file another complaint and another one. And if nothing happens, you get a lawyer and you sue the police force as a group. You file a civil liberties class-action lawsuit. If you can prove that the police ignored your valid complaints, you'll have a good case. And it's the captain who will take the heat. That's why you should trust him. If he gave you a complaint form to fill out, he's not going to ignore it. But if you don't fill it out, he can't take any action against that policewoman."

They didn't believe me, I could tell. And I didn't blame them. They could very well be right. So far, following the rules hadn't done them much good when it came to dealing with the world. Malcolm X may have been murdered, but so had Reverend Martin Luther King, Jr.

That day, after school, I stopped by Justin's classroom. I thought maybe he could give me some realistic advice to pass on to my students. Justin was busy straightening up, but he waved me in and I sat up on the ledge under the windows so I'd be out of his way. I told Justin about Cornelius and the other kids and how frustrated I was at my inability to convince them to use the legal system to fight the prejudice they encountered.

"Do you think I'm too idealistic?" I asked Justin. "Am I wrong to tell the black and Hispanic kids to file complaints? If I don't tell them to file a complaint, what should I tell them? Go shoot a cop? That's what Cornelius thinks they should do."

Justin's back was to me when he answered. "Tell them to get over it."

Surprised at the bitterness in his voice, I fell silent. Justin finished erasing the chalkboards, realigned the desks into neat rows, picked up the crumpled papers that had missed their mark and were lying on the floor near the trash can.

"Come on," he said. "Let's get a cup of coffee. I want to tell you a story."

Justin sketched in the background for me as we drove to a coffee shop in the shopping center just up the hill from the school. He and his friend Jack, a senior vice president at Xerox Corporation, had decided to take a trip home to Atlanta the previous summer to visit their folks and spend the last few weeks of summer getting in as many rounds of golf as possible on the beautiful courses in North Carolina.

"Jack is even bigger than I am," Justin said, as he ducked to enter the door of the coffee shop, "and it's a long drive from San Francisco to Atlanta, so he rented a big fat Cadillac for the trip.

Jack has more money than he knows what to do with, so it wasn't a big deal. We threw the clubs in the back and took off. We stopped in Palm Springs and played one round. I shot an eighty-nine and beat Jack by two strokes, so we were feeling cocky enough to get through Texas without sweating.

"Then we were getting close to home country, and we decided to take I-55 down to Jackson and hook up with 20 straight into Atlanta from the west," Justin said. "That was our first mistake. Our second mistake was stopping outside Pickens to stretch our legs. As soon as we cleared the exit ramp, the sheriff pulled us over."

"Speed trap?" I asked.

"Nope. Nigger trap. The cop looked like a cartoon character, big red nose, blubber belly, cigar stub in his teeth. And his name tag actually said Bubba Bodine. Sheriff Bubba Bodine. I started laughing, but Jack hit me upside the head so I shut up." Justin didn't open his mouth again until the sheriff asked them both to step outside the car and present their driver's licenses.

"I asked him why he needed mine since I was a passenger," Justin said. "Sheriff Bubba took the cigar out of his mouth, spit in the dust, and said, 'Boy, you ain't in California now. You're in Mississippi, and you do like I tell you unless you want to stay here permanent.' "

Bubba took both licenses, then asked them to open the trunk of their car. Bubba pulled out Jack's clubs, a personalized set with mahogany hand grips, took a good long look, and spat again.

"What you doing with these here clubs, boy?" he asked Jack.

"We're going to play some golf back home in Atlanta," Jack said.

"Is that right? I ain't never seen a nigger play golf. You boys sure you didn't steal these clubs?" Neither Jack nor Justin responded. The sheriff shoved the clubs back in and slammed the trunk. He looked them both up and down, once, twice, three times, then said, "I bet you boys date white women, too."

"I tried to keep my mouth shut," Justin said, "but I couldn't help it. I told him if he had a legal reason to pull us over, then I wanted to hear it. Otherwise, we were tired of wasting our time. The next thing I knew our butts were in the back of the patrol car on our way to jail. I couldn't believe it. We spent the night in there with that fat ass sleeping at his desk the whole time. Didn't want to risk leaving two such suspicious characters unguarded overnight. We might have sneaked out and played golf or something."

"I would have lost it and hit the jerk," I said. Justin nodded and stirred his coffee, which he hadn't even tasted. He just talked and stirred, mesmerized by the spoon swirling the deep brown liquid around and around in its cracked white china cup.

"I can't tell you how close I came to killing that man with my bare hands," Justin said. "But Jack told me if we made any kind of move that could be construed as threatening, even verbally, we'd be dead. Literally. I said I couldn't believe it. I said it was the 1980s, for God's sake, in the U.S.A. Jack told me to wake up and look around. He said, 'You see this cell where you're sitting right now? Well, that's where you live, whether you realize it or not. Black men are not free in this country or any other. You hand over your wallet and watch your back and you might live a little longer, but you will never be free. If you think you're a free man, you'd best get over it.'"

Justin rubbed the back of his hand across his forehead, then looked at me with the same stony stare I'd seen so many times in so many young faces in my classroom. "I got over it," he said. "Cornelius will, too, if he lives long enough."

I started to cry. Justin immediately reached across the booth and put his hands on my shoulders. "Hey, I'm sorry. I didn't mean to make you feel bad."

"I don't feel bad. I'm so mad I could spit, and there's nothing

I can do to change things and that makes me even madder. There's no place for the feelings to go, so I cry. I hate it when it happens, but I've always been like this."

"You can't let them get to you. If they make you mad, they own you." Justin squeezed my shoulders and gave me a little shake to emphasize his point.

In class the following day, I told Cornelius what Justin said about people owning you if they can anger you. I didn't tell him about Justin's experience with Sheriff Bodine, but I did tell him Justin's advice: Get over it.

"I don't want to get over it," Cornelius said. "Why do I have to get over it when it shouldn't happen in the first place?"

I had no answer. I asked the class if they had any suggestions. They decided that there is no way to deal with such anger. It can't be helped and it can't be avoided.

"You just have to build yourself up real strong inside," Toshomba said, "and stay strong so they can't get to you."

"I'm strong, but not that strong," Tyeisha Love said. "I don't even think you can be that strong."

"That's why you gotta join a gang," somebody in the back of the room said.

"Who said that?" I asked.

Leroy raised his hand. "I did. People be thinking we hanging out together looking for trouble when we just trying to make sure we got a witness when the cops come down on us."

"Yeah," Cornelius said. "Like you ain't alone."

These were not neglected children talking about joining gangs. Cornelius and Leroy and Toshomba all had mothers and fathers who were educated, employed, and dedicated to raising healthy, decent children. But these kids, girls included, seemed to think that gangs were a viable solution to their problems, which made me question all the newspaper and magazine articles I'd read that attribute gang activity to the breakdown of the family unit among minorities in America.

These kids didn't have broken families. Their parents and grandparents loved them dearly. But their families aren't there to argue when, in a hundred small ways, the world tells nonwhite kids that they are not normal, not okay, not entitled to feel proud or free to walk among society as bona fide members. They don't belong, they aren't welcome, and they know it. So they create a society where they do belong.

"I got a question for you." Cornelius interrupted my speculation. "I got a cousin who goes to Stanford, and he was telling me all about the fraternities and parties and shit. And we was talking about gang rape and date rape and how it be happening all over, and most of the time it's them fraternities that be doing that shit. So how come the police and everybody don't be freaking about those fraternities of white boys? They just like gangs. Bunch of dudes wear the same haircut and jacket and T-shirts with their tag on them, and they hang out and get drunk and rape girls. Cops don't dog them all day. But they be down on me and my friends because we hang out on the street, wearing our colors, just chillin'. We drink some beer, but we don't do drugs, and we don't sell drugs, and we don't kill nobody, and we sure don't be raping no women. How come they be all over us, when we're just making our own street fraternity?"

I didn't have an answer, but Tyeisha Love had a question.

"How come you can't just be your own man?" she wanted to know. "Why you got to join one of those gangs, anyway? You don't see me doing that."

"You're a cheerleader," Leroy said. "That's a gang."

"Maybe he's got something there," I said.

"You think cheerleaders are a gang?" Tyeisha asked. Both her eyes and her mouth formed big round O's.

On the chalkboard, I wrote: MASLOW'S HIERARCHY OF NEEDS. Beneath that I wrote the needs, in descending order—aesthetic, desire to know and understand, self-actualization, self-esteem, belongingness and love, safety, physiological.

"Abraham Maslow was a psychologist who studied human nature and came up with the list of needs that he thinks people have to fulfill in order to be happy. We all start at the bottom and work our way to the top. Some of us get there." Most of the kids sighed and stopped listening, but a few sat up straighter, so I kept going. One listener is enough sometimes.

"First you have to fulfill your physiological needs—like having food and water," I said. "If you're starving to death, for example, you don't worry about whether you're wearing cool shoes." A few kids looked up.

"If you have food and water, then the next thing you need is safety. If you have to spend all your time worrying and hiding so you won't get eaten by tigers or stomped by elephants, then you probably don't have time to worry about whether you did your homework." A few more kids looked up. Some laughed. Simoa Mariposa tossed her head, sending a shimmering black whip of hair over her shoulder.

"That's why I don't do my homework, Miss J," Simoa said. "I'm always hiding from my father so he won't stomp on me."

I made a mental note to talk to Simoa after class.

"After you have food and water and shelter and safety, then you start to look around and see what's up. That's when you get interested in the other people and whether they like you or not. Just like animals, people need to hang around with a herd or a flock, even if it's a little bitty herd or flock. Think about it. You know how bad it feels when you think nobody likes you? And how good it feels when they do?"

Lots of heads nodded, and the ones that didn't acknowledged what I was saying with their eyes.

"How many of us spend time with people we don't really like, or do things we don't really want to do, sometimes things we know are wrong—and we say to ourselves, I'm not going to do that again. Tomorrow I'm going to cut loose and hang by myself. And then we turn right around and go with those people we don't really like, who don't really like us, and we do things we don't really want to do. And we hate ourselves?"

Tyeisha waved her hand in the air. "That's me. I'm always going shopping with my sister and her friends, and they always steal stuff from stores and I say I'm not going to go with them, but I go with them anyway and I always wish I didn't. And the next day I do it again."

"That's because we all need to belong to something," I said. "It's human nature. We need to belong to something and feel appreciated for who we are. Some people get that from their families—but lots of us don't. How many people have a family, people who love you, but you don't feel like you really belong?" Quite a few hands flew into the air.

"You aren't the Lone Ranger. Lots of people feel left out from their families. But we're human and we have to belong to something. So you need to find something to belong to—a sports team, a hobby club, a karate studio, a church, a garage band, maybe even just two or three people you eat lunch with every day. But if you don't find something good to belong to, then you're a target for those negative groups, the gangs that are into vandalism and violence and drugs, or friends who aren't really friends and try to get you to do things you don't really want to do. So find something to join, even if you have to make it up yourself with a couple of friends. Otherwise, you'll never move up that ladder to happiness."

Cornelius leaned toward the boy sitting next to him and muttered, "I guess cops are happy. They got a great big group of dickheads to belong to."

I would have liked to hug Cornelius, to soothe at least one little smidgen of the hurt, but Cornelius would never allow me to hug him. He cringed whenever I approached him and stood fidgeting until I moved out of his personal safety zone. I tried not to take Cornelius's distrust of me personally. I knew that he wouldn't have let me hug him even if I weren't white; he wasn't the hugging type. He had worked himself into a frenzy on the few occasions when I had offered to shake his hand in recognition of his academic or athletic achievements. Hugging Cornelius was out of the question. So was forgiveness, as far as he was concerned.

He raved and pouted over the bald tire incident for two weeks, unable to come to terms with the unfairness of it all. He repeated his story over and over again, and many of the kids listened over and over again. But at least he got it out of his system, shouted it out, and got my attention, which he seemed to value more than my advice.

Looking back, I wonder whether Simoa Mariposa tried to get my attention, too, whether Cornelius and Rico outshouted her, or whether she simply slipped out of sight so quietly that I didn't even notice she was slipping until it was too late. And I wonder whether that's what happened to the other girls in the back of the class, the original Academy girls who had disappeared somewhere between their sophomore year and graduation. I wonder whether they believed they were less important than the boys, whether they simply accepted the pain in their lives with less protest. Or did I pay less attention to their protests?

Chapter 11

That'll Teach Me to Think

I like to believe that I would have heard Simoa ask for help, even if she whispered. But now I wonder whether that is what she did, whisper; whether that's what girls do, whisper while the boys shout; whether the girls whisper because they don't really want to be saved from themselves.

Boys drop out because they want to work, or because they can't tolerate taking orders anymore, or because they refuse to develop the self-control necessary to restrain themselves from smacking anybody who makes them mad, or because they are in a hurry to begin their careers as criminals. When they drop out, boys usually end up on the street or in jail, and they know this, so they make a lot of noise on their way out in the hopes that we will stop them. They create disturbances that can't be ignored: They get drunk and breathe in the principal's face, they beat each other senseless, they walk around with pistols in their pockets, they threaten to kill their teachers. They get our attention, and sometimes their subconscious plan works and we stop them.

Girls, on the other hand, usually leave school in search of True Love, or because they believe they have found it. They are seduced by sex into thinking that the happy ending is within reach, if only they didn't have to waste their time being educated. So they get pregnant and quit school, or quit school and get pregnant, or become so pregnant with their delusions that they quit school. Girls leave more quickly, and much more quietly than the boys do. Girls wring their hands in quiet desperation for a few weeks, then disappear.

Maybe this is just my perception, my rationalization for why so many girls silently slipped away from me. I don't know. But I do know that I will never quite forgive myself for forgetting to talk to Simoa after class that day when she said she worried about her father "stomping" on her. I still have the slip of paper, the one on which I jotted her name to remind myself to talk to her immediately, but I forgot about it until that night as I changed out of my work clothes and emptied my pockets. When I pulled the crumpled piece of paper out of my pocket and read it, I immediately grabbed the phone. Then I remembered that Simoa didn't have a telephone. If I wanted to talk to her, I'd have to drive to East Palo Alto and hope she was home. But I was in Woodside, in a tiny apartment over the meadow and through the woods, a thirty-minute drive and about as far from East Palo Alto as it is possible to get and still be in California. Tired and hungry, I decided it could wait a few hours. I taped a note to the front of my briefcase so I would see it first thing in the morning on my way to work when my mind was fresh and I would be less likely to forget.

As a pot of pasta was busy noodling water all over the top of my stove, I sat in the living room and read an article in an educational journal that cited several studies indicating that most teachers favor boys over girls in the classroom. Teachers spend more time with boys, the author claimed, and pay more attention to them during lessons.

That's entirely possible, I thought, and probably because girls usually get the message more quickly. A frown, a cough, a whisper is usually enough to convince the girls in class to put away their makeup, stop passing notes, or save the giggles for later. But boys very often view eyebrow raising and throat clearing as encouragement to continue their misbehavior, not as a deterrent. Boys will continue spitting staples at the girls unless the teacher stops the spelling quiz and specifically instructs the spitters to desist. And boys will go on merrily throwing candies at the overhead lights unless the teacher interrupts the reading lesson to remind them that the assignment is to read *The Merchant of Venice,* not to see whether it is possible to hurl a Gummi Bear straight up into the air with enough force to make it stick it to the ceiling tiles.

Teachers smile more at boys, the journal article said, and they call on boys more often to answer questions during class. And they tell girls to be quiet, even though, statistically speaking, girls spend less class time talking. The saddest thing, the article concluded, was that the teachers who favored boys most were the very teachers who took pride in their equal treatment of both genders.

That would be me, I thought. Was I one of those deluded teachers? Did I spend more time and energy on my male students? Was that why I hadn't noticed until graduation day that only five girls from the original Academy class left Parkmont High with their diplomas?

There were good reasons for some of the girls to have left, as Justin so kindly pointed out the night I realized my oversight. Some of them had moved away or transferred to other schools. I didn't question that. My question was: Had I fought as hard to keep the girls as I had to keep the boys? If I hadn't fought for them, why hadn't I?

I remember being especially proud that seventeen of our first twenty-seven Academy graduates were black or Hispanic males, more than the combined count for the rest of the high schools in our district. An admirable accomplishment, certainly. Even more admirable was that most of those boys went on to college, two with full four-year academic scholarships.

Of the five girls in that same graduating class, two were black, none was Hispanic. Nobody had ever mentioned those sad statistics. Sadder still, I don't think anybody, including me, had even kept count. Why hadn't I? After serving nine years in the macho, male United States military, where I witnessed and experienced daily doses of gender bias, from subtle slights intended to undermine my self-confidence to blatant abuse designed to make me give up and go home, why wasn't I more aware of gender bias at my own school, even in my own classroom?

All the water boiled away and my fettuccine glued itself permanently to the bottom of the pot as I pondered the possibility that I had somehow been brainwashed into believing that it was my job as a teacher of at-risk students to save minority males at all cost, to save white males whenever possible, and to let the females—regardless of race—fend for themselves.

As I dined on my emergency rations, tortilla chips and chocolate chip cookies, I drew a grid and wrote the names of the girls in the Academy down the left side. Across the top of the page, I labeled columns for academic progress checks, home visits, in-class conferences, career counseling sessions, and personal entertainment. Then I made a list of recreational and cultural events—plays, movies, concerts, shopping trips, restaurant lunches, nature hikes, horseback riding—and wrote a girl's name beside one event. Of course, I'd continue to take the boys out, too, just as I had always done, but from now on, the girls were at the top of my list and not the bottom.

Simoa Mariposa's name was first. One of the top students in the senior class, Simoa was both brilliant and beautiful, with the golden brown skin, thick black hair, and dramatic facial features of her native Tongan culture. For the first two years in the Academy, Simoa earned special awards each semester for perfect attendance. She was never sick, never cut, never missed a single class. Some students might have been embarrassed by the attendance awards, afraid that they'd be teased for "kissing up" to the teachers, but Simoa could take anything her classmates handed her and give it back double.

High grades and perfect attendance were as far as Simoa cared to go in fitting the stereotype of the ace student. In every other respect, she was a handful and a half, the first one to voice her opinion, the last one to give in during an argument. And Simoa definitely didn't hold her punches.

The day after I made my list, as I was handing out journals for a writing assignment, Simoa and Leroy Baxter both had headed for the same seat in the back corner near the window. Simoa got there first, plopped her books down on the desk, and flashed Leroy a big fat grin. With her hair twisted into an elaborate top-knot that emphasized her graceful neck, two earrings in each ear, and a diamond stud in the side of her nose, Simoa looked like a wooden carving of a tribal queen.

Cornelius Baker, who had scoped the seat next to Simoa's, snapped his gum at Leroy and slapped him on the back. I didn't hear it, but Leroy must have directed Cornelius to perform a particular anatomical function, because the next thing I heard was Simoa admonishing Leroy.

"No effing allowed in school, Leroy honey, and besides, look who you offering to do," Simoa teased Leroy. She jerked her head sideways to indicate Cornelius and shook her head. "You gonna get a bad reputation you going around making offers to get it on with big, ugly football players."

Leroy, caught off guard, stood with his mouth open, staring at Simoa while the students around him, who had overheard Simoa's taunt, repeated it behind cupped hands and exploded into snorts of muffled laughter. Before Leroy had a chance to come up with an appropriate insult, I hushed the other students and hurried them into their seats. As they rummaged in their pockets and backpacks for pens and pencils, I wrote the writing prompt on the chalkboard: You are engaged to be married to the love of your life. A week before the wedding, your fiancé/fiancée is involved in a terrible automobile accident and will now be confined to a wheelchair for the rest of his/her life. What will you do?

"Start writing," I directed the class. Familiar with the procedure for timed responses, they knew they were to begin writing and keep on writing until I called time at the end of five minutes, when I would collect the journals and we would discuss our responses to the question. Everybody started writing except Toshomba Grant, who asked how to spell *paraplegic*. A few seconds later, Joanie Fisher, who was sitting in the seat in front of Simoa, waved her hand. When I stopped at her desk, Joanie whispered, "Can a paraplegic have sex?" Joanie's whisper echoed across the room, where pens and pencils froze, poised above paper.

"That's a question I am not qualified to answer, I'm afraid," I told Joanie, trying to make my voice sound scientific and teacherly. "I'm sure it would depend on the nature and extent of the person's injuries." Joanie glanced around the room at the faces turned her way. Her own face flushed a bright pink.

"I just wondered if we could still have kids is all," Joanie whispered, softer this time, but not softly enough.

"I'm with you," Simoa informed Joanie. "I wouldn't marry no man who couldn't give me kids."

Simoa's reassurance seemed to ease Joanie's embarrassment, until Simoa added, "And I sure wouldn't sleep with no man who couldn't satisfy me. But if he could satisfy me, I wouldn't care if he couldn't move his hairy old legs." Simoa raised her eyebrows and glanced meaningfully at the boys in the class who were all staring at her, some glancing meaningfully back, most with their mouths hanging wide open.

"Simoa!" Tyeisha Love gasped. Tyeisha and Simoa were best friends, in spite of their many differences, or more likely because of them. Tiny but strong-willed, Tyeisha provided the stability and strong moral values that Simoa admired. And vo-

luptuous Simoa thrilled Tyeisha with her sexy, daring flamboy-
ance.

"At least a man with no legs won't go running around on you,"
Simoa informed Tyeisha, who promptly folded her arms and
turned her back in a huff. Tyeisha's hair was plaited into sixty or
seventy tiny braids, half with bright red wooden beads and half
with a tiny silver bells at the ends. As she whirled around, her
hair tinkled musically.

"Well, it's the truth." Simoa nodded her head sharply, stamp-
ing her seal on the subject, and resumed her writing.

If I hadn't been so flabbergasted by Simoa's comments, and
her precociousness, I would have stopped the discussion sooner,
but I was temporarily struck dumb, like most of the students in
class.

Cornelius Baker recovered first. He rolled his eyes at Simoa
and said, "Girl, how you gonna have sex with some dude can't
move his legs?"

Simoa rolled her eyes back at Cornelius and said, "I guess I'd
just have to do all the work then, wouldn't I?"

I recovered at that point and threatened two hours of after-
school detention for the next person who interrupted the writing
session. After the five minutes elapsed, I collected the journals
and pretended to have just remembered an important vocabulary assignment that had to be done immediately. I wasn't about
to attempt any further class discussion on the morning's writing
topic. And, after a moment's reflection, I deleted the topic from
the list of writing prompts.

When the bell rang, I asked Simoa to stay behind for a minute. She sighed loudly and collected her books. As she neared
my desk, I noticed that the area around one of her eyes was
much darker than the other side of her face. When she noticed
me looking at her eye, Simoa said, "I'm okay. Me and my cousin
got into it yesterday, but everything's all right now."

"Have you seen a doctor?" I asked.

"What for?" Simoa laughed. "It's just a little bump. You can't hardly notice it anyway." I had no reason to suspect Simoa's excuse, except that she had offered it before I asked.

"I'd like you to see the nurse, just to be on the safe side," I said. I fished in my desk for a pass.

She sighed again and shook her head. "I'm fine, Miss J. Honest. Just fine."

"I wouldn't bug you about it if I didn't care about you, Simoa," I said, as I filled out the form. "But you're special. You've got it all—brains, beauty, wit, creativity. You have a real future. And you're the only student who never cuts my class. Maybe you're the only one who truly appreciates me. I have to take extra good care of you."

Even Simoa couldn't resist that much flattery.

"Okay, I'll go to the nurse." She took the pass. As she started to step out of the room, Tyeisha Love stepped forward from her hiding place beside the bookshelf in the back of the classroom. Tyeisha and Simoa always walked to classes together, but I had assumed that Tyeisha was waiting outside while I talked to Simoa.

"I appreciate you just as much as Simoa does, you know," Tyeisha said as she stomped toward my desk. At first, I thought anger prompted her stomping, but as she neared my desk, I realized that Tyeisha's shoes, which were exactly the same shade of red as the beads in her braids and the stripes in her red-and-white tunic, had little bells knotted along their white shoestrings, and she was stepping down hard to make her shoe bells tinkle.

"You know Simoa doesn't come to school because she wants to," Tyeisha said as she reached my desk and stood next to Simoa. "She just comes so her daddy won't beat her stupid ass for cutting. That's how come she gets all those awards for attendance." She tilted her head and batted her eyelashes at

Simoa, who caught the comment in midair and snapped it back. "No wonder you got brown eyes, girl," Simoa said. "You so full of shit." She grabbed her pass and stalked out of the room. "She was kidding, wasn't she?" I asked Tyeisha. "She's not really mad at you?"

"I never know when she's playing," Tyeisha admitted. "I'll find out later, though."

For a few seconds, I considered having with Tyeisha the discussion about sexual abstinence that I had planned to have with Simoa, in the hopes that Cornelius would relay the message, but decided it against it in the hope that Tyeisha wasn't as experienced as her friend. No sense adding any ideas to her repertoire. With Simoa for a friend, I figured that Tyeisha probably had more than enough ideas to keep her occupied until well after she was twenty-one.

"Do you got a minute, Miss J?" Tyeisha asked me, as I was mentally debating the discussion.

"I always have a minute for you," I said. The last time Tyeisha had asked for a minute had been several months earlier when she wanted to know what I thought about the idea of her quitting school so she could work full time as a Jehovah's Witness. Fortunately, I had had managed to hide my dismay and help her make a list of pros and cons so she could decide for herself. At the end of our talk, I couldn't resist a little bit of emotional manipulation, though.

"I respect your right to choose your own life," I had told Tyeisha, "but I love you and I will miss you so much I'll probably cry every time I see your empty seat."

Tyeisha had decided to finish school so she could earn more money for her church and was considering attending college so she could earn even more. I assumed that she wanted to talk to me about her church, which is another reason that I decided not to discuss sex with her unless she asked me to. As long as she remained enchanted with her church and its rigid rules, there was little danger of her becoming an unwed mother or any other teenage statistic.

"What did you want to talk to me about?" I asked Tyeisha. We only had a minute left before the next class would start arriving, and then personal conversation would be impossible.

"I was just wondering can people catch being an alcoholic," Tyeisha said.

"Alcoholism is a disease. but not the kind you can catch from somebody else like a cold."

"I know that. But in safety ed we had this guest speaker who was a doctor, and he said you can get alcoholism if your parents have it. So I thought maybe I might have caught it from my mother."

"I'm sure what the man meant was that you could inherit the disease. If your parents pass down certain genes, you might be more likely to develop an alcohol dependency than somebody else would."

Tyeisha nodded and hugged her books closer to her chest. She still looked confused, so I asked her if she wanted to talk some more after school. She shook her head.

"My mother is picking me up right after sixth," she said. For as long as I had known her, Tyeisha lived with her grandmother, a strict but loving woman in her early fifties.

"Your mother?" I tried to sound casual.

Tyeisha nodded. "My mama just decided to come back and be my mother last week, on my sixteenth birthday. I didn't ask her where she's been for the past ten years."

I couldn't imagine what Tyeisha must be feeling, but I knew it had to hurt. During her first year in the Academy, she had written about the pain, page after page after page, of living with a mother who took drugs and drank and cried all night long about her dead husband, and who frequently told her only child that she hated her because she looked so much like her dead daddy.

Then, as if that wasn't enough hurt for one child to have to endure, when Tyeisha was six years old, her mother had walked out and left her with her grandmother.

"She never even said good-bye," Tyeisha had written in her final entry about her mother. After that, she had turned her attention to other subjects and never mentioned her mother again. This year, her senior year, Jehovah and fashion design shared top billing in her journal.

"Is your mother better now?" I asked Tyeisha, lowering my voice so that the students filtering into the room for my next class wouldn't overhear. I thought she might be embarrassed, but she didn't seem concerned at all.

"Oh, she goes to all the AA and Al-Anon and Weight Watchers and all the other meetings for drugs and drinking and doughnut eating," Tyeisha announced in her bright cheerleader voice, "but it never lasts. And I been thinking I probably got what she's got."

"Well, there's one way to make sure you don't ever become an alcoholic or a drug addict," I said.

"What's that?"

"Don't drink or take drugs."

"Everybody drinks, Miss J. Except the Jehovites."

"I don't," I said. "And I don't do drugs, either. I don't need to drink or do drugs. I was born crazy."

"I know that," Tyeisha said. "You're a teacher."

A group of students clomped into the room and started squabbling over the window seats. Tyeisha checked her watch.

"Can I have a pass so I can get into math class?"

As I wrote out the pass, I tried to make my voice sound casual as I asked Tyeisha whether she was serious about Simoa's father beating her if she missed class.

Tyeisha nodded. "Everybody's father does it," she said. "Don't they?"

When I didn't answer, Tyeisha complained, "We always tell

you our secrets and all kinds of personal stuff. But you never tell us. Do you think that's fair?"

"No, I don't," I admitted. I stepped outside the classroom, drawing Tyeisha with me. She didn't want to go, but I outweigh her by at least thirty pounds and I'm hard to stop when I decide to move. Behind us, moans and groans registered the displeasure of my class at being excluded from the excitement.

"Put me on your calendar for Sunday afternoon," I told Tyeisha. "There's a classical music concert over at this big beach house in Half Moon Bay. I'll pick you up at two thirty and we'll go to the concert and during the intermission I'll tell you all kinds of personal stuff about me."

"Classical music?" Tyeisha wrinkled her nose.

"Everything has its price," I said.

"All right. But you better remind me on Friday so I don't forget."

"You can count on it."

I had intended to ask Simoa to the concert, since her name was the first on my list of girls, but I didn't think it would hurt to pencil in Tyeisha and move Simoa to the number-two spot. I didn't think one more week would make that much difference. That'll teach me to think.

Chapter 12

Would You Do That to a White Girl?

There were lights on inside Simoa Mariposa's house, and I could hear loud voices and the boom of music with a strong bass beat coming from behind the door, but nobody answered my knock. As I stood on the front step, trying to decide whether to pound on the door or leave a note, I saw a movement in the picture window to the left of the door. A woman's hand drew back the curtain, and I saw a face, an older version of Simoa's face, for a brief second before it disappeared. As I raised my hand to knock a second time, the door flew open. A giant man with a flat, angry face glared at me with hard black eyes. "What?" he demanded. His anger struck me square in the face, and it took me a moment to recover.

"I'm Miss Johnson, Simoa's English teacher," I said, "and I just wondered if I might speak with her for a moment."

The man stepped back suddenly. He was bare-chested. On his right shoulder, a thick jagged scar snaked its away across the spot where his arm should have been. I tried not to stare, but I couldn't help it. The door swung shut in my face. I waited a minute, thinking he had gone to get Simoa, but then I heard the dead bolt clunk into place.

Tyeisha told me later that Simoa's father had been injured in an industrial accident at the manufacturing plant where he worked.

"He got his arm caught in this big machine, and it pulled it right off." We were walking up the steps outside the main office, and I stopped and stared up at Tyeisha, who was taking the stairs two at a time.

"*Pulled* off?" I was certain that she meant it had been mangled or cut off.

"Uh-huh. Some guy turned on this machine that he was supposed to holler first and see if anybody was near it, but he didn't and Mr. Mariposa's arm got caught in the machine and it ripped it right off. Then he sued the company and got a million dollars or something."

I stared up at Tyeisha as I tried to digest this appalling piece of news. She mistook my hesitation for disbelief.

"You can ask Simoa if you don't believe me."

"I believe you," I assured Tyeisha. "And I'd like to ask Simoa. But she hasn't been to school for a week, and I don't have any idea where she is. Do you?"

"No," Tyeisha shook her head. "Honest, I don't." She leaped up the last few steps. "Gotta get to my locker before the bell rings. Catch you later."

Nobody wanted to talk about Simoa, but I had a feeling, from the way they shuffled their feet and inspected their cuticles, that the kids knew more than they admitted.

"Has anybody seen or talked to Simoa Mariposa lately?" I asked every single class, every single day for two weeks straight. Nobody had seen her. Nobody had talked to her. Nobody wanted to talk about her, either, including the folks in the office. The Attendance Office monitor assured me that Mr. and Mrs. Mariposa had excused Simoa from school for an extended absence. The nurse and the guidance counselor agreed. Simoa wasn't truant; she was simply not at school. The principal's secretary, Cherry, said that as long as the parents excused a child, the school had no reason or legal grounds for filing a report. The local police dispatcher informed me that, although Simoa was a student at Parkmont, which was in the West Bay, the matter fell under the jurisdiction of the East Palo Alto Police Department, which was located in the East Bay along with the Mariposas' legal residence.

Every day for weeks, I drove to Simoa's house after school and knocked on the door, but nobody ever opened it. I left notes for her but never received an answer. After a while I stopped expecting anything. I stopped worrying about her grade point average and her attendance record and her missing credits. I started praying that she was alive.

About the time that Simoa disappeared, Araceli Andrade showed up on my doorstep with an application to enter the Academy. Normally, we don't take students after the first semester of their junior year because by then they are usually too far behind in credits or too far gone in attitude for us to help them. Araceli was a senior, and we were already into the second quarter of the school year, but there was no way I was going to let this girl walk away.

"I'll take full responsibility for her," I assured the other Academy teachers at our weekly staff meeting. Araceli had spent the first ten minutes of the hour with us, answering questions, then left us to decide whether to accept her application. She sat in her usual pose, arms and legs crossed, chin jutting belligerently into the air, eyes focused on the wall just above our heads, to avoid the danger of direct eye contact. But she answered every question without hesitation and didn't utter a single swear word. I was impressed. The other teachers were not, but they agreed to give her one chance. With her dismal attendance record and long list of suspensions, they didn't expect her to stay in the Academy very long. I expected her to stay, because I knew that Araceli was as stubborn as I am, and if she had made up her mind to succeed, that's exactly what she would do. What I didn't know was how much I would learn from her in the process. During four short weeks of summer school, Araceli had taught me one important lesson. Within four hours of joining the Academy, she taught me another.

Because the boys were so unruly and relished upsetting the girls, and because the only open seat was between Cornelius and Leroy, who were hanging halfway out of their seats in appreciation of Araceli's miniskirt, I rearranged the seating chart for first period so that Araceli could sit in the same section with Isabella Carrillo and Maria Hernandez and two other Hispanic girls. Isabella and Maria were straight-A students and kept tabs on the non-native English speakers in class.

Chubby Maria, with her baby face and tender heart, had designated herself the official translator for all the Spanish-speaking students who needed help understanding the assignments. When a question arose that Maria couldn't answer, she'd wave one pudgy hand in the air and whisper, *"Ayúdame, Maestra."* Help me. Isabella, small and thin, preferred to consult the Spanish-English dictionary that she always carried and was so soft-spoken that on the few occasions when she risked speaking in class, I had to go to her desk and stand directly beside her in order to hear. Maria and Isabella nurtured the girls in their group and mothered the boys, and I didn't doubt that the two girls would welcome Araceli into their group. It didn't occur to me that Araceli might not welcome the invitation.

When Araceli strutted over to her seat, Isabella kept her eyes on me, as she did every day, but Maria offered a warm smile to Araceli as she sat down beside her. Araceli didn't return the smile, which came as no surprise to me, since Araceli never smiled and rarely looked at her classmates. I handed Araceli a copy of "Busted" by David Haynes, a short story about a twelve-year-old African-American boy's initial experience with prejudice. As one of the students began reading aloud, Maria leaned over toward Araceli's desk and pointed out the paragraph being read. We finished the story and, after a short discussion, I assigned the class the task of writing an essay on their personal experiences or observations of prejudice. For once, nobody argued about the assignment. Nobody asked for an alternate topic. They wrote furiously until the end of the class period, and several asked if they could take their journals home to write more.

Araceli joined the line and tossed her journal into the bin beside my desk on her way out of the room.

"So, do you think you're going to like the Academy?" I asked, primarily in an attempt to assure Araceli that I was concerned and willing to offer whatever help she might need.

"Oh, yeah," Araceli said.

As soon as she was out of sight, I fished her journal from the bin and opened it, hoping her essay might give me some insight into Araceli's personality. What her essay gave me was a look at myself, and it wasn't a pretty sight.

My Experiance with Prejudice
by A. Andrade

My experiance happened today right now in this class. There was a lot of empty desks where I could of sitted, but just because I speak Spanish, my English teacher putted me with a bunch of other girls who speak Spanish, like just because we speak the same language we have to be best friends or something. But we do not even speak the same languages. I am from Argentina and we have our own kind of spanish and it is way different of the way that *gordita* girl talks. She sounds like she came from Tijuana or somewhere in mexico where the fruit pickers and cholos live. And that other one, the sad, skinny girl, she is from nicaragua. In case you are not knowing your geography, it is in central america which is a hole another continent from south america where my country is.

People always doing that, especial teachers, sticking all of the spanish speakings in one place like we have to like each other because we all eat frijoles and tortillas. But los americanos all eat hamburguesas and french fries and the teachers do not think they will always liking each other. And the teachers put los negros together, too, when they do not know each other. Why the teachers do that? Do they are thinking we are the same peoples because we all have black hair? Or they cannot tell us apart one from each other, so they putting us together so when they call our name they do not have to look at nobody, just look at our group and we are in it. Maybe you do not even know our names.

Quien soy yo?

You want us to write about a time we saw somebody be predjudice and how does that made us feel and what we think about it, well I cannot tell you all that because I do not know. But it is making me think. Would you do this thing to a white girl?

Lesson number two from Señorita Araceli Andrade.

Chapter 13

I Am Still Here

One hot, humid midsummer night during U.S. Marine Corps officer training in Quantico, Virginia, Drill Sergeant Bertie Hawke shouted us out of our bunks at 0300 hours and led us on a fast and furious fifteen-mile hike in full combat gear, with loaded utility belts around our waists and seventy-pound Alice packs slamming against our backs. As we tromped through the dense forests, the heat and humidity caught up with us, but the dampness did nothing to soothe my throat, which burned from sucking in so much hot air. Ignoring Sergeant Hawke's instructions, I drank the contents of both my canteens well before the halfway mark. A few hours later, as we approached our campsite, I collapsed in midstep, dehydrated and delirious, with an entirely new understanding of the word *fatigue.* My company mates picked me up and dragged me the rest of the way, with Sergeant Hawke growling in my ear, ordering me to keep on going.

Sergeant Hawke intended her lessons to last a lifetime, and they did. Even as a career civilian, whenever I have been tempted to quit, I still hear Sergeant Hawke's voice reminding me that "pain and fatigue are not valid reasons for stopping." No matter how hard I have worked or how far I have walked, I have always managed to hit the deck running when reveille sounded. Until I taught high school.

Until I taught high school, I had never experienced genuine pain and fatigue. Nothing in my past had prepared me for the pain of watching eager, ambitious children have the love of learning squeezed out of them slowly, one dangerous day at a time, until they finally learned the lesson that our educational system teaches: America needs poorly educated poor people to serve its well-educated wealthy people. I didn't know how to heal the hurt that prejudice and poverty inflict on innocent children, and because I couldn't heal it, I couldn't rest.

When I went to bed at night and closed my eyes, I saw Simoa Mariposa's bright, beautiful face fading silently into the shadows. When I woke in the morning, I'd remember dreaming about Raul Chacon eating and eating and eating and never filling the emptiness inside him. When I walked into the classroom, I saw Cornelius Baker's handsome face, twisted into an unnatural, perpetual scowl to protect his tender heart against police officers and store owners and teachers and bus drivers who were blinded by his black skin, unable to see the integrity and honor that struggled to stay alive inside him.

That kind of pain doesn't heal, and that kind of fatigue can't be overcome with rest. I gave it my best shot. Even Sergeant Hawke couldn't say I hadn't tried. But after four years, I finally hit empty. I slept straight through Thanksgiving vacation, but when classes resumed the following week, on a fine November morning, I couldn't drag myself out of bed. I lay in bed for an hour after the alarm rang, trying to motivate myself to move. When it was too late to call a substitute, I crawled out from under the covers, pulled on a pair of jeans, my old cowboy boots, and a sweater, and drove down the mountain to Parkmont. Toshomba Grant, who arrived ahead well ahead of the crowd, was waiting outside my classroom, as usual.

"What's up, Miss J?" Toshomba took my briefcase and waited

while I unlocked the door. He deposited my case on my desk and went to open the cupboard under the windows. He stuffed his bulging backpack inside, then turned around and rubbed his dimpled brown hands together as he took in my sloppy attire. "Are you sick?"

"Yes, I think I am, Toshomba."

"Did you go to the doctor?"

"The doctor can't fix what's wrong with me. I'm sick in my heart."

He frowned. "Did you have a heart attack?"

"No, but my heart hurts. It hurts all the time, and I don't think anything can make it stop."

Toshomba chewed his lower lip for a few minutes. When the other kids started to arrive, he hushed them and told them to sit down and be quiet. He held whispered conferences with various classmates in the back of the classroom and succeeded in shutting up everybody but Rico Perez.

"What's the matter, Miss J?" Rico demanded when everybody was seated and waiting for me to take roll. I hadn't stopped at the office to pick up the roll sheets, because it seemed too far to walk.

"Nothing's the matter. I'm just a little tired. Why don't you guys just write in your journals today and then take a break for the rest of the period."

"That ain't fair," Rico said.

"Okay, don't write, then. Do whatever you want. Just don't draw blood or light anything on fire."

"That's not what I mean," Rico said. "It ain't fair if you got a problem and you say nothing's wrong, but when we got a problem, we always gotta tell you."

"I'm sorry," I said. "I don't mean to be nosy. I just ask questions because I want to help you guys whenever I can."

"And that's why you gotta tell us," Rico insisted. "So we can help you."

"Thanks," I said. "I'll be all right."

Toshomba sighed loudly and shook his head. He held out his hands, palms up, and shrugged at Rico—I told you so. Rico slumped down in his seat and shoved his feet under the desk in front of him. Tyeisha Love stood up and walked to my desk. Without saying a word, she put both arms around me and held me for a minute, then patted me on the back and whispered, "It'll be all right." My mother used to hold me in her arms and say those same words to me when the world was too much to bear. When Tyeisha said them, I started to cry.

"Aw, man," Cornelius muttered. He tried to sound mad, but he looked like he might cry himself any minute. I hurried to grab a tissue and wipe my runny nose. I patted another tissue at the tears.

"Thanks, Tyeisha," I said. "I think that's what was wrong. I just needed a hug."

"It's okay, Miss J," Tyeisha said. "You gave me a lot of hugs before."

"I guess everybody needs one sometimes." As I looked at my senior class, I saw tears in so many eyes that, without intending to, I added, "If anybody else needs a hug, stand up."

Every single student in the room stood up, including Cornelius Baker. Starting at the first desk in the front of the room near the door, I walked up and down the rows of desks and hugged each of my students. Some of them grabbed me hard and held on like they were afraid of drowning; others gave me a quick, safe squeeze. When I reached Cornelius, he was still standing, but his arms remained pasted to his sides. Touched that he would risk such a grand gesture in front of the other students, I resisted the impulse to jump on a chair and grab him around the neck. I wrapped my arms as far as they would reach around his broad back and pressed my cheek to his chest for a second.

The students stayed on their feet until I had hugged everybody, then they sat down and wrote in their journals, as though nothing unusual had happened, as though they hadn't just breathed the life back into me.

During lunch hour, I left Rico in my room grading papers and went to the staff lounge to call my doctor for an appointment. The nurse said she might be able to squeeze me in right after school, so immediately after the last bell, I stacked three plastic bins of journals inside my office to read later and toted two bins out to my car to read at home.

Dr. Worth gave me some Valium after I described my sleeplessness and sense of despair, but he gave me only a few tablets.

"I'm going to refer you to a psychologist," he said. "I don't think this is a physical problem."

"Of course I'm crazy," I said. "Only crazy people teach high school."

Dr. Worth smiled, but it wasn't his usual hearty grin, and he didn't ask me whether I wanted to discuss birth control, as he usually did as his way of teasing me about what he referred to as my "unhealthy single status."

"I don't think you're losing it," Dr. Worth said, "but I think you need to learn how to take care of yourself better if you intend to stay in the classroom." He checked the chart on his clipboard. "You've been in twice this year already for sore throats, three times for sinus infections, and once for an earache."

"I've always had a delicate respiratory system," I reminded him.

"I know that. But stress can aggravate it."

"Okay. You're the doctor."

"Yes, I am," he said, as he handed me a slip of paper. "And so is Violet Howe. A very good doctor."

I imagined that a woman named Violet would be pale and frail, blond and blue-eyed, with a kind face and a soft smile. Dr. Howe was nearly six feet tall, with bright orange hair and hands big enough to palm a basketball. Her face wasn't unkind, but it didn't strike me as particularly kind, either. If there had been a couch in her office, I probably would have left, but she ushered me into a sunny room furnished with three big, puffy, upholstered chairs and two walls of built-in bookshelves. In the center of the room, a white wicker coffee table held several small figurines and a large box of tissues. Dr. Howe folded her big body into the chair nearest the door and invited me to sit across from her.

I sat down, feeling uncomfortable and entirely unsure that I wanted to be there. Dr. Howe didn't press me. She waited silently as I inspected the floral pattern in the arm of the chair, the rows of books on the shelves, the pale green carpet. When I finally looked at her, still unable to think of anything to say, she whispered, "You're feeling very sad."

A rocket scientist, I thought to myself, staring at the carpet. Dr. Howe cleared her throat softly. I looked up.

"You must let go of it," she said. "You can't hold it in. You've been holding it in too long, and your body and your mind are trying to tell you that it hurts."

I shook my head and said, "If I talk about it, I'll cry."

"What's wrong with crying?" Dr. Howe wanted to know.

"Because if I start, I won't be able to stop."

"Perhaps if you don't start, you won't be able to stop the pain," Dr. Howe suggested. "Why don't you tell me what it is that makes you cry so much."

So I told her about Simoa with her black eye and her angry one-armed father and how she disappeared one day and nobody seemed to care; and about Joanie Fisher's stepfather beating her mother and spending all her mother's money on cocaine, and so when I called Social Services they told me Joanie was seventeen, so she should leave and get a job because she was too old, nobody would take her in as a foster child. I told her about Isabella, who asked whether I could help her get a Social Security card because she and her mother left everything behind and moved to the United States so that Isabella would have a chance to get a good education and a job, and how they took backbreaking work for less than minimum wage and sometimes the man who owned the restaurant where they cooked and washed dishes paid them half of what they earned. And I told her that now Isabella needed an operation on her foot, but she had no money to pay for food, let alone the operation. I told her about Danny Richards, whose ex-Army-captain father drank and beat him up and made him sleep in the garage, even in the winter, if Danny's bedroom didn't pass inspection. And about Cornelius Baker, who was so talented and so smart but whose anger was eating him alive, and there was nothing I could do; I couldn't love him enough to make up for the rest of the world. And about Tyeisha Love, whose mother told her she couldn't love her because she looked too much like her dead father.

When I stopped—not because I ran out of things to cry about but because my throat hurt too much to talk anymore—both my hands were filled with clumps of soggy tissues and the box on the table was nearly empty. For a moment, I thought I saw a tear glint in Dr. Howe's eye, but if it was a tear, it dried very quickly.

"You have to let go," she said. "You can help your students. You can love them. But you can't save them."

"I know," I said. "That's exactly what I've been trying to tell you."

"I understand that," Dr. Howe said. "But your primary responsibility is to take care of yourself. Otherwise, you won't be able to help anybody."

For the longest time we sat there, Dr. Howe looking at me, me looking at the floor. Finally she said, "Perhaps you are drawn to these children because they allow you to work through your own issues."

I pointed out that racial prejudice and poverty were not my issues.

"No," Dr. Howe agreed, "but perhaps you can identify with feeling unloved and unwanted."

Fortunately, my fifty minutes expired about that time, so I didn't have to do any further soul searching. On my way out the door, Dr. Howe told me to work on separating my personal life from my private life.

"If I could do that, I wouldn't be here. That's the whole point. I can't close my door and forget about the kids. Sometimes I think I may be the only person who thinks about them at all."

"And one may be enough. Children who are traumatized by neglect or emotional abuse usually survive quite nicely if they have the good fortune to connect with an adult who believes in them and offers them unconditional love and acceptance. That love and acceptance become their lifeline, and they will hold on to it."

"You mean just by loving them and caring about them, it will make a difference?" I asked. "It will fix them?"

"Not all of them, but a great many of them. You need to concentrate on helping those who accept your help and stop expending so much of your energy on the ones who are beyond hope." This woman is the one who is crazy, I thought, if she thinks I can just forget about those kids.

"Just close the door and go home at night, right?"

Dr. Howe nodded and closed the door.

Hal Gray used to tell me the same thing, but Hal had a much better sense of humor, so I called him when I got home, hoping to catch him in between sailing adventures.

"I'm not really a teacher," Hal used to tell me. "I'm a sailor, but the kids don't know, so I don't disillusion them. They need their dreams."

Hal's dream, for as long as I knew him, was to retire and spend the rest of his life sailing the waters off the coast of the Pacific Northwest with his wife, Gracie, another retired teacher. Hal and Gracie weren't at sea when I called. Hal was in the hospital, dying of lung cancer. His walking and positive thinking couldn't combat the nicotine he poisoned himself with for thirty years. When I hung up the phone, after talking to Gracie, I felt as though I'd been cut adrift. Even though I hadn't seen Hal for months, I had felt a sense of security in knowing that he was out there somewhere, skipping over the waves, within reach if I truly needed him.

That night I fell asleep on the couch and woke up in the morning with red, puffy eyes, but I thought I could pass it off as another sinus infection, if anybody asked.

Araceli didn't ask. "You been crying," she said, an accusation. I considered denying it, but Araceli was an expert at denial and would know I was lying, so I nodded and busied myself with my lesson plans, shuffling papers from one drawer of my desk to another.

"How come you been crying?"

"Oh, I don't know. It's probably PMS." I smiled, but Araceli didn't. She just watched me with her relentless eyes until I added, "And I'm worried about Simoa." I didn't say, "And I'm worried about you, too, and half of the other kids in the Academy because you know your lives are lousy but haven't got a clue about how bad they'll be later on."

Araceli watched me for a few seconds, her black-rimmed eyes narrowed, her painted mouth pushed into a pensive pout. She left without saying anything but returned after school with Tyeisha Love in tow. She nudged Tyeisha with her elbow and jutted her chin in my direction.

"I know where Simoa is," Tyeisha said softly.

I was out of my chair and standing in front of my desk before my chair, which I had kicked over in my haste, hit the floor. "Is she all right? Where is she? Why didn't you tell me?" I fired questions at Tyeisha. When I finally slowed down to catch my breath, she shrugged her shoulders, and I realized that in my excitement I had grabbed both Tyeisha's upper arms in a killer grip as though I intended to squeeze the answers out of her.

"Sorry," I said, as I dropped my hands. I walked toward the first row of desks and motioned for Tyeisha and Araceli to come and sit with me. Tyeisha shook her head and looked nervously toward the door where Araceli stood, arms crossed, a miniature but effective roadblock to any student who happened to stroll past my classroom.

"Is Simoa all right?" I asked.

Tyeisha nodded. "Far as I know, she is."

"What happened to her? Where is she?" I asked, more gently this time. Tyeisha's eyes stared into mine, trying to read the answer she needed.

"If you know something, you gotta tell, don't you?" she asked. I frowned, trying to figure out what prompted Tyeisha's question.

"I mean, like if somebody gots a gun and you find out, you gotta tell the principal and the police because you're a teacher and all. Right?"

"Yes," I nodded. "That's what I'm supposed to do."

Tyeisha sighed. "Then I can't tell you nothing."

"You know I don't always follow the rules," I reminded her. "And have you ever heard about me telling somebody's secrets?"

Tyeisha tilted her head and tucked the tip of one of her many braids into her mouth as she considered my confidentiality track record.

"I haven't," she said, then turned her head toward the door. Araceli gave the slightest shrug in answer to Tyeisha's unspoken question.

"I won't tell," I said. "I give you my word. No matter what you tell me, I swear on my honor that I won't tell."

"And you won't tell that I told you?"

I shook my head. "Word of honor."

Tyeisha said, "Meet me at the library in ten minutes. I know

nobody gonna see us there." She and Araceli were out the door
and down the sidewalk before I had time to ask any more questions. When I reached the library, I saw them in the far corner,
near the reference book section, probably the safest spot at
Parkmont for a private conversation. When Araceli saw me coming, she got up and moved to a table between us and the door. I
sat down across from Tyeisha.

"I don't know if I should tell you," she said, "but Simoa is in
big trouble." She stopped.

"Maybe I can help her."

"Nobody can't help her," Tyeisha said sadly. "It doesn't matter anyway, because she ran away."

"Where did she go?" Either San Francisco or San Jose, I expected, both within an hour's drive from Parkmont.

"Tonga."

"Tonga?"

"That's where her grandma lives. She's going back there to
hide because her daddy's going to kill her when he find out that
man taped Simoa and him having sex."

I held up both hands. "Wait a minute. You're losing me. What
man?"

"This man who got her drunk and had sex with her. You know
Simoa like to shake her bootie." I nodded. I hadn't known, but I
might have if I had paid proper attention.

"She didn't know it but he taped the whole thing, and then
afterward he told her she got to have sex with some other men
and if she don't then he gonna show that tape to her daddy and
her daddy will kill her for sure. You ever seen him?"

I drew a deep breath and let it out very slowly. The one-
armed man with the flat face.

"Maybe he's lying," I suggested. "Did Simoa actually see the
tape?"

Tyeisha nodded. "That's exactly what I said, Miss J. I said,
'You know for sure that man got a tape?' Cause you know how

boys always be lying about what they getting. Simoa said she
didn't see the tape so I thought maybe he was making it up, but
then I heard Charlie Chu telling a bunch of boys to come on
over his house and see the tape. Simoa heard the word and ran
away so her daddy won't kill her. That man is mean. You know I
told you about how he got his arm ripped off?"

I nodded. Not the kind of thing I was likely to forget.

"Well, they gave him a bunch of money and now he stay home
all day, watching the soap operas and talk shows and drinking
beer. That's how come Simoa never cut classes, because he be
sitting right there in the living room if the office calls up. If they
call up, he just sits there and waits, and when Simoa walks in the
door, he starts beating on her. He gonna kill her for real if he
find out about that tape. So Simoa had to run away."

Tyeisha stopped. She drew a deep breath, then puffed up her
cheeks and blew the air out in a long, low stream. I asked her
how Simoa expected to get to Tonga. Where would she get the
money for such a long trip? And how did she expect to make
such a long journey alone at her age?

Tyeisha shook her head and raised both hands, palms up, in a
graceful shrug. "I don't know."

I searched the library for a scrap of paper and scribbled my
phone number on it. I folded the paper carefully and handed it
to Tyeisha.

"Tell Simoa to call me whenever she can, day or night. I'll figure out something."

Tyeisha put the paper into her pocket and patted it. "I'll give
it to her—if I see her." She stood up to leave.

"Simoa's lucky," I whispered. "You're a good friend."

"Yeah, well, I hope she thinks so," Tyeisha said.

As soon as Tyeisha and Araceli were safely outside the building, I rushed from the library to the principal's office. Dr. Delgado was out, but Mr. Simms, the new vice principal in charge of
discipline, was in. Mr. Simms and I had met only once, and I

didn't have a firm fix on his personality, but I didn't have any other options. I explained the situation as coherently as I could, which was difficult with him interrupting me every few seconds to repeat something so he could jot down a note on a long yellow pad of paper. As I talked, I kept searching his face and eyes for a clue to his reaction, but I couldn't get a reading.

"Who gave you this information?" he asked, when I finished my story. He held his pen poised above the pad.

"I can't tell you," I said. "I gave my word."

Mr. Simms opened his hand, and the pen plopped onto the pad. "Then there's really nothing I can do. You can't even tell me this man's name. And what proof do you have that there is a videotape? I need some sort of evidence before I accuse Charlie Chuton. You realize that these are serious accusations that you're making?"

"Mr. Simms," I said, not unkindly, "I know you haven't been at Parkmont very long, but ask anybody. Charlie is the biggest dope dealer on campus."

"That may be so," Mr. Simms said, "but we have no evidence, no proof that a tape exists. We can't search a student's locker, much less his home, without some sort of proof."

"Can we call the police and get a warrant?"

"And what would we tell them, Miss Johnson? That some future dropout"—he paused—"I assume that your source is one of your Academy students?"

I stared at him, too angry to speak. It had taken us three years of college scholarships, honor roll GPAs, and high-paying jobs to shake the stigma of the "at-risk" label attached to our program—and our students. It was bad enough that the student body prejudged the Academy kids, but it was inexcusable for staff to write them off without giving them a chance. And I don't know why, exactly, but I felt it was somehow even more heinous for Mr. Simms, an African-American man, to stereotype my students. If I had known how to articulate what I was thinking, I would have, but I was too angry to do anything except stare at Mr. Simms.

He continued. "Shall we tell the police that we want a warrant based on the fantastic story of some unidentified child? We need something concrete before we call in the authorities. Surely you understand that."

"No, I don't."

"Then at least you must understand that this is not the sort of incident the superintendent would prefer to see publicized unless—"

I stood up and walked out before I hit the man. I stomped down the stairs and across the rectangle of grass that separated the administration building from the classroom buildings. As I turned to go up the sidewalk toward the teachers' lounge, for some reason I looked back over my shoulder. Mr. Simms was standing in his office, watching me from the window behind his desk.

It was five thirty by then. The teachers' lounge was deserted, so I decided to call the police immediately, instead of waiting until I got home. Parkmont's campus spans the intersection of two separate villages but is nearer to Edgewood, so I called the Edgewood Police Department and asked for assistance. The dispatcher told me I would have to call the East Palo Alto precinct, since Charlie Chu lived there. With the familiar feeling of talking into a void, I repeated my story to the East Palo Alto officer who answered my call.

"I could come over there and make a statement, if it would help," I offered, as I concluded.

"That won't be necessary," the officer said. "Mr. Simms has already called to let us know that the Parkmont administration will conduct an investigation starting tomorrow. And Mr. Simms has offered to handle this case personally, on behalf of the school. So you don't have to worry. It's being taken care of. But thank you for calling."

The following morning, I stopped by Mr. Simms's office and asked him if he had heard anything. He said he hadn't but would keep me informed. Then he surprised me.

"I know you think I'm acting like an insensitive bureaucrat. My job carries certain responsibilities, and I take them seriously. But I promise you that I will do everything I can to help Simoa. Her safety is my number-one priority." Taken completely off guard, I nodded dumbly at Mr. Simms. "If you happen to see her," he said, "please tell her that I need to talk to her personally and get a statement so I can take some action on her behalf."

Relieved, I picked up my roll sheets and headed for my classroom. I called the roll for first period, read the announcements, and handed out the student journals. When everybody was busy writing, Tyeisha sauntered to the pencil sharpener and ground her pencil down to half its original size, then stopped by my desk on her way back to her seat. "I got a note for you," she whispered.

I held out my hand, but she shook her head. "Later."

When the bell rang, Tyeisha took extra time stowing her notebook and pen in her backpack. When everybody except Araceli was gone, she pulled a piece of white paper from the zippered pocket inside her purse. I reached for it, but Tyeisha didn't hand it over immediately.

"She said I can't give you this unless you promise to tear it up and burn it after you read it. And you can't show it to anybody, neither."

I promised. I locked the door to my classroom and raced down the hall to the staff bathroom, the only place I could be sure I wouldn't be interrupted while I read Simoa's note.

Dear Miss J,
You can't imagine for even one minute what a mess my life is. Tyeisha told you some of it, but she doesn't know that my whole family hates me now because I saw my father mess-

ing around with some hore and I told my mother and she told my father she was leaving and he beat her real bad and almost killed her and now all my aunts and cousins hate me because of my mom and because there her sisters and if she leaves then they don't get none of my dad's money. They all said it's my fault my parents are splitting up and they said if they see me, they'll kill me, and they ain't lying, so I got to go to Tonga because my grandma lives there and she'll let me go and live with her. And that's only part of it. I can't even tell you the rest but if I can't go to Tonga, I'm going to kill myself before somebody else does it for me.

I know you want to help me, but I don't think there's anything you can do because you don't know my dad he has all these friends and stuff and they rule the Gardens. So, I just wanted to tell you thank you anyway for trying to help me. I wish I could come back to school. I miss my friends and I miss you, too. I wish you were my mother. Then I wouldn't have this shitty life.

I was tempted just to hop in my car and forget about the rest of my classes, but I had 145 other students counting on me, so I waited until after school and called Tyeisha.

"Can you get a message to Simoa?" I asked.

Tyeisha dropped the phone. I assumed she went to get a pencil, but she went to get Simoa. When I heard Simoa's voice on the phone, I was so thrilled I kissed the receiver.

"Oh, Simoa," I said. "I'm sorry about your mother and all your problems, but I think we can handle it. But I can't help you if you run away. And besides, Mr. Simms said if you come to talk to him, he can help you."

"For real?" Simoa asked. "He's gonna help me?"

"For real," I assured her. She agreed to come on the early bus the following morning, half an hour before the first bell, and meet me behind the bleachers where we could talk privately.

My classroom was too public, with kids in and out and the phone ringing every few minutes.

I didn't tell Mr. Simms the details, but I did tell him I had talked to Simoa and she had agreed to come and talk to me. I told him I would try to convince her to talk to him. He thanked me and shook my hand.

"You're a big help, Miss Johnson," he said. "I appreciate your cooperation."

For the first time in weeks, I slept through the night instead of lying awake worrying. The next morning, I parked off campus, walked through the side gate on the far side of the gymnasium, and stayed in the shadows of the bleachers where I had a clear view of the bus loading area and the administration office. Tyeisha was the first student to dance down the steps and off the bus. When I saw her, I raised my hand to wave at her and started to step forward, but something in her face made me stop. Just in time. After the last student debarked from the bus, the doors hissed closed. A few seconds later, the doors reopened to drop off two more passengers—Mr. Simms and a uniformed police officer.

As I stared from my spot in the shadows, Tyeisha walked directly toward me and passed without looking at me, her lips a hard, straight line that cut across her face. On the other side of the blacktopped driveway, Mr. Simms and the police officer crossed the loading area and headed up the steps of the administration building.

Tyeisha cut my class that day, and when I tried to track her down, I found that she had cut all of her classes. Araceli was on contract so she couldn't afford to cut; if she cut, she'd be dropped from the Academy. I didn't have a chance to talk to her before or after class; she hurried in and out so fast that I thought she must have lost faith in me and decided to hate me, too.

But Araceli never did what I expected. A few minutes after the last bell, as I was sitting at my desk trying to decide whether to keep my appointment with Dr. Howe or ditch the whole idea of trying to cure myself of caring so much about everything, Araceli came in.

"You fucked up, *Maestra.* Yes?" Araceli said by way of greeting as she clomped into my room. She had traded in her tank tops and miniskirts for baggy jeans and combat boots.

"I know. I'm really sorry. I never thought Mr. Simms would double-cross me like that."

"It is not your fault," Araceli said.

"No, but Tyeisha will never trust me again."

"She will forgive you."

"I hope so. In the meantime, I guess I'll have to find somewhere else, someplace really private, away from school, for Simoa to meet me."

Araceli shook her head. "Simoa she is gone."

"Where?"

"I don't know. When Tyeisha saw Mr. Simms waiting at the bus stop, she runned and told Simoa don't to come. So Simoa she ran and I do not think she will be coming back. If this was me, I would never come back."

I was too sad to cry. Besides, I'd be in Dr. Howe's office soon. I did some of my best crying there. I was too tired to confront Mr. Simms and too ashamed to track down Tyeisha. I gathered my gradebook and my purse, my lunch box and my briefcase, and turned off the lights.

"I give up," I said as I stepped outside. "Every time I try to help somebody, I make a mess out of it. I quit." I turned and waved for Araceli to step outside so I could lock the door. She stood in the darkened classroom, her face hidden in the late afternoon shadows. She took one step, then planted her black combat boots solidly on the gray tile floor.

"You cannot quit, *Maestra.*"

"Come on, Araceli," I said sharply. "This isn't a good time to play with me. I had a shitty day. Tyeisha hates me. Simoa's gone.

I'm tired. And I'm late for an appointment."

"I am still here, Miss J. And many other students. What about us?"

"What about you?" I really wanted to know.

"We are here, and you are our teacher. But sometimes you are getting so busy and worrying about one *estudiante* and it fills up your whole head and you are forgetting the rest. Everybody."

She wasn't telling me anything I didn't know, but I wasn't in the mood to hear it.

"What about us?" Araceli repeated. She didn't raise her voice; she knew I'd listen. "If you will quit, what will we do?"

You're all so much tougher than I am, I thought. But I didn't say it. "You'll survive," I said over my shoulder.

"Probably we will. But you?"

"Me? Don't worry about me."

"But you are the one. What if we quitted? The students? What will you do without us?"

How did somebody who is only sixteen years old get to be so much smarter than I am? I turned back, intending to give Araceli a hug and thank her for putting me in my place, but Araceli stepped outside and closed the classroom door behind her. With one look she squelched any thoughts of hugging her. This was serious business and, just like Dr. Howe, Araceli kept her professional distance.

I stood on the sidewalk, staring at Araceli's receding back, as she and her boots clonked down the sidewalk, around the corner, and out of sight.

Mr. Simms was the last person I wanted to talk to about Simoa, but the police wouldn't talk to me and I couldn't just forget about her. I waited a couple of days before I went to see Mr. Simms, until I was confident that I had enough control not to slug him on sight.

"Have you found out anything about Simoa's situation?" I asked. He gave me such a long, stern look that, for a moment, I wondered whether he had seen me hiding behind the bleachers the day she was supposed to come to school.

"Have you?" he bounced the question back to me.

"I have good reason to believe that she's run away."

"Why?"

"You know why. Because of the videotape."

"Which you haven't seen," he reminded me. "And we can't be certain that tape—or the man who supposedly made it—exists."

"Oh, he exists," I assured Mr. Simms. "His name is Lando and he lives in Oakland."

"And where did you get this information?"

"What's the difference? You said you needed a name. Now you have one."

"But I also need to know who told you the man's name," Mr. Simms held his pen poised above his memo pad. "Before I call the police, I need to be sure that my information comes from a reputable source."

"Trust me, it does."

"I trust you implicitly, Miss Johnson. It's your source I'm concerned about."

"I can't tell you. I gave my word of honor."

"Then I can't help you or Simoa." The tone of his voice was businesslike, as though he were denying my request for extra pencils. I tried to remain calm, to stay seated in the hard little wooden chair facing Mr. Simms's desk, the same chair where students sat to receive their punishment.

"What difference does it make who told me?" I asked. "You said you needed the man's name. I got it for you. Can't you at least call the police and find out whether there is such a person and whether he has a record of dealing drugs and seducing little girls and forcing those little girls into prostitution?"

I hadn't intended to stand up and lean over Mr. Simms's desk until my face was so close to his that I could see the little specks of green in his brown eyes, but that's where I was when I stopped shouting. In the tense quiet that followed my outburst, as my questions echoed off the walls and I sat down, Mr. Simms stood up, walked briskly around his desk and across the carpeted floor, and opened the door of his office. Outside his secretary was sitting at her desk, staring at us, one hand pressed to her lips.

"Thank you very much for stopping by, Miss Johnson," Mr. Simms said. "I'll check into the matter and get back in touch with you."

He shut the door very softly behind me, and I knew he was proud to be able to do so, because we both knew that given the reverse situation, I would have slammed the door hard enough to crack every window in the office. Thoroughly disgusted with myself, I resolved to stay away from Mr. Simms.

But my curiosity took me back through that same door, a week later, again without an invitation or a welcome.

"Have you heard anything?" I asked. Mr. Simms looked up at me and smiled, so I prepared myself for bad news. He took off his black-rimmed glasses and popped one earpiece into his mouth as he nodded for me to sit down.

"I was not surprised to learn, although you may be, that your source was wrong. Mr. Lando did not have intercourse with or make a videotape of Simoa Mariposa."

"How do you know that?"

"I asked him."

"You just called the man up and asked him?"

"As a matter of fact, I did." He smiled again, a small, mean smile that drew his full lips into a thin, hard line. "And he denied it. He said he did know who Simoa was, and he wasn't surprised that some less scrupulous man had taken advantage of her, given her precocious nature and her looks, but that he had plenty of grown-up lady friends—more than enough to occupy his time—

and he had never found it necessary to ply any woman with alcohol."

"He has an impressive vocabulary for a drug dealer," I said. "Or did he also deny that?"

"He did."

"And you believed him."

"Why not? I have no proof to the contrary, and he sounded like a very reasonable and intelligent man."

Unlike you, I wanted to say. I wanted to say it so badly that I bit my tongue hard enough to draw blood. I was halfway out the door before Mr. Simms stopped me.

"Miss Johnson?" I turned, but didn't respond. "I trust that this matter is over and will be forgotten."

"It may be, as far as you're concerned. If you don't want to risk the reputation of the school, that's fine. I understand, that's your job. But I have nothing to lose."

"Except *your* job." He said it so softly that I almost didn't hear him.

"Excuse me?" I walked back into the room, right up to the edge of his desk. He stood up and faced me from the other side, his hands curled into fists that rested on the slick, hard surface.

"You're treading on dangerous ground, Miss Johnson. You have no idea what men like Lando are capable of."

"I thought you said he sounded like a reasonable, intelligent man," I reminded Mr. Simms. He sighed and sat back down in his chair and pressed the fingertips of both hands together. He rolled his hands forward, toward the chair where I had been sitting.

"Sit down, Miss Johnson. I want to tell you a story."

Not long ago, perhaps a few weeks, Mr. Simms said, one bright, sunny Monday morning, he had confiscated three thousand dollars in cash from a freshman student on campus and had turned the money over to the police. That very afternoon, as the students were gathered at the bus loading zone, a white stretch limo with a gold antenna and heavily tinted windows rolled up the driveway and pulled to the curb where it sat, motor purring, as Mr. Simms watched from his post at the top of the steps above the loading zone.

"Even the students sensed that they should stay away from the car," Mr. Simms said. "They stood back and watched as all the doors flew open and four big men stepped out, leaving the driver in the car. They were all dressed in black, with big gold rings, Rolex watches, diamond earrings."

Mr. Simms noted my expression and nodded.

"I almost laughed at them myself, until I saw the Uzis lying in the backseat of the car."

One man had stood beside the car, his hands in the pockets of his leather jacket; another stationed himself a few feet in front of the car, ensuring a clear exit. The two largest men, both well over six feet, walked directly to Mr. Simms, took him by the arms, and escorted him up the stairs and into his office, where they shut the door and pulled the blinds shut.

"One of them stood in front of the door, and the other one stood in front of the windows with his arms crossed. His arms were twice as thick as mine and covered with tattoos. They demanded the money I took from the boy. I said that I had turned it over to the police.

"They told me it was rent money, and the boy had collected it for them to give to their landlord. The one near the windows, who was closest to me, grabbed me by the throat and threatened to throw me out the window if I was lying." Mr. Simms stopped and straightened his collar and tie. "He would have done it, too, if I hadn't recognized one of his tattoos and convinced him that I knew one of his fellow gang members. We grew up on the same street."

The two men let him off with a warning but promised that if he ever interfered with their business transactions again, they would visit him at home. His story finished, Mr. Simms gave me what clearly was meant to be a meaningful glance.

"What are you saying?" I asked. "Are you trying to tell me that some big, bad gangsters are going to drive their big, bad car up to my house and shoot me just for asking questions?" I smiled at the improbability of the image.

"No," Mr. Simms said. "They'll hire somebody else to do it."

I hadn't thought of that. For a minute, I was scared, but only for a minute.

"I've never liked bullies, Mr. Simms, and I've never been afraid of them. The more talk, the less action. And they make me sick." I picked up my purse and started for the door. Once again, Mr. Simms stopped me with a quiet question.

"How long have you been teaching here, Miss Johnson?"

"Three years."

"You may be granted tenure this year, then. Is that right?"

I didn't bother to answer because it wasn't really a question. It was a reminder that Mr. Simms was in charge of the committee that would evaluate my performance and decide whether to grant tenure.

"I honestly do appreciate your concern about your students, Miss Johnson," Mr. Simms said, in a thin, tired voice, and for once I believed him. "But you have many more students to worry about. I told you I would take care of this matter, and I will. That's my job. Your job is to teach. Period. If you interfere with my job, you won't have a job to worry about. And if you aren't here, you won't be able to help any of those students you love so much."

Araceli, Cornelius, Rico, Toshomba, Tyeisha, Joanie, Danny, Julio, Sean, Leroy. Their faces, and a hundred others, flashed across my mind, a continuous slide show, one face melting into another.

I closed the door softly on my way out. At home that night, I called the Oakland police, but they had no record of anybody named Lando; they said I needed a full name.

"He don't need a whole name," Tyeisha insisted when I asked her. "Everybody know who Lando is."

Not ready to admit defeat, but not willing to jeopardize my job, either, I put Simoa's picture on my piano to remind me to continue to check on her in whatever way I could without drawing attention from Mr. Simms or Lando's oversize business associates. Then I turned my attention to my personal recreation plan. It was mid-December, five months of school to go after vacation, and I had made it only one-third of the way down my list of students. Time and money were both running short.

Chapter 14

The Play's the Thing

Yuck!" Danny Richards opened his mouth and aimed his index finger toward his tonsils, miming a gag, when he found out he was among the six lottery winners whose prize was an evening at the theater. I had switched to a lottery system after Isabella Carrillo and Maria Hernandez tiptoed into my classroom one day after school and stood silently watching me grade papers until I glanced up and noticed them standing patiently a few feet from my desk. When I asked them what they wanted, they exchanged nervous looks and blushed. Finally, Isabella blurted, "You are taking every student to some place?"

"Yes. I plan to take each one of you someplace special, a play or a concert or a nice restaurant—someplace you wouldn't ordinarily go."

Maria clapped her hands and spun around in a circle, grabbing Isabella in a hug. Maria whispered something in Spanish, and Isabella shook her head quickly.

"What?" I asked. Isabella frowned at Maria, who stared at her feet. "Don't be afraid. You can tell me."

"We were wondering do you like us very, very much, *Maestra*?"

"You know I love you, you silly rabbits." They both giggled. "Did I do something to make you think I don't like you?" Perhaps I had inadvertently insulted one of them. Sometimes one of my jokes misfires and scores a direct hit on somebody's tender feelings. Isabella shook her head.

"We only want to know if you are going to take every *estudiante*," Isabella said. I showed them their names on my list. They thanked me a thousand times and scurried out of the room. After they left, I replayed our conversation a few times in my mind, trying to decide whether they were simply curious or whether I had done something to make them think I didn't like them. Then it dawned on me: They thought I was inviting students to go out with me in some order based on how much I cared about them—the ones I loved would go first, and so on.

After that, I used a lottery system to select the students for the special outings. The first prize was a pizza dinner and an evening at the theater. Pizza was always a winner, but a play was another story. None of the kids looked too thrilled about seeing a play, although Danny was the only one who refused to go. Danny lived for the final bell when he could jump into his souped-up Camaro and peel out of the parking lot, eager to get home and gap his spark plugs or polish his chrome. I might have taken him horseback riding, or for a ride in a hot-air balloon, or something that involved movement, but I never would have considered taking him to a play if I hadn't pulled his name out of the prize box. The more I thought about it, though, the better I liked the idea. It would be a stretch for both of us, and that was the point of the excursion.

"You don't even know the name of the play yet," I said.

"It doesn't matter," Danny said. "I ain't going. How come you can't take us someplace fun like drag races or Great America or something?"

"Because you can go those places by yourself," I explained. "I'm trying to introduce you to new things, new experiences that you might not otherwise have."

"I don't want no experience where everybody goes around

talking backward and the men wear women's clothes."

For the next two days, Danny adamantly refused to consider attending the play. He thought I was trying to trick him and the other kids into watching Shakespeare in their spare time, or something equally horrendous, but I assured him that this was a modern comedy called *Angry Housewives,* about a group of women who form a punk rock band.

"Okay," Danny finally agreed, "but if anybody says 'where goest thou' or if any men got them leotard things on, I'm out of there. I'll hitchhike home."

The newspaper reviews had described *Angry Housewives* as a comedy about a widow whose husband dies with no insurance, leaving her to raise her punk-rocking son alone. Desperate for money, the mother and three friends, unable to find employment, form their own punk rock band and enter a contest. The housewives win first prize and become a screaming sensation. It sounded like just the ticket for my students—an example of somebody using brains and talent instead of stupidity and violence to overcome adversity.

As I watched their faces in the glow of the stage lights, I was delighted to see that the kids were caught up in the drama, even Danny Richards. Earlier that evening, Danny had reminded me that he planned to leave if any men appeared on stage wearing tights. I promised to drive him home if that occurred. As we had waited on line to enter the lobby of the theater, Danny sighed and ran one permanently grease-stained hand through his blond curls.

"I still don't see why couldn't you take us to someplace fun, if you're going to spend your money anyways," he muttered.

"I told you. I'm trying to help you expand your cultural horizons."

Our cultural horizons were broadened far beyond my expectations. The *Angry Housewives* theme song turned out to be "Eat Your Fucking Cornflakes." When they launched into their song, the kids whistled and stomped their feet, delighted to hear dirty words shouted in public by adults. I had visions of Joanie Fisher going home and singing the song to her mother, the librarian at Saint Ann's Elementary.

"Maybe we should leave," I suggested at intermission. "I'm not sure your parents would approve of some of the language."

"Right," Joanie said. "Like we haven't heard it before."

"I've heard a lot worse than that," Danny claimed, and immediately started spouting a list of extremely creative obscenities in a loud, clear voice. Joanie joined in, and the others clamored for a turn as I herded them outside and threatened to take them home immediately if they didn't shut up.

"If you let us stay for the end of the play, we promise not to tell anybody," Joanie offered. The others agreed that her plan was splendid, and after handshakes all around to seal our pact, we stayed for the final curtain.

Danny, who flunked every spelling and vocabulary test and claimed he couldn't do any better because he just couldn't memorize anything, sang the lyrics to "Eat Your Fucking Cornflakes" word for word at least ten times the following day at school. When I reminded him of his promise, he insisted that he had agreed not to discuss the song lyrics with his parents, and that he had kept his word.

"All right," I said. "I won't argue with you, but I won't accept anything less than seventy percent on your spelling and vocabulary tests from now on."

"Man, Miss J," Danny said, "you never quit, do you?"

"Never."

The next prize was dinner at a trendy restaurant in Menlo Park and another play, this one a drama at the Golden Gate Theatre in San Francisco. Tickets were expensive, so I could only afford to take one student. One of the seniors, Julio Escobar, won the lottery but he said he didn't want to go. I thought he might have the same concerns as Danny Richards had had.

"It isn't Shakespeare, I promise," I told Julio. "It's a play about a teacher at a school for boys who hate school. It has rap music and dancing. I think you'll like it."

Julio insisted that he was too busy to go, but I told him to think it over for a few days before he made up his mind. In the meantime, I asked Rico Perez to find out the real reason why Julio didn't want to go.

"He doesn't got a tuxedo to wear," Rico reported later that day.

"A tuxedo?"

"Yeah," Rico said. "He said he seen an ad in the *Chronicle* for that play and the people going in the theater was all wearing tuxedos and fur coats and big jewelry and stuff."

"Then what should I wear?" Julio wanted to know when I told him he didn't have to wear formal clothes.

"Wear something you would wear to church," I suggested. I expected him to show up in a pair of polyester pants, a cheap cotton shirt, and an old necktie with a lopsided knot. When he walked into the restaurant to meet me, I honestly didn't recognize him. He was wearing baggy black pleated trousers, black and white wingtip shoes, a starched white shirt, black silk tie, and black suspenders. He looked like a model from the cover of *GQ* magazine.

Julio's taste in food wasn't as sophisticated as his taste in clothing. After he read the menu, which featured an assortment of exotic dishes with lots of truffles, sun-dried tomatoes, and fruit-based sauces, he looked stricken.

"I hope it won't embarrass you if we leave," I whispered, "but I don't see anything on this menu that appeals to me at all. Would you mind if we just leave a small tip for the waiter and go get some Chinese take-out?"

I listed our choices—a park, my living room, the BART station. Julio chose to eat in the BART station, since he had never ridden the train, although he had lived in East Palo Alto for seventeen years. We drove to the Daly City station and ate our kung pao chicken and fried rice as we sat on a cement bench on top of the elevated platform overlooking the rows of ticky-tacky houses.

Julio hardly ever talked in class, but he did his assignments and behaved well, so I respected his right to keep his personal life private. But as we ate, he seemed to relax and forget that he was talking to a teacher, so I asked him about his future plans.

"I'll probably go to prison," he said. I laughed, thinking he was kidding, and choked on a mouthful of rice, but there wasn't a trace of laughter in his dark eyes.

"You're serious, aren't you?" I asked as soon as I could speak without coughing. Julio shrugged, as though the truth was obvious.

"Why would you say such a thing?" I wanted to know. "You aren't in trouble, are you?"

"No," Julio said, "but all my brothers and uncles and most of my cousins are in San Quentin, so I'll probably go there, too."

"You can choose not to go to prison, you know," I said. "You're intelligent and handsome and charming."

Julio stuffed a giant bite of chow mein into his mouth and watched me while he chewed. He swallowed and started to wipe his mouth on his shirt sleeve, but I handed him a napkin.

"I forgot what I was wearing for a minute," he said. "You really think I'm smart and all that stuff?"

"Yes, I do." I did.

Julio gazed out over the rooftops, thinking, for a long while. Then, suddenly shy again, he looked at his lap and mumbled, "I can't hardly read."

"I know that."

He glanced up, too surprised to stay shy. "Why didn't you say nothing then?"

"What did you expect me to say?"

"You could've told me I'm stupid and yelled at me."

"But you're not stupid, and yelling is unattractive. I hate yelling. You know that."

Julio nodded. "Yeah. You don't hardly yell at us, even when we act stupid. How come you're so nice to everybody, even Cornelius and that Anglo boy who sits in the back?"

"I treat people the way I would like them to treat me."

"So if I treated you bad, you'd be mean to me?"

"No, I would still be nice to you, because that's how I would like to be treated."

"But if somebody disrespects you, how come you still treat them good? It doesn't make no sense."

"Because I refuse to allow other people to control my behavior. I make my own rules, and I follow them. I don't waste my energy getting mad at people I don't care about."

Julio nodded. "That's cool. But I don't think it's for me. I'm always getting mad at Dr. Delgado or Mr. Simms or somebody."

"I know what you mean." It was cowardly and hypocritical not to admit to Julio that I, too, often lost my temper, especially when dealing with Mr. Simms, but sometimes I'm a cowardly hypocrite. As the train raced along the track toward the city, Julio was engrossed in watching the scenery flash by. I spent the time trying to analyze my behavior toward Mr. Simms. I had told Julio the truth in a sense—I did try not to allow myself to waste energy on people I truly did not like or respect. In that case, since I reacted so strongly to Mr. Simms, and vice versa, there must be something more to our disagreement than mutual dislike. As the conductor announced our arrival at the Union Square station, it occurred to me that perhaps I was guilty of the very thing of which I considered myself most innocent. Simply because he was a black man, I expected Mr. Simms to disregard his primary duty as an administrator and break the rules to help minority kids. Because he didn't do what I expected, I wrote him off as some kind of race traitor, without acknowledging that intertwined with my anger was a grudging respect for a man who refused to compromise his principles.

When we entered the theater, Julio seemed to shrink into himself, looking younger and smaller than seventeen, but the longer we stood in line at the box office waiting to pick up our tickets, the taller he stood. At first, he risked only quick sidelong glances at the people near us, as though he expected them to protest his presence. Before long, he was scrutinizing every detail of their clothing, which ranged from rumpled linen to raw silk. The longer we stood on line, the more confidence Julio projected, and I realized that, from his point of view, rumpled linen looked more wrinkled and sloppy than nonchalant, and raw silk looked much more raw than it did sleek and expensive.

After we got our tickets, Julio squared his shoulders, puffed out his chest, and offered me his arm. He escorted me proudly to our seats in front row center, where he sat, straight and stiff, his eyes riveted on the stage, until the lights came up to signal intermission. He insisted that I remain seated while he went to buy cookies and coffee.

After the final curtain, I asked him what he thought of the performance, and he said, "I liked it a lot. This is my favorite kind of play."

Surprised, I asked him what other plays he had seen.

"This is the only one I ever saw, but it's my favorite kind."

On our way back to the BART station, I stopped at a store in Chinatown and bought two postcards. I gave one card to Julio and fished two pens out of my purse.

"You write a message and send this one to me, and I'll write one to you." I handed him his pen. "Then we'll mail them at the train station and, in a few days, we'll get them in the mail and we'll have a nice memento of our night at the theater."

Julio asked for my address and copied it on his card, painstakingly, in block letters. Then he told me to stay where I was because he couldn't write anything if I was looking at him. He walked halfway down the block to where a row of newspaper vending machines lined the curb and used the top of one of the machines as a desk. I dashed off a quick thank-you to Julio for escorting me to the theater and a wish for his successful future. He bent over his card for several minutes, frowning, the tip of his tongue protruding from between his teeth, as he concentrated on writing. When he finished, I walked to him and held out my hand, planning to take his card and drop it in the mailbox with mine.

"No," Julio said. He put the hand holding the postcard behind his back. "I gotta mail it myself so you can't read it. It should be a surprise." He stuck it in his pocket and promised to mail it later.

Julio spent most of the ride back to Daly City admiring his reflection in the windows of the train, turning his head this way and that, adjusting his collar so that it stood exactly so, and spent the ride from Daly City to East Palo Alto playing with the buttons on my car radio, seeking and scanning his way across the spectrum of stations several times. As we pulled to the curb in front of his house, he switched off the radio and looked at me for a few seconds. I thought he was probably trying to think of a way to thank me, and I was about to break the silence by telling him how much I had enjoyed his company, when he said, "Can I come to your room after school and do my homework? Maybe you could help me a little bit if I get stuck."

I didn't trust myself to speak, so I nodded and gave him a quick hug.

I thought he might have had second thoughts, but Julio arrived at my room a few minutes after seventh period ended the following day and took a seat in the back row. I stayed at my desk in the front of the room, respecting his need for distance, and graded papers. Every couple of minutes, Julio would call out a word and ask me what it meant.

"I told you I can't read too good," he said, after the sixth or seventh word.

"Reading is like any other skill. If you don't practice, you don't get better at it. You play basketball, don't you?" He nodded. "Well, think about how many times you had to practice before you could make a shot from the free-throw line."

"Yeah, but basketball is easy."

"So is reading, if you practice."

"Do you really believe that?"

"I would never lie to you," I said. *"Nunca hablo a ti con la mentira. Siempre hablo a tie con la verdad."* I sang the lyrics to one of the only songs I knew in Spanish.

Julio grinned. "I remember that song. You sang it once for me and Jesse."

Julio and Jesse, his next-door neighbor and best friend, had joined the Academy during their junior year, a year later than the others, and they didn't know anybody except each other. Jesse's response to the threatening new situation was to pretend he wasn't there. Every day he sat in the same seat in the back row of the room and stared at the chalkboard. Julio, taking his cue from Jesse, did the same. For a week I let them sit, hoping they'd realize there was nothing to be afraid of, but the realization never struck them, and all of my attempts to involve them in the class failed. One day, as I circled the room, answering questions about the literature assignment the students were working on, I paused in the aisle between Julio and Jesse and whispered, "You get credit in this class for trying. And you might be surprised how well you do if you try. Don't be afraid to try." At the word *afraid,* Jesse snorted and his gaze swept from the chalkboard to the ceiling, avoiding me entirely.

"I promise never to embarrass you in this class," I said. "You don't have to read out loud. Nobody else will see your essays. You aren't competing with anybody but yourselves. And I know you're intelligent, even if you don't know it."

Jesse stared at the ceiling, but Julio peeked at me out of the corner of one eye. Thrilled by what I considered a major breakthrough, I started singing, *"Nunca hablo a ti con la mentira."* I will never lie to you. *"Siempre hablo a ti con la verdad."* I will always tell you the truth. As I concluded the verse with *"Tu vives en mi pensamientos, ahora me arrepientos, que yo te hace llorar,"* you are always in my thoughts and I'm sorry that I made you cry, Julio's cheeks started to twitch, holding back his smile. When the smile escaped in spite of his efforts, he shook his head and looked at Jesse.

"She's *loca,*" Julio whispered, grinning. Jesse looked at Julio, then at me. I winked broadly and whispered, *"Loca* about you, baby," and continued on my rounds of the room.

Jesse held out longer than Julio did, but by the end of the quarter, they were both completing most of their assignments.

"How come you sang that song?" Julio asked, happy to have an excuse to take a break from his reading.

"It's hard to hate somebody who sings pretty songs to you in Spanish, isn't it? It makes you smile, and then you don't look so tough."

"Yeah," Julio agreed. "But that ain't fair. That's taking advantage."

"I'm so sorry."

"No, you aren't. And you just told me you wouldn't never lie to me. See why nobody trusts teachers?"

Chapter 15

The Lonely Tycoon

S hakespeare had been such a surprise hit with the first Academy class that I added *The Taming of the Shrew* and *The Merchant of Venice* to my standard syllabus. My students fell in love with Mr. Shakespeare's stories, although it had taken a handful of dollars and a briefcase full of candy bars—my "reader rewards"—to convince them to even attempt to read the first scene of *The Taming of the Shrew*. Once they got started, there was no stopping them, and it was their idea to read the second play.

Cornelius's class had enjoyed *The Taming of the Shrew,* just as the previous class had, but nobody suggested reading another play. This time it was my idea, and the kids weren't exactly thrilled about it.

When I handed Cornelius Baker his copy of *The Merchant of Venice,* he held the book gingerly between his thumb and index finger, as though he were holding a dead mouse by the tail. He wrinkled his nose and whined, "How come we gotta read this ancient stuff?"

"It's a good story," I told Cornelius, "about two guys who are best friends. One of them is rich and one is poor. The poor guy borrows a bunch of money from the rich guy, and the rich guy signs a paper that says the moneylender can cut a pound of flesh out of his body if his friend doesn't pay the money back."

"*Ee-uu.*" Cornelius looked at the book with even more distaste.

"I bet the guy doesn't pay up, right?" Tyeisha Love said. "You shouldn't've told us the story, Miss J. Now it'll be boring."

"Oh, no, it won't. I didn't tell you whether he pays, and I didn't tell you what the poor guy wanted the money for in the first place."

"Drugs, probably," Toshomba said. Seeing my expression, he raised both hands and said hurriedly, "I was kidding. I was kidding."

"Sex, I bet," Cornelius said, grinning wickedly, recovered from his initial shock at the prospect of reading Shakespeare.

"Close," I said, surprising Cornelius. "But it does have something to do with a beautiful woman."

"Yeah, but I still don't see why we gotta read this old stuff." Cornelius flicked his fingers at the book, which he had dropped onto his desk. "Why can't we read the modern version?"

"There isn't one," I said. "If there was one, I'd let you read it. But nobody ever wrote a modern version."

"So we could write it," Cornelius said.

"Cool," Toshomba said. "Can we?"

"You'd have to read the original version first, or you wouldn't know the story," I explained.

"So what?" Toshomba said. "It isn't a very fat book. We can finish it fast."

I expected the others to object to the idea of reading the entire play and then rewriting it. It would be twice as much work and twice as much time spent studying Shakespeare. I glanced around the room, but nobody else said anything.

"I'll make you a deal," I said. "We can make this your class project for the whole quarter—January through March. No spelling tests. No vocabulary. No reading assignments. But everybody has to agree to work on this. You have to read the

entire play, rewrite it, design your own costumes and props, and
perform your play for me to earn your grade. If you do it, everybody who participates gets an A for the quarter. If you quit,
you're in big trouble. Everybody."

Toshomba and Tyeisha exchanged glances, nodded, and
turned to look at Cornelius. They knew from experience that if
Cornelius didn't want to do a particular project, he would sabo-
tage it for everybody else.

"It was my idea in the first place, wasn't it?" Cornelius asked.

"Fine," I said, hiding my surprise. "Does everybody agree?
Raise your hands." I was even more surprised to see Rico
Perez's hand shoot into the air before anybody else's. They
didn't know I knew it, but Rico and Cornelius lived on opposite
sides of East Palo Alto and both ran with neighborhood posses
that promoted race pride, which translated into bashing the
heads of anybody who wasn't of their specific ethnic background. They did know that I would not tolerate any outward
show of racial prejudice in my classroom or in the Academy, so
they kept to their respective corners of the room and pretended
not to notice each other.

"You're up for this, Rico?" I asked. "Julio? Jesse?" All three
boys nodded their heads. Cornelius spread his arms like a
mighty black thunderbird and said, "It's unanimous, of course,
because these guys are smart enough to recognize a brilliant
idea when I say it."

I almost reneged on my offer, because I was afraid it would do
irreparable damage when they quit halfway through the book, as
I was sure they would. Perseverance wasn't their strong suit, and
I didn't think they had the resilience to recuperate from another
in a long line of failures.

"A deal's a deal," I said. "Let's get started."

Cornelius took the role of Bassanio, the young lover, and assigned the other roles to his classmates. Julio surprised everybody, even himself I think, by volunteering to read the part of

Antonio, the merchant and friend who lends Bassanio his money.

"Good for you," I told Julio. "I'm proud of you. It takes guts to read Shakespeare."

"I figured it was so hard that nobody couldn't read it very good, so it would be a good time for me to practice," Julio said. "They won't even know if I mess up because they don't know all them weird words neither."

We were deep in the middle of Act II, about the time that Bassanio arrives at the beautiful Portia's doorstep with the money he has borrowed in Antonio's name, when the door of my classroom flew open.

"I'm back!" Raul Chacon announced as he made his grand entrance, jeans riding low on his hips in a "sick sag," baseball hat jammed on backward, his hands hidden inside the too-long sleeves of his baggy black Oakland Raiders jacket.

Delighted at the interruption, the seniors applauded Raul's appearance. He removed his hat and swept it through the air as he bowed to the class.

"Don't worry, Miss J," he said, "I won't interrupt your class."

"Are you cutting school?" I asked. The last time I had seen him, Raul had been on his way to Foothill Community College to enroll. He assured me that he had plenty of time, hours to spare, before he was due in class.

Raul took a seat in the front row, which usually had a few empty seats. Like churchgoers, my students headed for the back of the room, as though the closer they were to the front of the room, the closer they sat to the hellfire that school threatened. As he sat down, I offered Raul a book.

"I remember this," he said. "It's about that dude who borrows the money from his homie and the money guy tries to cut his—"

I interrupted him by placing one finger against his lips. "They haven't read that far yet," I said.

Raul stood up and held out both arms. "Sorry, guys," he said to the class. "I didn't mean to wreck it for you. It's a pretty good book."

Cornelius nodded, as if the compliment were for him.

Raul read along with the class and stayed in his seat after the bell rang and the seniors raced outside. I sat down next to him and checked my watch. We had six minutes before my next class started. Raul, seeing me check my watch, said, "Don't worry. I got time. I don't even gotta go to class, anyway."

"Of course you have to go."

"No, I don't. I'm flunking everything." Earlier that year, when he had rattled off his list of classes, I thought he might have trouble with American literature and freshman composition, but I was certain that he'd do well in weight training, his favorite subject at Parkmont.

"How can you flunk weight training?"

He shrugged. "I always cut."

"But I thought you liked weight training. You aced it when you were here."

"I do like it. But every day this homeboy who's in my class says, 'Hey, Raul, let's go get some lunch. I'm buying.' So I go. You know how I like to eat."

"I know." I nodded. Same old Raul, still ninety-five pounds, still hungry. Seeing him sitting there, in his old seat, I realized how much I missed him.

"College is too hard, Miss J. And I miss being in your class. Maybe I should've flunked, and then I could stay here with you."

"But it's time to move on," I said. "You're twenty-one years old. You're a college man now. And you have a good job." He made a face. "Aren't you still working at SLAC?"

Raul and Gusmaro had both landed jobs at Stanford Linear Accelerator Center during the summer before their senior year of high school, and both were offered full-time jobs after graduation.

"Yeah, I still work there," Raul said, "but it's just a dumb job in the dumb warehouse where the dumb ugly people work because we're too dumb and ugly to work in the main office."

I had thought he would get over his envy of Gusmaro, who landed a job as a receptionist and then moved into personnel. Raul thought Gusmaro got the better job because he was taller and smarter. I didn't know how to explain to Raul, without pushing his self-esteem even lower, that it was his own lack of self-confidence that sabotaged his job interviews. I had tried several times to discuss it with him, but each time he had insisted that it was his ugliness that kept him from succeeding.

"How is Gusmaro doing?" I asked.

"Did you know him and his girlfriend had a kid?"

"But his girlfriend is only fifteen."

"Don't worry," Raul said. "They're getting married. They got their own apartment in Sunnyvale and they don't have to share it with anybody and they got two cars and everything. I guess Gusmaro puts all his money in the bank or something."

"You could do that, too," I said.

"Get married?"

"No. You could put your money in the bank and save up and move out of East Palo Alto and live in a nice place."

"All my friends are in EPA, Miss J. And I can't save my money. I keep trying, but every time I get a check, I end up spending it on girls who dump me because I'm ugly and stupid."

"I wish you'd stop saying those things about yourself. It makes me want to cry. And it isn't true. You aren't ugly and you aren't stupid. But if you tell yourself those things all the time, you believe them."

The bell rang and we had to interrupt our discussion until the next break, when Raul told me about his latest love affair. He got this girl's phone number from a friend and called her for a date. She agreed to go out with him, and he took her to a dinner and a movie. Then she asked if they could go to the mall and window-shop. As they were walking through the shopping center, she complained repeatedly about being cold, so Raul bought her a coat. Then she said that she really liked him and would like to be his girlfriend, but she wanted to be sure she never missed his phone calls so would he please buy her a beeper. He did.

"The next day, I called her up and she said she liked me and everything, but she already had a boyfriend so she couldn't go out with me," Raul said. "That's how come I think I'm stupid— because I believed her."

"We all make fools of ourself for love," I said. "I have plenty of times." Raul's eyes lit up at the prospect of learning about my love life, but I directed the conversation back to his breakup.

"Don't spend your money on girls unless you've known them a long time," I advised Raul.

"That's what my sister said. So her and my cousin Nina told me don't let that girl rip me off. They told me let's go get all that stuff you bought. So we went to the girl's house all the way out in Cupertino, and when we got there and I told her I wanted my stuff, she just laughed and shut the door and stayed in her house. My sister wanted to break the windows, but we didn't because it was a rich neighborhood and we knew they probably had alarms and stuff."

"Well, that was smart," I said.

"Yeah, but then I messed up because I was so mad that I let that girl put me down in front of my sister and my cousin, so when we were driving back on the freeway, I started going real fast and then this guy in a Camaro tried to race me and I crashed my car."

"At least you didn't get hurt."

"My cousin got hurt pretty bad. We went off the road, and the car flipped over on top of a tree. I gotta pay for the tree, too."

"Is your cousin all right?"

"Yeah. But now my uncle and aunt hate me and so does everybody else because I don't got no insurance and they have to pay for her hospital and everything. And since I don't got no insurance, the cops will probably throw me in jail because I can't pay for the trees and stuff."

I asked Raul why he didn't have insurance.

"I can't afford it."

"But how did you register your car without insurance?" His pained looked told me the answer. His car wasn't registered.

Raul stayed through the next class and asked for a piece of paper so he could write when the students wrote in their journals. I handed him a sheet of notebook paper.

"You better give me a couple," Raul said. "I gotta a lot of stuff to write down."

When I collected the journals at the end of the class period, Raul made no move to leave.

"Don't you have a class coming up soon?" I asked, hinting that he should leave but careful not to make him think I was trying to get rid of him. He drew in his breath and released such a sad sigh that my heart ached. He stood up and held out his hand. I took it and pulled him to me and hugged him until I heard him gasp for air.

"Sorry," I said, as I let him go. "I didn't mean to squeeze you so hard."

"You can squeeze me anytime, Miss J. Nobody ever hugged me as good as you."

As my fourth-period class filed in, I sneaked a peak at Raul's journal entry.

Hey, Miss J,

I remember one time when we had to write about what if we could have one magic wish and I don't remember what I wrote, probably something stupid like always. But if I had a wish right now, I would wish that I was still at Parkmont in the Academy so I could be in your class because you always told us every day that we were special and smart and lovable and handsome and charming and I believed it when I was in your class. I still be saying them little affirmations like you told us to, but they don't work to good when I don't got your class. I'm still just a dum stupid motherfucker but I keep on trying because I know you wouldn't lie to me and you said I could make it if I work hard. If you say I can make it, I know I can but I just wish it wouldn't take so long. I'm getting real tired.

Raul had done so well during his senior year and I had been sure he'd succeed once he had a decent job and a chance to go to college, but it didn't seem to be the case. I wondered whether Hal Gray had been right, as he had so often been, when he warned me that I was hurting Raul and my other students by helping them too much.

"If you solve all their problems for them and never give them a chance to fail, they'll never learn to take care of themselves," Hal had told me in one of our last conversations before he retired. "They'll be cripples, always looking for somebody to take care of them."

With the echo of Hal's words and Raul's example in mind, I decided not to help my seniors rewrite *The Merchant of Venice*. If they failed, it would hurt their grades, but they would have another quarter to recoup their loss, which might even turn out to be a better learning experience than their original project.

When he realized that I wasn't going to lead the class, Cornelius took over. He hurried everybody into their seats and directed them to open their books to the appropriate passage. Usually, when reading any literature, my students resist analyzing the story, pretending they don't understand anything, dragging each discussion out as long as possible, fighting the inevitable return to the text.

This time, they rushed me through the reading, competing for the chance to offer their own interpretations of difficult passages, instead of shrugging their shoulders and staring blankly at the pages in front of them, waiting for me to grow impatient with their silence and fill in the missing pieces for them as I usually did.

"Why would Portia's father make such a strange will?" I asked one day. "Why would he make his daughter agree to marry the man who picked the treasure chest that had the real treasure in it, even if she didn't love the guy?"

"He was a psycho," Tyeisha suggested, "and he doesn't want her to have his money after he's gone."

"No," Toshomba said, "I think he's just pretending. He's not really dead, so he doesn't want her to get married."

Even Maria, who never participated in class discussions because she was afraid people would laugh at her accent, had a suggestion.

"I think the father doesn't thinks there is very many smart mans. So he makes a hard question and only a very smart man can answer it. So his daughter will get a smart husband and if he is smart, probably he will be nice and the daughter will love him." Breathless with excitement at having spoken in front of the class, Maria patted her chest and fanned her flushed face with a cardboard folder.

"That's pretty good," Rico said, nodding his head and looking around the room to see whether the others appreciated the contributions of his brilliant fellow Mexican-American. It was the first time Rico had participated in the discussion about the play, and I took it as a sign that he and Cornelius were still honoring their truce. I didn't stop to think that it might signify just the opposite, that Rico had spoken out to emphasize the lack of attention paid to the Mexicans and other Hispanic students in the class.

By the end of January, they had read the entire play and discussed it great detail, and they had all written two-page thesis papers based on a central idea or character in the play. It was the first time that every single student in the class had completed a writing assignment. I was delighted and so impressed by their progress that I decided to take another step back and let them organize the rewrite on their own. Cornelius assigned each person several pages to translate and held a lottery to pick the name of the person who had to transcribe their version and type it on the class computer, an ancient Apple IIe.

I was in my office, a tiny cubicle at the back of the room, when the conversation in the classroom suddenly exploded into a loud, violent argument. I rushed into the room and found Rico and Julio facing off against Cornelius and Leroy. Joanie, Tyeisha, Araceli, Violeta, Isabella, Toshomba, Jesse, Danny, Sean, and the others sat in the middle, watching. I stood between the two pairs of boys and held up my hands.

"Back up," I said. Nobody moved. "Back up or it's over and everybody flunks." They backed up a few inches, but that was enough to satisfy me. If they were able to listen and respond, there was hope for a peaceful solution.

"What's the problem?" I asked.

Cornelius waved his hand at Rico and Julio. "These Mexicans said we are discriminating them because we named all the characters and stuff," he indicated himself and the other African-American students in the class. I was about to interrupt and instruct him to include the others, but Cornelius waved his big hand in the air to quiet me.

"They got a point," he said. "We did take over, so here's what we're going to do. We going to let the Mexicans pick two names. Go ahead." He nodded at Rico.

"Does that sound fair to you?" I asked Rico. He glared at Cornelius, unwilling to lose face by accepting the first offer.

"Three," Rico said. He braced his feet and jutted his chin into the air.

"Cornelius? Leroy? How does that sound?" I asked.

Leroy nodded, and Cornelius said, "Okay. Go ahead."

After a discussion that involved fierce whispers and emphatic hand gestures, Rico, Julio, Jesse, Isabella, and Violeta decided to name the main character, the rich merchant, Pancho, and his poor young friend Juanito.

"And that Portia lady should be named Isabella," Rico pronounced, "because Isabella never says nothing in class, so she should get somebody named from her name."

Toshomba, who had drawn the honor of scriptwriter, listed the names on the chalkboard. Pancho, Juanito, and Isabella, followed by Shapiro as Shylock, and Muhammed and Hakim as the friends of Pancho.

Leroy wanted to title their version *The Player Who Got Played*, but Tyeisha's title got more votes, so their play was dubbed *The Lonely Tycoon*.

As soon as they settled the names and title, Cornelius suggested that I go back into my office so that my presence wouldn't make them feel too nervous to think.

"If we need you, we know where to find you," he said.

I graciously withdrew to my office and worked on lesson plans and graded papers, expecting to be called for consultation at any given moment. They never called. Although I was surprised and delighted by their maturity and responsibility, I felt a pang of disappointment as I realized that this new class of seniors would move on in a few short months, as the class before had done. I consoled myself with the thought that this class would be more self-reliant than Raul Chacon and his posse had been.

They spent the next month writing their play and memorizing lines, and two weeks creating props and costumes. Julio sat in the corner, quietly sketching scenes from the play, until Maria peeked over his shoulder one day. With a squeal and a mouthful of giggles, she led Rico to the desk where Julio sat.

"Hey, Vato!" Rico shouted, as he picked up the drawing Julio was working on. "This is good, man." He circled the room, holding the drawing by its edges so that everybody could admire it.

Julio's sketch showed Pancho (Antonio) standing straight and proud, his head thrown back, his shirt torn open to reveal a broad, muscular chest, as a leering, malevolent Shapiro (Shylock) prepared to carve out Pancho's heart.

"Could we make a poster of that?" Cornelius wanted to know. "It should be like our movie poster." I promised to find a way to enlarge and reproduce the sketch and asked Julio if he wanted to be the official artist for the production. He agreed, on the condition that he didn't have to take a speaking part in the final production. Reading a role out loud from the book had been enough for him.

Julio's poster looked beautiful. Unfortunately, he never got to see it. A week before the end of the quarter, on the opening day of *The Lonely Tycoon*, Julio disappeared. Rico swore he didn't know what had happened, yet Julio's mother seemed less upset than I was about his disappearance.

"If you hear anything, please call me," I asked her.

She never called, and I headed into an emotional tailspin. First Simoa, now Julio. Who was next?

Unlike Simoa, Julio didn't disappear without a trace. He showed up at my classroom one evening a couple of weeks later, when I stayed late to catch up on grading journals.

"Hey, Miss J," he said softly from the doorway.

"Julio!" I didn't know whether to jump up and hug him or slug him for making me and his mother worry so much. I couldn't decide, so I just sat and stared at him.

"I knew you'd be here," he teased. "You're always hiding out here. You should get a man, you know, so you got a reason to go home at night."

"I'm doing just fine by myself, thank you very much."

"There you go again, lying to me."

"I'm serious. And I'm really mad at you for going off like that. Don't you know I worry about you?"

Julio shrugged and turned around. He shuffled to the back row and sat in his usual seat. He sat up straight and gripped the front edge of his desk with both hands.

"I'm sorry, but I didn't have a phone where I was."

"Yeah, right. And where is this unlikely place that has no phone?"

"Jail."

I choked on my surprise and started coughing.

"Not real jail, just the county detention center," Julio assured me. "I had to do some community service because I got in a little bit of trouble. But I only got one more week, and then I can come back to school."

"They can't just pull you out of school," I protested.

"Yes, they can," he said, "because I'm eighteen already."

"You are?" I asked, ashamed, remembering Emilio Lopez who had been arrested shortly after his eighteenth birthday, which I had also missed.

"It's no big deal," Julio said. "I wish I wouldn't've had a birthday, because that's how I got in trouble."

He told me he had bought a giant diamond ring for his girlfriend so he could give it to her on his birthday and ask her to marry him.

"A real diamond?" I asked. He nodded. "Where'd you get that kind of money?" I crossed my fingers behind my back, hoping he wouldn't say he had earned it selling drugs or stealing cars.

"I bought it from Sean Collins," Julio said.

As soon as I heard Sean's name, I knew the rest of the story. Sean had stolen the ring from a jewelry store a long time ago, but it was very expensive and still on the records when the police found Julio with it.

"If my girl would've kept it, none of this would've happened," Julio said. "But she broke up with me and I was so mad I went out and got drunk and punched in some windows in a store and I had the ring on me when the police busted me."

"Oh, honey, I'm sorry she broke up with you. You've been going together a long time, haven't you?"

"Two years," he said, his eyes filling with tears. He walked to the doorway and stood with his back to me. I could see his shoulders shaking. I went and put my arms around him. "I really loved her," he whispered.

When he could trust himself to talk, Julio told me the rest of the story. He didn't want to rat on Sean, so he took the bust himself, even though Sean would have gotten a lighter sentence because he was younger.

"Sean obviously doesn't care what happens to you," I said. "Why don't you tell the truth and let him answer up to what he did?"

"Because I'm not a stupid skinny white boy who doesn't have any friends," Julio said.

I started to cry, primarily out of anger because this was the second time that Sean's thieving had jeopardized somebody else's future. First Rico and the Colt pistol, now Julio and the diamond ring.

"Hey, don't cry, okay. I'll only be gone another week," Julio said. "But I wondered could I take my book and practice reading?"

I picked three novels from my bookshelf and handed them to him. "You can keep these, if you like them."

"Thanks, Miss J. And don't worry about me. I'm still going to graduate, even if I am old. You know that guy who came to our class last week—what's his name?"

"Raul Chacon?"

"Yeah," Julio nodded. "If Chacon can graduate when he's already twenty, then I can graduate when I'm nineteen. And besides, if I have to come back next year, at least I'll get to be in your class."

Julio shook my hand and thanked me again for the books

before he disappeared into the darkness outside. I wanted nothing more than to rush to Sean Collins's house and smack him silly, but it wouldn't change anything. I could only hope that Sean felt the same twisted knot of despair in his gut that I felt in mine.

Chapter 16

It Shouldn't Never Happen

Araceli Andrade tried to shrug off her plummeting grades by insisting that she had changed her mind and no longer wanted to become a trained cosmetologist.

"Who cares?" she demanded when I pointed out, during a meeting with Araceli and the other three Academy teachers, that she had dropped from all A's and B's to all C's and D's in less than a month.

"We care," Don Woodford told Araceli. "All of us care, or we wouldn't be sitting here with you, giving you our undivided attention." Jean Warner and Jim Bergie nodded.

We were sitting in the tiny Academy office, which barely held four chairs and a desk. Araceli had pushed her chair as far away from ours as possible, against the back wall of the room. Clad completely in black, including her lipstick and fingernails, despair seemed to be her latest fashion statement.

"We want to help you," Jean said softly, "but we can't help you if you won't let us, honey."

Maybe it was the word *honey,* or simply Jean's motherly manner of speaking, but whatever it was, it broke through Araceli's shell. She continued to sit straight in her chair, but tears streamed down her cheeks, leaving black rivulets of melted mascara.

"I know you be trying to help me and everybody," she said between sniffles, "and I appreciate it you helped me find out how to be a real hairdresser and all that, and how to get a loan to pay for school and everything, but I changed my mind. I don't want to go no more."

"I don't believe you," I said. I didn't. "You're a good actress, but not that good. You weren't making it all up. You were really excited about getting your cosmetology license and starting your own shop someday. What happened?"

Araceli inhaled slowly. "My father—" she started, but her voice cracked and she stopped and closed her eyes.

"What about your father?" The other teachers and I exchanged knowing glances. We had met Araceli's parents once, during Back to School Night. The entire Andrade family had made the visit, Mr. and Mrs. and three daughters. The girls stayed close to their mother, who, eyes downcast, walked a few paces behind her husband. Mr. Andrade hadn't said more than a few words, but his message had come through loud and clear: I am the master of my world and the women who live in it.

During summer school when I had first met Araceli, I had sensed that she was a lot like I had been as a teenager. When I met her father I realized why. Araceli and I had grown up twenty years and three thousand miles apart, but we came from the same family.

"What about your father?" I prompted Araceli again.

She squeezed her eyes shut even tighter and bit her lower lip to try to stop the trembling.

Jim Bergie shook his head and made a motion to end the meeting. Jean, Don, and I nodded. We wanted to help Araceli, not make her miserable. Jim cleared his throat.

"It's okay, Araceli," he said. "You don't have to talk about it right now. Maybe you could—"

Araceli's eyes flashed open. "He say only bitches and whores go to college and get their own business and stuff. He say good womens stay home with their husband at night and don't be going out noplace. Like my mother. She been going to school at night trying to get her GED because my dad, he can't work very much because he got a disability at work and we don't got enough money, but my dad he get real mad and call her a dirty whore every time she leave the house. And he don't want me to go to vocational school or college. He say I got to graduate high school so people knows he got a smart daughter, and then I got to learn how to act right so somebody gonna marry me. So now I got to go right home after school. I got to be in the house five minutes after the bus gets to my corner, and I got to go right home and cook the supper and wash the dishes and clean the house and wash the clothes and iron the clothes and wash the floor. I can't do no more homework at home, and I can't read no books or nothing."

After Araceli dried her tears and left with our assurance that we'd figure out a solution, the four of us created a plan. We arranged to take turns bringing a brown bag lunch for her so she could do her homework in our classrooms during lunch hour. We also added a seventh-period class so that she would have an extra hour to spend at school. The only class offered during seventh period was art, not Araceli's first choice, but she agreed that drawing and painting would be better than scrubbing the floor by hand.

By the end of the quarter, Araceli was back on track with A's and B's in all of her classes, and an A+ in art. I stopped by Mr. Hidalgo's room to thank him for taking Araceli into his art class in the middle of the term. Mr. Hidalgo, who was on his hands and knees wiping a large blob of blue paint from the floor in the corner of his classroom, stopped and looked up at me, his thin face surrounded by a cloud of gray hair. He stood up and wiped his hands on his smock and then walked across the room and picked up a canvas that measured about two feet by three.

"Look at this." He turned the canvas to me. A giant green fire-breathing dragon straddled an ocean bay, its tail curled gracefully among a range of soft purple mountains, its menacing eyes trained on a ship filled with muscular sailors.

"Jason and the Golden Fleece," I said. "We're reading that story in my class right now."

"I know," Mr. Hidalgo said. "Araceli painted this."

"My Araceli? By herself?"

Mr. Hidalgo nodded. "She said it was a makeup project to bring up her grade for your class. She was supposed to write a summary or draw an illustration for one of the myths you read in class. She asked me if I thought this would be good enough to submit for a grade."

Usually, student artwork for the myths consisted of a picture copied out of a reference book, or a crude sketch of an anemic warrior or a dragon that looked more like an overgrown dog with enlarged nostrils. Araceli's painting was far beyond anything I had ever expected or received.

"What did you tell her?" I asked Mr. Hidalgo.

"I told her I thought she should let you look at it and then put it in a portfolio and start thinking about applying for a scholarship in the Art Department at San Jose State."

"It's already March," I said. "Isn't it too late to apply for this fall?"

"For this kind of talent," Mr. Hidalgo said, "people make exceptions."

When Cornelius Baker saw Araceli's painting, he hired her on the spot to design a program for *The Lonely Tycoon* and declared the finished product "a million times better than those lame little pictures on the programs over at the real live theater." He posted a copy of the program on the wall outside our classroom beside Julio's poster of Shapiro (Shylock) preparing to carve a chunk of flesh out of Pancho's (Antonio's) chest.

Julio and Araceli might have stolen the stage from the "real live theater" artists, but the actors were in no danger from the

Tycoon cast. None of them had been able to memorize the lines, and their costumes consisted of bedsheet togas, cardboard crowns, and aluminum-foil swords. The three treasure caskets—spray-painted shoe boxes—looked much more likely to contain old tennis shoes than precious jewels.

Aesthetics aside, the play was a hit and kept remarkably close to the original story line, with one exception. In the final scene, instead of declaring that Shapiro must give up his beloved Jewish religion and give all his money to his daughter and her Christian husband, Pancho intervenes.

"Shapiro shouldn't've messed with his daughter's business, telling her she can't marry a Christian and all that shit," Cornelius declared, in his role as Pancho. "So I'll take his money and give it to his daughter, but Shapiro gets to keep his religion. Nobody has the right to take away what a man believes in. That's like making somebody give up their culture. It shouldn't never happen."

Although they seemed to enjoy their moment in the spotlight, the *Tycoon* players refused to repeat their performance for parents or friends.

"You said we just had to write our own play and put it on for you," Rico reminded me, "and we would all get an A. We did it, just like we said, so it's time to pay up. You're the one who always says, 'A deal's a deal.' "

I paid up, but I could have kicked myself for not having figured out a way to hide a video camera to tape their one and only performance. In another sense, though, I feel even more blessed because I was the sole recipient of such a precious gift.

Encouraged by their enthusiasm and talent, I decided to try another creative project. After reading poetry samples from our literature textbook and listening to song lyrics, including rap, I assigned the seniors the task of writing and illustrating a poem of any length or form, from haiku to rap. As I distributed multicolored marking pens and drawing paper, I noticed that

Cornelius had retreated to his old seat in the far corner of the room, where he sat with his back to the class. When I placed a sheet of paper on his desk, Cornelius "accidentally" bumped it with his knee and pretended not to notice as it floated to the floor. I picked it up and placed it on his desk again.

"Is something wrong?" I asked. Cornelius shook his head but didn't look at me.

"All you have to do is try, and you pass this assignment," I reminded him. "It doesn't even have to rhyme."

"I can't."

"Of course you can."

"No," Cornelius insisted.

"Why not?"

"I just can't. I ain't got nothing to say."

"You don't have any feelings about anything at all?" I asked. Cornelius shook his head.

"But something must make you happy or sad." Cornelius continued to shake his head, slowly, back and forth, left to right to left to right. "Then make a poem about something that makes you mad." His head slowed down enough to allow for a quick glance out of the corner of one eye. I dropped to my knees and clasped my hands in front of my chest.

"Please don't make me beg," I said, batting my eyes at Cornelius. "It's so unattractive."

He snorted softly and shook his head harder at my silliness.

"Come on," I pleaded. "I know you can do it."

"I ain't hanging it up on the wall."

"You don't have to," I said, trying not to sound too eager. "You don't even have to show it to anybody. Just me. And as soon as you show it to me, you can rip it up and throw it away. As long as you do it, you get credit."

Cornelius lifted one large hand and placed it palm down on the paper I had placed on his desk. "Don't look," he whispered.

I quickly made my way to the other side of the room and

pretended not to be watching Cornelius as he frowned and chewed the eraser end of his pencil. At the end of the period, I drifted back toward his desk. Once again, he sat with his arms crossed, his back to the class. At first glance, I thought he had changed his mind and decided not to write a poem, but when I reached his desk, I saw the poem, written in tiny letters in the center of the drawing paper.

"It's a haiku," Cornelius explained, as I bent to read it. "You said it don't gotta rhyme, just five syllables, seven syllables, five syllables. So this is a haiku, right?"

"Right," I whispered. "It's a haiku."

> Ice cold blue black steel
> Red blood running in the street
> Gun is man's best friend

Maybe it was a warning, or a plea. At the time, I was too stunned to do anything except enter a grade for Cornelius in my gradebook and watch him shred his haiku into tiny pieces and sprinkle them into the trash can like the ashes of a cremated body. Two days later, Mr. Simms called me into his office and told me that Cornelius had been expelled. He and two other boys had been caught on campus with a loaded gun in their vehicle. None of the boys would admit owning the weapon, so they were all being expelled.

"Is there anything I can do?"

Mr. Simms had started shaking his head before I even asked the question. "Concentrate on the ones who are here. That will keep you busy enough."

I wrote a letter to the school district superintendent, vouching for Cornelius. I explained that he had joined the Academy as a sophomore with failing grades and a miserable attendance record. During the next two and a half years, he had earned a 2.8 GPA, improved his attendance, and had worked for the past two years as an office clerk in a small law firm in Palo Alto. I said that

I would personally vouch for his character and integrity.

"If Cornelius says the gun was not his, then it wasn't. I know that in my heart," I concluded my letter. "Cornelius Baker is not a liar, and I would bet my life on that."

The following Monday, Cornelius walked into my sixth-period class as though nothing had happened. He took his seat in the back and pointedly ignored me, which I interpreted as a sign that he was delighted to be back in my class. I returned the compliment by ignoring him, except for one brief pat on the shoulder as I just happened to walk by his desk at the end of class.

My supervisor, Madeline Richards, the director of the Academy program at the district level, called me that afternoon to ask whether Cornelius Baker had been in class.

"Yes, he was," I said, "and I was so happy to see him. I thought he was expelled."

"He very nearly was," Madeline explained. "I was at his expulsion hearing, and I wouldn't have given two cents for his chances. He wouldn't answer any of the questions, wouldn't even look at the members of the board. He just sat there, with his arms crossed, staring at the floor. The superintendent told him that they had found out the gun belonged to the boy who was driving and that there was a very good chance that Cornelius and the third boy had been telling the truth when they claimed they didn't know it was there."

"If they found out it wasn't his, then why didn't they let him go?" I asked.

Madeline said they were upset because he had refused to cooperate with the police or the school officials in even the smallest way. He told the arresting officer that he didn't know anything about the gun, and that was the last thing he said. He wouldn't talk to his parents, either.

"At the hearing, the superintendent told Cornelius that all he had to do was ask for a second chance and he could have it," Madeline said. "But he acted like we weren't even there. Then the superintendent brought out your letter and read it out loud. When he finished, he asked Cornelius if he had anything to say in response. The kid still didn't say a word, didn't move a muscle. But he was crying. I've never seen anybody cry like that, without making a sound. He just sat there, tears streaming down his face. He didn't even try to wipe them away. We all felt like crying. We knew he wasn't too far gone to save if he could cry over your letter. That's why we sent him back to you. I just thought you should know."

Chapter 17

Peoples Needs to
Learn This Things

T he coolest thing that happened in Tonga was when my old granny took us to the graveyard at night and we dug up some old bones to take a curse off our house," Simoa Mariposa informed her classmates with a mischievous grin. "It was real dark and there was all these weird sounds in the night, like *oooh* and *eeegh*." She paused to grab her throat and gag for effect, delighted at the screams from some of the other girls. "We sprinkled some stuff on the bones and put them back in the ground and went home. And that's the end of my speech. Thank you very much." After an exaggerated bow and much finger waving, Simoa strolled to her seat.

Simoa had simply walked into the room on the first day of the final quarter of the school year. When I saw her, I was struck dumb, standing at the chalkboard, my hand poised in midair. For the life of me, I couldn't remember what I had been about to write.

"Did you miss me?" Simoa asked as her tawny face flowered into a full-bloom smile. At first glance, she seemed to look the same as she had the day she disappeared so many weeks earlier. And for a few days she managed to put on a convincing show, but as she relaxed into the familiar flow of the school day, she dropped her guard, and I realized something significant had changed. I asked her to stay after class for a minute.

"It was just a bunch of lies," she insisted when I gently broached the subject of Lando and the videotape. "You know how men be lying like dogs all the time. Don't pay them no never mind. I'm fine." She grinned at me, but the sparkle was missing from her brown eyes and her grin looked stiff, more like a grimace than a real smile. Impulsively, I hugged her. She hugged me back for a just a second, then suddenly pulled away, but it had been long enough for me to feel the telltale bulge in her belly. She was pregnant.

"I got a lot of things to take care of," she said, as she grabbed her books and took off down the hallway.

As far as I could tell, I was the only one who knew Simoa was pregnant. Her baggy pants and oversize shirts and jackets were the latest style. She didn't seem upset by her condition and clearly didn't want to discuss it, so I left her alone. I didn't want to push her away now that she was finally back, safely, in school and scheduled to graduate on time.

"I got a whole bunch of extra credits," she had explained when I asked whether missing an entire quarter of school was going to jeopardize her graduation. "I took seven classes instead of six in my freshman and sophomore years."

"That was pretty smart planning," I complimented her.

"No it wasn't," she said, with her usual blunt honesty. "I didn't plan nothing. I just didn't want to go home."

I was trying to think of something to say, some word of advice or encouragement, but nothing came to mind. Simoa patted my shoulder and smiled, this time a genuine smile.

"Don't worry about it, Miss J. I'm all right. Shit happens, you know, but I can handle it. Honest. You'll see. I'm gonna graduate and get out of here and go back to Tonga and live with my grandma. I'm gonna take my sister with me, too, so nobody can't hurt her. We got family. We'll be okay. You're the one who ain't got nobody here if you need something. Maybe I should be worrying about you."

"I'm fine," I assured Simoa.

"Then how come you got them big bags under your eyes and you look like you ain't slept in a week. You got a new man or something?"

It was my turn to plead too much work to stand around chatting. Simoa shooed me away with a graceful wave of one carefully manicured hand. At least she was healthy, and she seemed in control, and she hadn't dropped out of school and given up like so many pregnant girls do. And with Simoa back in class, all but two of the senior girls had made it through the year. Genee Sutherland, whose parents had threatened to kick her out of the house if she didn't stop dating her thirty-four-year-old boyfriend, had quietly arranged to take the high school proficiency exam. She aced the exam, found a job, rented an apartment, and enrolled as a full-time student at a local community college. Tenille Murray, a brilliant, beautiful girl buried beneath a mountain of fat, had transferred to an alternative program rather than put up with the constant teasing and humiliation of the boys at school.

Tenille had written a letter to me in her journal the week before she left the Academy.

Dear Miss J—

You probably think I'll miss Parkmont, but I won't. Nobody likes me. They don't even want to know me because I'm fat, like they think it's contagious or something. People always tell me I have a pretty face if I would just lose some weight, but I've tried everything and I can't do it and I think it's better to just be me than to get anorexia and kill myself like all those stupid girls. But thanks for being nice to me anyway. You're the only person who never gave me advice about going on a diet. It's like you didn't even notice I was fat. You just noticed me. Thanks.

Since Genee already had an equivalency diploma, and Tenille would graduate from alternative school, Simoa's return brought us back to 100 percent retention for the senior girls—quite an improvement from the previous year's pitiful showing. And this class was bigger than the first Academy graduating class. Twenty-seven of the first fifty kids graduated the previous year, with only five girls in the group. This year, we would have thirty-two, and the split was half male and half female. Definite cause for celebration.

When the scholarship awards started to arrive, there was even more reason to celebrate. Two of the boys received football scholarships to Lawton University in Oklahoma, and Maria Hernandez and Isabella Carrillo both received full-tuition academic scholarships, Maria to San Jose State and Isabella to Foothill College. And even though Araceli's application was late, she received a partial scholarship from the Fine Arts Department at San Jose State.

"I cannot believe this!" Maria squealed when she opened the letter and read the good news. "I have been praying every day for this to happen and now my prayers has come true. I am so happy, Miss J, my heart is too full." She pressed her chubby hands against her chest and puffed her cheeks full of air. She held her breath for a second, her eyes wide, then expelled her breath in a burst of giggles. "I think I will faint!"

Isabella rummaged in her purse for a cotton hankie and handed it to Maria, who waved it wildly back and forth in front of her flushed face.

Isabella opened her letter, read it silently, smiled, crossed herself, carefully refolded the paper, and returned it to its envelope.

"Do you remember when we were first in your class for the students who did not speak the English?" she asked me.

"Yes, I remember you very well."

"I also remember you," Isabella said. "And I always think of what you said to me when I cried and told you I cannot do the hard work in your class. Do you remember what you told to me?"

I shook my head.

"That is fine," Isabella said. "You do not have to remember it because I will never forget it. You told me that if I make one hundred mistakes before I learn something, then I will have learned one hundred and one things. But if I learn something right the first time, I have learned only one thing. I think I have learned one million things already."

To celebrate their scholarships, I took both girls out for a milkshake after school on Friday. Neither of them wanted to be impolite and sit in the front seat, leaving the other in the back, so they both squeezed into the tiny backseat of my Fiat for the ride to East Palo Alto. As we approached the corner of Isabella's street, she tapped me on the shoulder.

"Please drive slowly here," she said. I checked the pavement ahead. EPA is almost as famous for its potholes as it is for its high homicide rate. The road looked smooth. I glanced in the rearview mirror and caught Isabella's eye.

"I want my neighbors to see me riding in a car with my beautiful teacher," Isabella explained, as she tossed her long black hair away from her face, sending it flying in the wind like an ebony flag. Beside her, Maria beamed, a raven-haired cherub.

The next time I saw Maria and Isabella, they were both sobbing. Their clothes were dirty and torn, their faces scratched and bleeding. They had run into my classroom during lunch break, followed by a flock of their friends who explained that Angie and Berta, both seniors, had attacked them in the bathroom. Why? Because Maria and Isabella were graduating and going to college. Angie and Berta were coming back for another year, their third time around as seniors.

"Let's go see Dr. Delgado," I told Maria and Isabella, as soon as we had dried their tears and disinfected their scratches.

"We already have seen Dr. Delgado," Isabella said. "He told to us that we will be suspended if we are fighting again."

"That's ridiculous!" I said. "He must have misunderstood." Maria and Isabella exchanged knowing glances but shrugged and followed me to the office.

"That's correct," Dr. Delgado said when I asked him if he had threatened to suspend the two girls.

"But they weren't fighting," I argued.

"It doesn't matter who starts the incident," Dr. Delgado explained. "Anybody who is involved in a violent altercation on school grounds is automatically suspended for three days. That's district policy."

"So you mean if somebody is getting straight A's and I'm jealous and I walk up and knock her upside the head, she's going to get suspended, too?"

"That is correct." Dr. Delgado held up his hands, palms down, as though warning an overexcited puppy to sit. "I know it may seem unfair to you, but it's the only way to maintain an orderly campus."

"It doesn't *seem* unfair. It *is* unfair. They aren't fighting. They're being attacked. Don't you make any differentiation?"

"I'm sorry, Miss Johnson. I don't make the rules. Feel free to take this up with the district superintendent."

I'll do better than that, I thought to myself. Out loud, I said, "Thank you so much, Dr. Delgado. It's been a most informative conversation."

He smiled and nodded as I stomped out of his office and down the hall, Maria and Isabella, silent and pale, scurrying behind me.

Before I sent the girls to their fifth-period class, I called Maria's mother and asked her to meet us in my classroom after school that day. When she arrived, I took a clean journal out of the supply closet and labeled it "Official Record of Incidents Involving Angela Herrera and Berta Chavez." I showed the girls and Mrs. Hernandez how to log every conversation or other interaction involving the two girls, by recording the exact time and date, exactly what occurred, affixing their legal signatures, and getting any witnesses to sign and date the page.

Next step was to call the EPA police dispatcher and file charges against Angie and Berta for assault, since they were both over eighteen. The officer who took the call suggested that we call the East Palo Alto Law Project and make an appointment to get a restraining order against the girls. We made the appointment for the following afternoon, and Mrs. Hernandez promised to pick up the girls and deliver them to the appointment.

"Now watch carefully," I told Maria and Isabella. "This is what I want you to do the next time Angie or Berta or anybody else tries to get in a fight with you at school. You put your palms together like this." I raised my arms above my head and placed my palms flat against each other. "Let me see you try."

Isabella performed the movement easily, but Maria had trouble bringing her short round arms together above her head. She had to strain to make her hands meet. Mrs. Hernandez moved her hands in her lap, and I could see that she was mentally rehearsing the same procedure.

"Close enough," I said. "Now you keep your hands just like this and you scream your head off like this." I screeched like a cat with its tail caught in a screen door. Maria and Isabella giggled delightedly, and Maria danced up and down.

"Come on," I said. "Let's hear you scream." They tried, but Maria's scream sounded like she was gargling with mouthwash, and Isabella's was inaudible.

"Try it again. I'll help you." I let out another scream and nodded my head at them until they joined in, timidly at first, but gaining confidence and momentum as I started hopping up and down, whooping and hollering. Finally Maria managed an acceptable yell, and Isabella promised to practice at home.

"It feels funny and looks stupid," I said. "But if you do this, everybody will see you and they will know that you are not fighting. You can't fight with your arms straight over your head, can you?" They shook their heads.

"Right. And if Dr. Delgado suspends you from school for fighting when you are clearly not fighting, then I will quit my job, and we will file a lawsuit against the school."

Both girls stopped giggling and stared at me with wide, frightened eyes.

"Don't worry. It isn't going to happen. And if it does, we'll sell our story to the television news and get rich." Their fear turned to shocked delight. "That isn't likely to happen either, so don't get your hopes up." I closed the journal and handed it to Mrs. Hernandez. "Take good care of this because we'll need it if we have to go before the school board or the court." She took the journal with both hands and clasped it to her chest in the same familiar gesture I had seen Isabella use so many times.

"*Gracias por* helping this girls," Mrs. Hernandez said. "You are very good nice person for them."

"I love them," I said. "And I don't want them to go through their lives being victims. They are good girls, but they need to know how to protect themselves from people who aren't good."

Mrs. Hernandez nodded slowly. "Many peoples needs to learn this things."

"Well, now you can teach them."

"I will be the *maestra*." Mrs. Hernandez's shy smile revealed two rows of tiny, perfect teeth.

The next day, as we were grading papers during his clerk period, Rico Perez said, "Hey, Miss J, what's this I heard about you helping Maria and Isabella get some kind of police thingie on those crazy girls who were beating on them?"

I explained that a restraining order makes it illegal for somebody to come within a certain distance of the person who files
the order, if the court accepts it.

"Do you think I could get one against Omar?" Rico said. "You
remember that guy I was gonna kill?"

"I definitely remember," I said. "I tried to get you to request a
restraining order before, if you recall, but you said you'd rather
shoot him."

Rico nodded. "Yeah. I would've, too, except for Tio. But I
been thinking about what you said, and what Tio told me, and
Omar's been bugging me again, and I thought maybe we could
try doing it your way this time. Just to see if it works." I was on
the phone before Rico had a chance to reconsider, dialing the
law project office. When I hung up, I dialed the EPA police dispatcher and handed the phone to Rico.

"Talk," I said. "You're a law-abiding citizen, not a criminal.
Stay that way."

Rico told the police office about Omar and agreed to make a
police report, since the officer offered to send a dispatcher to
meet him at whatever location they agreed on.

"Pretty cool," Rico said, when he hung up. "I don't even have
to go to the police station, so nobody will see me go there and
spread the word that I'm a rat."

"You aren't a rat. You are a decent person. Omar is the rat."

"Yeah, yeah. But you know what I mean."

He tapped the telephone receiver lightly with his fist. "You
know, that cop wasn't too bad to talk to. He was even pretty
nice."

"Imagine that," I teased. "You might be surprised how many
people would be nice if you gave them a chance."

"Like who? You? I give you a chance to be nice to me every
day. That's nice of me, right?"

"Yes, and I appreciate it more than I can tell you," I said. "Dr.
Delgado and Mr. Simms can be nice, too."

"Is that right?"

"Yes, it is. Why don't you give them a chance sometime and see for yourself?"

"I'll think about it."

While Rico was busy thinking, I paid a visit to Dr. Delgado's office and told him about Omar stalking and repeatedly threatening to kill Rico.

"Have these incidents occurred on campus?" Dr. Delgado wanted to know.

"No. I believe they have all taken place in East Palo Alto."

"Good."

"Excuse me?"

"What I meant was that it is good that this man hasn't followed Rico to school where the lives of other students would be endangered." Which translated into: As long as it isn't on my campus, it isn't my problem.

"But what about Rico's life? He's a student at Parkmont, even though he lives in EPA."

"Still, the matter falls under the jurisdiction of the East Palo Alto Police Department. There really isn't much we can do here at Parkmont, other than take our normal security precautions."

"You mean you think Casey's I-Spy sunglasses and Radio Shack walkie-talkie are going to protect Rico from a crazy crackhead armed with an automatic?"

Dr. Delgado checked his watch and informed me that he was late for an appointment thank you very much for stopping by to inform me of this situation I will keep it under observation.

I called the Parkmont Police Department and tried to file a complaint against Omar for threatening Rico, but they agreed with Dr. Delgado that it was a matter for the East Palo Alto police. However, if the alleged perpetrator perpetrated anything on school property, I was to let them know immediately and they would take appropriate action.

I thanked the officer kindly and went home to bed, secure in the knowledge that the public school system administrators and the local police were getting a good night's sleep because the perpetrators were busy on the other side of the freeway, picking on the poor people.

Chapter 18

Sueños con los Angelitos, Maestra

You gonna be there for a while today?" For a second, I couldn't place the familiar voice. I hadn't heard from Julio for three weeks, since he had stopped to tell me about getting busted for buying the stolen diamond from Sean.

"I'm grading papers. I'll be here until about five," I said.

Julio didn't respond. I heard shouts, the ground-shaking thump of a low-rider sound system, then a dial tone.

A half hour later, at about four o'clock, after the buses had left and most of the staff and students were gone, a dark green Chevy pulled into the parking lot outside T-Wing. I didn't recognize the car or the five boys who climbed out and headed straight for my classroom. One of the boys was walking with crutches. I didn't recognize him until he hobbled into the room and said, "Hey, Miss J, did you miss me?"

Two of Julio's escorts stood outside my classroom, flanking the doorway, and the other two stood inside, facing the windows that overlooked the parking lot.

"What happened to you?" I asked Julio.

"Got bit by a dog," he said, grinning.

"Must have been a pretty big dog."

"I was just kidding. I got shot."

"Right." I started to laugh, until I realized he was serious.

Julio hobbled over to the student desk where I had been grading worksheets and turned so his right side was facing me. He pointed to his right leg. As he moved his arm to point, I noticed the clear plastic hospital ID bracelet on his right wrist.

"Look," he said, tapping his finger against his thigh where two round red spots and a couple of dark brown stains marked his khaki pants. "My leg is still bleeding. The doctors said they can't take the bullet out because it's too close to my nerve."

"What happened?"

"A drive-by. You should see my car, bullet holes everywhere. Man, I was lucky I just got one in my leg."

Lucky wasn't exactly the word that came to my mind. And now that I could see Julio's face clearly, I knew it wasn't the word he was thinking of either. If his friends hadn't been with him, I knew he would have thrown himself into my arms and cried like a baby. I made a motion to stand up, but he stopped me with the slightest movement of his head.

"I just wanted to let you know I was all right since I know you probably been worrying about me and everything," he said. "I got done with my community service and I was gonna come back to school, but then this happened."

"When?"

"Last night. I just got out of the hospital when I called you."

"Why?"

"I don't know," Julio said. "Honest. I think it could have been some guys who thought I was my cousin because I got this cousin who gets in a lot of fights and they might've been trying to get a payback. Or else it was the Sac Street gang retaliating for a drive-by last week. Who knows? But I seen the guys who done it. I know them, even."

"You know them?"

"They go to Parkmont. Jaime Gonzales and Lupe Cardenas. You probably don't know them. They ain't in the Academy or nothing. They're too stupid to be in your class."

"Did you tell the police?"

One of the boys inside the room turned sharply and looked at Julio, who quickly shook his head. "They won't do nothing. They don't even care, really. We got so much stuff going down in EPA. You could stand right on the corner in the middle of the day and shoot a hundred people and the police probably wouldn't even come."

"Well, you have to report it to somebody."

"No." Julio shook his head. "I just gotta find someplace to hide out because they'll probably come after me since I know who they are."

"Then you have to call the police. Don't be stupid." I stood up and headed for the telephone in my office, but Julio lifted one arm and blocked my way with his crutch.

"Don't," he whispered. One of the boys near the door muttered something in Spanish, too quickly for me to catch what he was saying, but all four of Julio's bodyguards were beside him in less than five seconds. "I gotta get going," Julio said. "I'll be okay, Miss J. Honest." Bodyguards and crutches notwithstanding, I grabbed him and hugged him tightly.

"You have my number?" I whispered.

"Yeah, sure."

I stepped back and held him by both shoulders until his eyes met mine. "Call me if you need anything at all."

"Okay. But don't worry. I'm cool."

He didn't look cool limping out to the car with his friends, and he didn't sound cool when he called me several hours later, in the middle of the night.

"They're sitting outside my house waiting for me," he whispered when I picked up the phone. "Jaime and Lupe. They been out there since after school. They even took a shot at me when I was coming home, but I got inside okay. I thought they'd take off, but they been sitting out there ever since—" His voice cracked.

"What kind of car do they have?" I asked, already half dressed in the jeans and sweater I'd dropped on the chair by my bed.

"A white Camaro. Real low."

"Don't move. Don't go near the windows. Don't do anything. Just wait. They have to leave sometime. They can't stay there forever."

Julio's bravado broke, and I heard him swallow a sob.

"They'll get hungry or have to go pee or something eventually, won't they?" I asked.

He laughed through his tears. "Yeah, I guess."

"Okay, then, listen. I'll be sitting right here by the phone. The second they leave, you call me and I'll come get you. In the meantime, you pack some clothes and whatever else you need. Do you know where I live?"

"No."

"Good. You can't tell anybody where you're going, not even your mother. I'll talk to her when I get there."

"Thanks, Miss J," Julio whispered, then hung up.

The Escobars' kitchen was filled with women and children—sisters, aunts, cousins, and nieces—when I arrived. I almost asked where his father was, but then I remembered that he had told me all of the men in his family had either been killed or were in prison. Mrs. Escobar was sobbing hysterically, clutching Julio's arm as two little girls wrapped themselves in the folds of her long skirt and peeked through their fingers at me.

"*Mijo*," Mrs. Escobar sobbed. Julio was her only living son. Instinctively, I crossed the kitchen and took the tiny woman in my arms.

"*No te preocupes*," I said. "*Nadie voy a molestar su hijo ahora. El voy a estar conmigo.*" She stopped clutching Julio's arm and collapsed into my arms. I held her head against my chest and smoothed her hair back from her face, as my mother had always done when I came to her scared and crying. Tears in his own

eyes, Julio watched for a moment, then motioned that he was
ready to go.

"Are you packed?" I asked, glancing around for a suitcase or a
bag.

Julio held up a plastic garbage bag and nodded. "I got everything. Let's go."

Neither of us breathed as we bounced across the poorly paved
streets of Julio's neighborhood. I left the lights off until we
reached the freeway entrance at the edge of town, then I flipped
on the lights and floored it. We weren't sure we had escaped
without notice until we crossed through Menlo Park and started
up Sand Hill Road toward Woodside. There were a few lights
traveling behind us, so I cut across Portola Road to Mountain
Home Road, a winding, tree-lined street lined with heavily
wooded estates. A single pair of headlights followed at some distance, but by the time we crossed through downtown Woodside
and started up the back side of the mountain via Kings Mountain
Road, I knew we were safe. Kings Mountain is a five-mile
stretch of road through the giant redwoods of Huddart Park, a
series of tight switchbacks that test the traction of any car, and
most people make the entire twenty-minute trip in first or second gear. Driving by instinct, I took the tight curves in second
and the wide curves in third, and we were at the top of the
mountain in ten minutes. There was no way that a larger car,
much less a bulky low-rider, could have followed us without
pitching over the side of the road and down the dark side of the
mountain.

That night, with Julio bundled in blankets on my couch and
me tucked under my covers in the next room, I learned how
Julio had lived for eighteen years, how so many of my students—
Raul, Gusmaro, Cornelius, Tyeisha, Toshomba, Leroy—still
lived every night of their young lives. I learned what mortal fear
feels like, what it sounds like. The sigh of a tree, the whisper of a

leaf skittering across the gravel drive, the soft tread of a squirrel scampering across the backyard—every normal night sound became the killer who lurked outside, waiting for his chance. I couldn't sleep, so I was awake when Julio started to scream in his sleep. When I woke him, he clutched my arms with both hands, and I could feel his entire body shaking as I hugged him. He hadn't been very big in the first place, and he had lost quite a bit of weight. I could feel the bones in his back and shoulders. Without thinking, I picked him up and carried him to my bed, where he curled up like a baby and slept in the safety of my arms while I stared at the blackness outside my bedroom window, wondering what was out there waiting for this frightened child.

He slept straight through the alarm and the noise I made getting ready for work the next morning. I hated to leave him alone, isolated on the top of a mountain, with a bullet lodged in his leg, but I had to go to school and make sure the word got to Jaime and Lupe that Julio was out of town, gone for good. If they believed he was gone, they'd stop looking for him and find another target for their frustration and anger.

"Don't worry about me," Julio said. "I'll be okay. The doctor showed me how to clean the wound so it won't get infected. And I'll call around to find somebody to take me to Mexico. That's what my mom wants me to do. We got a lot of family there. I just gotta find somebody who can come and get me 'cause my mom don't got no car and she don't drive anyway. Is it okay can I use your phone while you're gone?"

"Don't tell anybody where you are," I warned, as I headed out the door.

"I can't," Julio said, " 'cause I don't even know where I am."

Julio might not have known where *he* was, but Jaime and Lupe knew exactly where *I* was. That afternoon, shortly after the final bell, I was getting ready to lock up my classroom and leave when the ground started to rumble beneath my feet and the windows rattled. At first I thought it was an earthquake, but the rumbling grew louder and stronger, pounding with a rhythmic pulse that sent shock waves from my feet up through my body.

A white Camaro crawled around the curve at the end of the driveway that led to T-Wing and crept toward the far end of the building, stopping directly opposite my classroom. I was standing about three feet from the bank of windows that lined the outer wall of the classroom, watching the Camaro through the smeared, dusty glass. As the music continued to blast and pound, four large figures stepped from the car and walked slowly toward me. They were dressed in identical outfits—black jeans, white T-shirts, oversize black and red flannel shirts, black watch caps pulled down low on their brows.

Looking back, I wonder why I didn't run to the phone and call security when I saw the Camaro. I don't remember being scared. I don't remember feeling anything as I watched those four boy-men stalk across the blacktop drive and over the trampled, half-dead grass outside my room. When they reached the building, they lined up on the other side of the windows, so close that I could have reached out and touched the one directly in front of me if it weren't for the glass that separated us. When I close my eyes, I can still see his hard, cold face, his dark eyes that stared, unblinking, like the blank black button eyes of a teddy bear.

They stood for several moments, watching me. Then, on some silent signal, they all turned and walked back to the car. The driver, the last one to step into the car, raised his right hand and pointed his index finger at me, his thumb in the air, his other fingers bent back, imitating a gun. He "aimed" it straight at me for a long second before he dropped his hand and slid behind the wheel. As soon as the Camaro drove out of sight, I called Dr. Delgado. He suggested we meet the following morning, but I convinced him to give me fifteen minutes that afternoon. I explained everything that had happened, except that Julio was hiding out in my apartment.

"Where did the shooting take place?" Dr. Delgado asked, although I had already told him where.

"East Palo Alto."

"Then it's out of our jurisdiction," he said. "Unless the incident occurs on school property, it's a matter for the local police where it happens."

I had a sickening sensation of déjà vu. This was the same conversation we'd had about Rico Perez when Omar threatened to shoot him. I knew it was useless, but I had to try.

"Julio Escobar is a student at Parkmont," I said. "Don't you think we should do something?"

"Miss Johnson, we provide the best possible security for our students while they are on this campus."

"I'm not saying you don't. But I think we need to do something about this. We can't just let these kids run around shooting each other."

"Unless Julio files charges, we have no grounds to take any action against the other boys. Do you have any idea what kind of lawsuit the school could get slapped with if we accused a minor of assault with a deadly weapon with no proof to back up the claim?"

"Or the damage that this kind of publicity can do to a school's reputation?" I added. "We wouldn't want Buffy and Jody's mama to find out there are real live guns at her children's school, would we? That might make us look bad."

Dr. Delgado cleared his throat. "We do need to consider the effect that news of this sort of incident might have on the parents of our students. But, in any case, we need Julio to come in and fill out a report before we can take any action."

"He can't come in. He's gone."

"Where?"

"I don't know."

"Is he coming back?"

"I don't think so."

"Well, then," Dr. Delgado rubbed his palms together. "We don't really have a problem then, do we?"

"You have a serious problem, sir."

"I beg your pardon?"

"Nothing."

Julio stayed at my apartment for two weeks, until we could arrange for somebody from Mexico to pick him up in San Jose. Although we stopped jumping at every sound, we never really relaxed while he was there; every time we heard a car engine or a thump outside, our eyes would search each other out and we'd stare, holding our breath, praying that this wasn't the moment when somebody would break down the door and riddle us both with bullets. After a short time had passed, taking our fear with it, we'd grin sheepishly at each other and pretend we had been playing, that we hadn't really been scared.

The day Julio left, I packed his clothes in one of my suitcases while he was in the other room saying good-bye to his mother on the phone. The leather suitcase was expensive, but I hardly ever used it and I thought it might make him feel better. His things didn't even fill the small bag: tennis shoes, two pair of jeans, four undershirts, three pair of boxers, two and a half pairs of socks, a black Raiders jacket, a picture of him and his girlfriend at the prom, and a worksheet from my class with a sticker and a heart on it. In the same tattered envelope with his prom picture were the postcards from Chinatown that we had written on the night we went to the play. My card to him was postmarked with the date. His to me had never been mailed. My name and address were printed in the address block, but on the message side he had started several times, then crossed out each word with heavy black strokes. The only word that was legible was *love*. That was enough for me. I was tempted to keep the postcard, but he had so few things that I couldn't steal one of his precious possessions.

"Where's my bag?" Julio asked when I handed him the suitcase. He glanced around the room, as though he expected to see the torn black plastic trash bag slouching in the corner.

"I threw it out. You can keep this suitcase." He wrinkled his nose and made a soft *"tsk"* of annoyance under his breath.

His lack of gratitude annoyed me. "You could say, 'Thanks, Miss J, for packing all my stuff so neatly and giving me your very own suitcase.' "

Julio quickly recovered and said, "Thanks, Miss J, for packing all my stuff." He pretended to like the suitcase, but I could sense his dismay. It didn't occur to me until I dropped him off in the parking lot of the Red Lion that he had probably wanted to hang on to anything and everything from his past because he might never return. That old garbage bag had held his entire past.

I helped Julio out of the car, but he insisted that I just shake his hand and drop him off, let him walk across the sidewalk to the wooden bench by himself.

"If you start saying good-bye all over again, you'll make me cry," Julio had said. "And besides, we already said everything already."

With the suitcase tucked under one arm, leaving his crutch dangling, he hopped up the sidewalk toward the bench then turned around and lifted one crutch in a salute.

"Te quiero, Maestra," he called softly.

"Tu vives en mi pensamientos, Estudiante."

I stood several yards away and watched until a red Honda Civic with Mexican plates pulled to the curb opposite Julio. Two women emerged from the car and covered Julio with hugs and kisses, their hands waving, their words flying past me in a flurry of unfamiliar Spanish. Julio glanced over his shoulder as they bundled him into the car. One last look. We both knew it was the last one we would ever share.

Chapter 19

Maybe I'm Crazy

I wasn't there at the school bus loading zone when Omar Corona showed up and started waving a loaded pistol in the air, hollering, *"Donde está Perez? Donde está Perez?"* I heard at least six different versions of the story, from the administration, the police, and the students, so I'm not exactly certain what happened, but everybody who told me the story related the same basic plot.

Omar was already close to the edge from frying his brain on street drugs and cheap wine for so many years, and when Rico went to the police and got a restraining order against him, Omar became infuriated. Instead of hanging around the neighborhood, waiting for a chance to harass Rico, he bought a semiautomatic handgun and drove his beat-up old Plymouth to Parkmont. Omar arrived shortly after three o'clock, just as classes were dismissed for the day, and parked his car behind the last school bus in line. As the kids poured out of the school and headed for the bus zone, Omar jumped out of his car and ran into the middle of the crowd, waving the gun and shouting, *"Donde está Rico Perez?"*

Kids hit the dirt, screaming, and Rico raced for the office to tell Dr. Delgado, as he had promised me he would do. When he burst through the double doors of the admin building, one of the secretaries tried to stop him, but he pushed her aside and ran down the short corridor to the principal's office. The door was closed, but Rico threw it open and yelled, "There's a man out there with a gun who's trying to kill me!"

I will give Dr. Delgado this much benefit of the doubt and nothing more: I don't think he understood that Rico meant the man was outside at that very moment. I think he believed Rico was referring to just another incident in East Palo Alto.

"You can't just charge into someone's private office without knocking," Dr. Delgado told Rico. "I'm in a meeting right now. You'll have to wait outside."

"Fuck you," Rico yelled, and took off down the hall toward Mr. Simms's office.

The same thing happened. Rico burst into the office, Mr. Simms protested that he, too, was in a meeting and refused to listen to Rico. Mr. Simms's visitor was one of the local police officers who often stopped by the school and spent a few minutes walking around, providing a visible police presence that was supposed to reassure the community.

"Fuck you, too," Rico said, and started to run back outside, hoping to find a security guard or someone who would help him get Omar. Mr. Simms, enraged by Rico's outburst, followed him down the hallway, yelling, "Come back here, young man. You can't swear at the staff and administration of this school. You're suspended as of this minute and I want you in my office right now while I call your parents."

Rico ignored Mr. Simms and continued elbowing his way through the crowd that had gathered in the office. Among the crowd was Rico's sister, Anita, one of our Academy sophomores. Infuriated by the principal's reaction to her brother, Anita grabbed Mr. Simms by the lapels of his suit jacket and screamed, "What's the matter with you? My brother is trying to tell you that there is a man with a gun out there by the buses

RIGHT NOW and there's a million kids out there who could get killed. You're so stupid you don't even listen."

They listened to Anita, but by the time Mr. Simms had summoned the security guards and the local police, Omar was long gone. Rico was held after school while Mr. Simms called his parents to report his outburst, and he was suspended for three days. Because it took so long to contact his parents and fill out the proper paperwork to punish him, Rico had to take the late sports bus home to East Palo Alto. Nobody but football players took the last bus because it didn't arrive until dusk and few kids wanted to face the neighborhood alone in the dark. Anita waited with her brother and rode home beside him on the bus. Nobody had stopped to consider that Omar might sit outside the main gate where he had a clear view of the administration office and the bus loading zone. Nobody expected him to follow the late bus back to East Palo Alto and grab Rico when he stepped off the bus.

But that's exactly what he did.

"I'm going to kill you, muthafucka," Omar muttered, as he grabbed Rico by the neck and pressed the pistol to the boy's temple. I have no doubt that Rico would be dead today if the policeman in Mr. Simms's office hadn't decided to disregard procedure and follow the bus. He managed to distract Omar and disarm him. Omar ended up in jail, and Rico spent three days at home, where he was supposed to take time to consider the importance of showing proper respect for the adults who worked so hard to provide him with an education.

I found out about the incident the following day when Rico failed to show up for class. When Anita told me what happened, and Toshomba Grant assured me that she was telling the truth, I called the office to ask whether it was true that Rico was suspended.

"Yes, he is," Sherry, the principal's secretary, said, "but I don't think it would be a very good idea for you to argue about it right now. Things are a little touchy around here, if you know what I mean."

I had no intention of going to the office, but not because I was afraid the principal would be in a bad mood. I didn't go because I knew if I did there was a good chance I would punch Dr. Delgado or Mr. Simms, or maybe both. Instead, I called Dr. Howe and made an appointment. I hadn't been to see her in several weeks, but something in my voice must have warned her that I was about to detonate.

"You must find a way to deal with your anger and frustration," Dr. Howe said, after I explained what had happened to Rico. "You must learn to accept the world and its imperfections."

"But it's unacceptable!" I yelled. "How can you just sit there? Why don't you want to scream and yell and smack people for being so damned stupid and insensitive?"

She didn't answer for quite a long time, but waited for me to stop ranting and sit down.

"You can't change the world," she said, finally, in her irritatingly calm voice. "You can do only what you can to help those you love. But if you don't learn to control your temper and your emotions, you won't be able to help anybody."

Those were almost the exact words Mr. Simms had used when he threatened to fire me if I didn't stop trying to force him to do something to help Simoa Mariposa. And, just as I had then, I sensed that there was some truth in what they said—if I lost my job, I wouldn't be able to help any of the kids. But another voice, this one from inside me, said that I was right to care, to try to help, that if everybody learned to accept this unacceptable world, it would never change.

"Maybe I'm crazy, according to your books," I told Dr. Howe, "and maybe I'm wasting my time and energy trying to change things that can't be changed. But I have to try. Because if I don't try, it will kill me inside, just as surely as Omar would have killed Rico."

Dr. Howe clicked her pen and made a note on my record.

"Write this down, Doctor," I said. "Write that I think you've got it backward and upside down. It isn't me who is crazy because I cry when I see a starving man eating out of a trash can. It's the the people who can walk past that man and find some way to rationalize it and accept it who are crazy. And maybe I won't be able to be a teacher forever because I can't understand why we don't have any paper in our school, and no money for books, and they cut the library hours in half and then turned around and painted all the railings and landscaped an acre in front of the school, and when I asked them why, the answer was: it's a different budget. Maybe I'm crazy because I can't understand that kind of thinking. Maybe the very thing that makes me able to connect with the kids—my heart—is the thing that will make me unable to keep on teaching. But I can't stop caring just because it hurts."

"I thought you'd be happy to see me go," I told Mr. Simms. After I filed my letter of resignation, he had called me into his office to say good-bye and tell me he was sorry I was leaving Parkmont High. "I know I've been a pain in the butt."

"Maybe," Mr. Simms admitted, "but I knew you were doing it on behalf of your students. There are a lot of teachers here who never argue with me, never cause a bit of trouble for me, but some of those same teachers take out their anger and frustration on the students. I prefer your method. You may have been a pain in the butt, as you put it, but your heart was always in the right place. Unfortunately, my job doesn't allow much leeway in that particular area."

He took off his glasses and held out his hand for me to shake.

"Let me know if you ever decide to come back to California."

"So you can move away before I get here?"

"Something like that," Mr. Simms said.

He asked why I had chosen New Mexico, and I told him I had friends in Albuquerque, which was true, but it wasn't the real reason. I chose New Mexico because it is one of the least populated states in the country, and I needed peace and quiet and space.

"I hate the desert," I had told my friend Diane when she suggested New Mexico as a possible new home.

"Have you ever been to the desert?" she asked.

"No," I admitted, "but I grew up in Pennsylvania and I've lived in northern California for ten years. I need trees, lots of them, and green grass and rolling hills."

Then, on her invitation, I visited Las Cruces, which is about an hour north of El Paso, and fell in love with the smell of sun-baked earth and the cactus-dotted horizon that stretches for miles in every direction until it crashes headlong into a purple-blue-brown mountain range that erupts from the earth, piercing the clouds and shooting straight for heaven.

I applied for graduate school and received an offer to teach freshman composition at New Mexico State University in exchange for my tuition. Although I knew it was time for me to go, I felt guilty, as though I were abandoning my own children.

"Think of it as giving blood for five years straight," Justin Bernard said when I asked him if he thought I was a quitter. "You paid your dues. You need to recharge your batteries and let somebody else take up the good fight for a while." He gave me a long, searching look. "But you know something?"

"I know a few things," I said. "But I keep forgetting them."

"I don't think you'll last very long."

"Are you kidding? Teaching college will be a vacation after this."

"Exactly. As soon as you get some rest, you'll get bored and start looking for another challenge. And my money says you'll end up back in high school, bitching and moaning, driving the administration crazy, and loving every minute of it. I'll give you two years max."

"Fifty bucks." I held out my hand. "Put your money where your mouth is, Mister."

"Fifty bucks? I know teachers are underpaid, but that's not even worth talking about. Let's make it a hundred even."

"I'll see you and double your bid," I said. "Two hundred is my bet, take it or leave it."

Justin grabbed my hand before I could change my mind, but I wasn't worried. I knew I'd win the bet. For five years I had given every ounce of physical, emotional, and mental energy I had to my students. I couldn't have done any more to help them, but I couldn't have done less, either. By the end of that fifth year, I felt so exhausted and empty that I often had the sensation of becoming transparent, almost invisible. When Simoa had disappeared, it had broken my heart, and even though she returned, my heart never really mended, just as hers never did. Then, when Julio was shot and had to run for his life, and Rico was nearly killed because of pure stupidity, including my own, something seemed to break inside me, even deeper than my heart. It sounds melodramatic to say that my soul was wounded, but that's how I felt. I loved teaching teenagers, but it hurt too much.

I hadn't planned, at first, to tell my students that I wouldn't be back in the fall, because I knew that many of them would take it personally. But I also knew that they had had so many heartbreaks, so many broken promises already, that they deserved to know, so they could spend the summer getting used to the idea that they'd have a new English teacher. For weeks, I tried every day to tell them, but each time a smiling face or a pair of innocent eyes would stop me short. I ended up breaking the news to each class at the end of their final exam period.

The sophomores accepted the news more gracefully than the juniors did, probably because they had been in the Academy program for only one year and weren't quite as attached to me as the older kids were. The juniors sat in stunned silence, until finally Anita Perez said, "What's gonna happen to us?"

"You're going to continue getting good grades and you're going to graduate," I said. "You're going to be successful people, and you're going to make sure your own children finish high school. That's what's gonna happen to you."

"But you're the only teacher who really likes us," Anita said. "Nobody else gives us a hug or a magic pencil on our birthday or takes us to lunch or calls our parents to brag on us."

"Leave her alone," a voice ordered from the back of the room. Bradford Baker, younger brother of Cornelius. "You just making her feel bad." Bradford had spent his first year in the Academy sitting in the far corner, in the same seat his big brother had sat in for three years. And like Cornelius, Bradford sat with his arms crossed, observing the rest of the class, as though it was an experiment conducted for his benefit.

Bradford was right. I did feel bad—until graduation day arrived, until I watched Maria and Isabella and Tyeisha and Joanie and Simoa and Araceli and ten other Academy girls parade past the podium, their stiff new high heels clicking across the make-shift stage, to collect their precious diplomas. At that moment, I knew it wouldn't matter if I never taught another class, or that I couldn't save all the children who need saving. I had helped my girls. I had made a difference in their lives, and it would affect them forever. They would not be helpless victims, but successful young women. I was so proud and grateful, and so certain that the Academy girls would march off that stage and keep on marching toward their dreams of college or careers, that I would not have hesitated to do it all over again—relive every fear, face every heartbreak, cry every tear. It had been a long three years and a difficult journey for all of us, but it had been worth it. Unlike the previous year, the girls had not been left behind. This time, when we gathered behind the grandstand to take a group photo of the new graduates, instead of a few tiny white clouds dotting a sky of royal blue robes, the girls' gowns created a brilliant shining white star in the center of the blue horizon.

After repeated hugs and thank-yous and pictures and promises to write, I escaped from the crowd to take one last walk across campus. I had already packed my personal belongings and turned in my keys, but I stopped at my classroom to peek in the windows and make sure I hadn't left anything behind but my heart. The empty desks and bookshelves looked so forlorn, like the faces of my students as they had shuffled to my desk to drop their final essays into the assignment basket. Hoping to make our parting as positive as possible, I had assigned them to write about what they had learned about themselves or how they had changed during the past year or two. I thought writing about their growth might leave them with a good feeling, one of accomplishment, instead of feeling a loss.

In some cases, my plan worked. Luis Gonzalez wrote about how much the Academy had helped him stop cutting class and raise his grades.

> I know I'm going to do better next year so I can graduate and while I'm writing this journal, I would like to thank you for all your help you gave me that help me a lot and for helping to think of going to college and about other things and for be a successful person in the future.
>
> Your student that loves you,
Luis Gonzalez

Luis's friend, Juan Garcia, drew a picture of a gun-toting gangster with a goatee, a hat pulled down to his brow, and a bandanna almost covering his eyes. This was supposed to be his former dream, I guessed, but he explained that being in the

Academy program had made him feel more mature and helped
him "get his act together."

> Now I am even thinking on going to college before I
> wouldn't think of that. All I wanted to do was get out of high
> school and start working, but now I have a job and I go to
> school and working right there where I work getting five
> dollars and fifty cents an hour made me realize I don't want
> to be working in a restaurant like that when I grow up.
> That's why I am working harder right here on high school
> so when I grow up I would be somebody important.
> Miss Johnson, that's all I have to say and I wish you
> would stay, so I wish you good luck and I want you to know
> you are the teacher that I really liked on all these years that
> I have been in school.
>
> —Juanito

Several other students ended their essays with a wish that I
would stay. LaShana Ross, who frequently threatened to quit
the Academy if I didn't get off her case, surprised me. She said
she wanted me to know that she admired me.

> You come to school every morning and take our shit
> which is something you don't have to do but you do it any-
> way because you care about us making something of our-
> selves. You give us that extra push that we need in life for
> us. You are really like an extra mom and I appreciate that.

After a handful of such thank-yous, my resolve began to
weaken and I started thinking that maybe if I took the summer
off, I could stay one more year if I made a supreme effort to
leave the kids' problems at school when I went home at night
instead of spending my evenings trying to save them from themselves and my nights dreaming of ways to solve their unsolvable

problems. But by the time I finished reading the other half of the essays, I knew it was hopeless. As much as I loved them, I couldn't take any more of their pain.

Sean Collins wrote about how horrible his life had become since his stepfather got a new job and the family was moving—without him. He would stay with a friend or go to San Francisco to live with his father and stepmother. To make it worse, he had recently hurt himself during an outdoor education class.

> I lost my glasses when I took a 20-foot freefall plunge into the shallow creek, I landed right on a small stump which fractured my ribs. I came home and first thing I hear is, "We're moving" and I said, "No, you're moving." I've been pretty depressed this last week, why did it have to be during finals? I think I failed Mr. Ryan's class and if I did then I might as well drop out of school.
>
> Sometimes I feel like shooting myself, but of course I don't. It's just that I think I'm intitled to a normal life and lot of people say life's not fair, well fuck that! I'm sick of all my family's shit. In some ways I want to move to my friend's house and get away from this Irish drunken large family. Well, thanks for listening to my problems. I'll really, really, really, really, really, really, really miss you.
>
> Love, Sean

My heart started sinking when I read Sean's journal, and hit somewhere near my gut when I read Blanca Armendariz's description of how it felt to be cast out of her family for becoming pregnant. A beautiful sixteen-year-old with shining ebony hair and an irresistible smile, Blanca had earned very good grades before she had her baby, but afterward her grades had dropped out of sight. She put up such a good front that I didn't realize her spirits had dropped along with her grades until I read her journal.

I left my home and now I'm living alone because I get in fight with my aunt because I get pragnant. I never wanted to tell anybody who was the father of my baby and I always keep everything to myself and that's bad for me. I have no friends like last year when I had lot of friends. Now I just going from my house to school and I not going out no place. I'm not give my phone number to anybody. I know I'm wrong and I need help but I'm not looking for it. Now I'm leave to Mexico a place where I don't know anybody and I'm going to leave far away from my family because I always knew that they hate me. They didn't tell me but I know that. I have a daughter and she is the only one that I'm sure and I know that she loves me and this is the only one who will be with me forever. She is the only one who gives me energy for living because she if the only reason I have for being somebody in this life, for keep going to school, and look for professional help because I think in my problems and I damage myself.

Keisha Brown's story was even sadder than Blanca's. Like Blanca, Keisha had been a lively, likable girl and a good student who suddenly stopped participating in life. But Blanca's problems began with a birth and Keisha's began with a death. Her father died from AIDS during the last semester of her junior year, and she never recovered. Unfortunately, nobody notified the teachers of what had happened. All we knew was that she had been absent for a week and then stopped working. She refused all offers of help and shut out everybody, including her closest friends. If I had known what happened, I might have been able to refer her to the school psychologist or to some sort of community program that offers counseling. But I didn't know what had happened until I read her essay, after she had already decided to drop out of school.

Miss Johnson, this past year I have seen a change in me. Lately I have been feeling three words—I don't care. I seem not to care about anything that is going on. I don't care what my mother says. I don't care what my friends say. I don't care what my teachers say and sometimes I don't even care about myself. I don't even care enough to talk to you and I know you would of helped me, but I didn't care enough to talk to you and now it's too late because you won't be here anymore.

You probably think I'm crazy, but I think I am crazy, too. Like when my father died, you know what, I didn't even care. I know that's wrong to say and feel, I know that, but I can't seem to help it, and I don't have any feeling for anything these days. I seem to have feelings just for cats. I know this is really going to sound crazy but I really do think I'm crazy. Can you believe that when I found out about my father that he was dead, I didn't even cry, but when I was driving down the street and saw a dead cat in the road, I started to cry. Miss Johnson, I have a problem and I don't know if I will ever get over it. Damn, Miss Johnson, have you ever heard of anything like this before in your life. If you have, please help me.

keisha

Keisha had informed me as she dropped her journal into the basket that she wouldn't be in the Academy next year because she wasn't going to go to school and her mother couldn't make her go. At the time, I thought she had simply had an argument with her mother, or was mad at me for leaving. I had no idea she was in such pain. I called her as soon as I read her journal, but there was no answer.

Keisha's journal was the next to last in the pile. I almost skipped the last one because it belonged to Curtis Bell, who had gone from a likable, mischievous class clown to a rude, obnoxious, unlikable punk. He refused to do assignments, disrupted classes, bragged about his repeated suspensions, got kicked off his beloved baseball team, and failed almost all his classes. Nothing the Academy teachers did seemed to get through to him, and he went out of his way to antagonize us. At the end of the year, we resorted to the threat of dropping him from the Academy, which usually produced immediate results. Academy students shared four classes with the same group of kids and developed solid friendships that they cherished. Curtis informed us that he didn't give a shit about the Academy and walked out of the meeting. I chalked it up to hormones and adolescence, until I read his essay.

> This year, I really turned myself around for the better the first semester and earned a 3.23 GPA for the first time. I think it was because I was really thinking about going to college and becoming an educator. You really helped me out and I am grateful. That is until about three weeks into the second semester. I know you noticed the change along with my other teachers and coaches.
>
> Well, some night in January my dad (my real dad) came out from Washington D.C. like he always does, but this time it was totally different. He didn't have to go right home in a few days and he wasn't out on business. He spent a week and a half out here with me and my brother.
>
> It seemed like something was wrong because he was always saying no matter what he will always be here. He said that before, but not with tears in his eyes and when we went out to dinner, he would always ask me to bring my girlfriend. But that night he said we should go eat by ourselves because I guess he had to tell me something. I thought he was gonna tell me he was getting married again for the 4th time, but no, he told me that my mom had been infected

with the HIV when she had been in the hospital for a heart operation. That's why I think my grades slipped. I guess that's why I'm an asshole to everybody. I guess that's why I don't care about college and I guess that's why I don't give a *fuck* about the Academy next year.

Even if Curtis's journal hadn't been the last one, I would have had to stop at that point. I couldn't help blaming myself for not noticing that Blanca and Curtis and Keisha had been in so much pain. It's always been my theory that students act terrible to get out attention, that their two primary operating emotions are fear and rage. Even knowing that, I had missed their clear calls for help.

I had left the journals in the bottom drawer of my desk, thinking that maybe they would help the new Academy English teacher find the best approach for each student. But things had a way of disappearing during summer vacation, so I walked over to the custodian's office and waited for Casey to return from monitoring the facilities for graduation. I asked him to let me into my room to get the journals.

I promised Casey I would turn off the lights and shut the door securely behind me, so he left me alone in the room. I took the journals out of the drawer and sat in my empty classroom with them on my lap, patting them softly, as though the gesture might soothe some of their pain, or mine. I sat in that empty room full of memories until I was sure that all the new graduates and their families would be off celebrating and only a few workaholics would be left behind, too busy to notice me. I didn't want to talk to anybody about anything. I sneaked around the back side of T-Wing just to make sure I wouldn't bump into anybody and hurried across the blacktop parking lot to my car.

A torn, crumpled, brown paper grocery sack sat on the hood of my car. Muttering to myself about disgusting pigs who were too lazy to throw their trash in the Dumpster that was a short walk across the parking lot, I picked up the bag, intending to toss it in the trash, but it was heavy, so I opened it out of curiosity. Inside the bag was a large silver trophy inscribed 1988 RAVENS-WOOD DISTRICT CHAMPIONS and a note.

Dear Miss J—

I was going to throw this away but then I thought maybe you'd like to have it, even if it is just a dumb old trophy from when I was in junior high. It's the first one I ever won but I got a lot more from high school so I don't need this one any more. If you don't want it, you can just throw it in the dumpster and forget it. I know I gave you a hard time this year, but you didn't never let that stop you from trying to help me. If it wasn't for you, I'd probably be out on the street, waiting for some dude to take me out. You're the only teacher I had who wasn't afraid to make me work. The rest of them were afraid of me just because I'm big and strong and black. They probably thought I would kill them or something stupid like that. But you weren't afraid. I'm glad I got to be in your class for the whole three years. I wish my brother could of had you for three years because he needs somebody to keep him in line, but at least he got you for one year and it helped him a lot. I know he would of got a lot worse already if you wouldn't have been his teacher.

Peace,
Cornelius Julien Baker

Chapter 20

Someplace Like This

I guess if you gotta go, you gotta go," Raul said when I told him I was moving to New Mexico. I had called and asked him to stop by my classroom so I could break the news and say good-bye in person. He walked to the window and stood with his back to me while he considered the idea for a few minutes, then turned around and gave me a serious look. "I don't think it's a good idea for you to be driving all those hundreds of miles all by yourself, Miss J."

"I've driven all the way across the country by myself," I assured him. "Three times. And I didn't have any problems."

"Yeah, but you was younger then, wasn't you? You said you was gonna be forty on your birthday. That's pretty old. You wouldn't be able to run too fast if somebody was chasing you. And you probably couldn't even change the tire if you got a flat because it would be too heavy."

"Is that right?" I said, catching his mischievous grin and flashing it right back at him. I knew what was coming, but I asked anyway. "And I suppose you have the perfect solution to the problem of my decrepit old age?"

Raul nodded. "You need a navigator to help you read maps and look for road signs and stuff so you don't get lost."

"And, of course, you have somebody in mind?"

"I already packed my suitcase."

We left on the last Saturday in June, towing my Fiat Spyder on a trailer behind the Ryder rental truck. I put Cornelius's trophy on the dashboard of the truck to use as a lucky charm. It would also come in handy if I needed to knock out a would-be mugger or car jacker en route. The weather was relentlessly sunny, and Raul spent the first hours staring out the window, watching the landscape change from velvety brown hills to desolate desert as he filled me in on the details of his love life since he'd left Parkmont.

"Every week, I get a new girlfriend and I spend my whole paycheck on her and then she dumps me," he said. "And I always say I'm through with women and I'm going to put my money in the bank and save it, but then somebody gives me another girl's phone number and I call her up anyways, because I always think this one will be different."

"Well, at least you keep trying," I said. "One of these days, you'll find somebody who appreciates you."

"Do you really think so?"

"Yes, I do."

"Well, if you think so, then I guess it might happen, because you're pretty smart. But I hope I don't meet no more pregnant girls like the last one I called up. She lived all the way over in Sacramento, and I called her up one night and she said to come on over and visit her. So I got in my car and drove all the way there and got lost and finally found her house, and she came to the door and she was pregnant. I still would have talked to her anyway, but she said she had a boyfriend, so I asked her why did she tell me to come over and she said she wanted to see what did I look like. I guess she thought I was ugly because she didn't invite me in her house or anything even after I drove all that way."

"You're not ugly."

Raul sighed and shook his head. "I know you been telling me

that since you met me, but I must be ugly or why don't I have a girlfriend? And how come I get the dumb job in the warehouse where nobody has to look at me?"

I explained that he probably got the warehouse job because he knew how to use the computer for inventory, and that if he wanted to get promoted, he should go to work every day instead of taking off every other Friday to go to Reno and gamble.

"Yeah, I know," he said. "I gotta start going to work every single day, but nobody in my family never had a job like that. They just get a few days' work and then they get a paycheck and go out and party. So it's hard to get used to going someplace every single day. It's boring."

He stared out the window for a while, then muttered, almost too softly for me to hear, "But I'm ugly and nothing can't change that."

I smacked my palms against the steering wheel. "Why do you keep saying that? You *aren't* ugly. I wouldn't lie to you. You're handsome. You have beautiful hair and pretty eyes. Look at yourself." I reached up and turned the rearview mirror so it faced him.

He shook his head. "I know how I look, and I believe you think I'm handsome. But I don't look regular."

"What's regular?"

"You know, like them guys in the magazines and catalogs. And in the movies. None of them look like me, except the gangsters."

"Well, none of the women in the magazines looks like me, either. I'm not tall and blond and skinny with big bazoobas."

Raul snickered. "You're a trip, Miss J." He paused. "Can I ask you something personal?" I nodded. "How come you don't got a boyfriend? I mean, for real? You always say you got your heart broke and you don't want to fall in love again, but I think you're real pretty and you're nice and you got a good body and a job and your own car and everything."

"I wish I could answer that question," I said, "but I don't know myself."

"It's okay if you don't want to talk about it," Raul said, but I could tell he was hurt. He shifted in the seat so that his forehead pressed against the passenger window. I thought about all the personal details of his life that he had shared with me through his journal and our conversations, and I realized how unfair it was to take so much and give so little. So I talked to his back. I told him about running off to join the Navy at age nineteen and eloping a few months later with a boy I hardly knew, ending up in an abusive relationship that dragged on for seven years before I found the strength to end it. I told him about burying my feelings as deep down inside as I could and transferring to the Marine Corps, where I welcomed the constant physical and mental demands and earned high praise for keeping my emotions out of sight and under control. When I left the service a few years later and started teaching, I intended to maintain my cerebral approach to life.

"If I had known I would love you kids so much, I never would have taken the job," I said. "But I wouldn't trade the last five years for anything, even if you guys did break my heart a thousand times."

Raul didn't say anything for several minutes after I stopped talking, and I thought he must have fallen asleep. In one sense, I was relieved, because I didn't like the vulnerability that comes with sharing my private thoughts, but in another sense, I was disappointed that he would never know I had tried to balance our lopsided friendship.

About ten miles down the highway, Raul sat up and stretched his arms. "You shouldn't of gave up," he said.

"What?" I didn't know what he was talking about.

"Just because that guy broke your heart, you shouldn't of gave up. Look at me. I must of got my heart broken a hundred times at least, and I'm still out there trying."

The highway hypnotized us both for a while, and we sat in a comfortable silence punctuated by the rhythm of the tires clicking across the seams in the concrete. I don't remember who spoke first, but we started talking just outside of Bakersfield and didn't stop until we hit Barstow. By the time we reached the Mojave Desert, we were out of stories. We were also almost out of gas, but neither of us noticed until we passed the blue sign that read: NO SERVICE NEXT 100 MILES.

We crossed our fingers and our legs, since we had drunk a six-pack of Coke between us before starting the climb through the high desert mountains. The gas supply held out, but our bladders didn't. We had to pull off the road and take turns squatting behind a tiny bush.

When we finally rolled into a gas station, the gas gauge was in the red, far below the E. After we filled the tank and pulled back onto the highway, Raul said, "That was the funnest part of the trip so far."

"Running out of gas is fun?"

"Not that. The fun part was watching you pee behind that bush. Wait'll I tell the guys." I started to protest, but he raised both hands to silence me. "Chill, Miss J. Chill. I was only joking. Your secret is safe with me." After a few minutes, he said, "All your secrets are safe with me, don't worry."

The rest of the hours flew by like the mile markers on the highway. By the time we reached Albuquerque, we were both tired of being cooped up in the cab of the truck, so we got out to take a short walk.

"This is pretty nice." Raul inhaled deeply and held out his arms. "I thought it was gonna be hot like that desert we been driving across. I never been anyplace where it was hot even in the middle of the night like that."

I agreed. The sun was shining, the sky was perfectly clear and blue, and the temperature was in the mid-eighties. "It isn't much different from California, is it? Except for the traffic and smog."

We climbed back into the truck and headed down Interstate 25 toward Las Cruces. The pine trees and grassy meadows gave way to scrawny, twisted mesquite bushes and clumps of gray grass that seemed to be trying to escape from the sand surrounding them. For every mile we drove down out of the mountains, the temperature rose another five degrees. By the time we reached the tiny town of Hatch, a short drive from Las Cruces, we were parched. My skin was so dry, I felt like a human potato chip. We stopped at a Dairy Queen to get an ice cream but made the mistake of taking our cones outside. Before we had taken ten steps toward the truck, we were both holding sugar cones filled with melted ice cream that dripped down our hands and immediately disappeared into the thirsty ground beneath our feet. In the few minutes that it took us to wash our hands, the temperature inside the truck had risen to over one hundred degrees. Raul turned the air conditioning on high and said, "I hope that place you rented gots a shower and a air conditioner."

"It does," I assured him. I had subscribed to the Las Cruces *Sun* for two months before moving and had rented a place over the phone from an elderly couple, Herb and Retha Young. Two bedrooms, two bathrooms on five acres, ten minutes from the college. And only four hundred dollars per month, less than half the rent for my apartment in Woodside, California.

When we reached Las Cruces, I called the Youngs from a phone booth outside the Sonic Drive-In on North Main Street. Herb told me to drive out Main Street toward the mountains until I came to Holman Road.

"Take a left on Holman and come down about five miles until you reach the end of the blacktop," he said. "I'll meet you there. I'm driving a blue Dodge minivan. Can't miss it."

As we headed toward Holman Road, we drove directly toward the Organ Mountains, which painted a beautiful backdrop for the cattle grazing on the open mesa.

Herb flagged us down and waved his arm to indicate that we

should follow him. He took off in cloud of dust down Holman Road for another quarter mile, then turned onto a narrow dirt road.

"Looks kind of like my street in EPA," Raul said. His street was unpaved and filled with potholes, and the road we were driving on did seem like Garden Street, until we hit the first washout. It was like driving over corrugated metal, with deep ruts that shook the truck so hard I could feel my teeth rattle, even in low gear. Up ahead, Herb skirted a deep pit in the center of the road and bounced across the desert, spraying sand for a few yards, until he dipped back down onto the road. We crawled over three more miles of rocks and potholes until the road took a ninety-degree turn to the right and headed into a dead end. Directly in front of us sat a single-wide aluminum trailer, dusty pink, with a giant satellite dish squatting in the front yard.

Raul looked at me and raised his eyebrows, and I knew he was thinking the same thing I was: I hope the inside looks better than the outside. It did. Clean carpets, modern plumbing, incredible views from the bedroom windows—one on each end of the trailer.

"It's awful hot in here," Raul told Herb, who had unlocked the door and escorted us inside. Retha had reached through the van window to shake my hand but opted to stay where she was.

"I thought this place had a air conditioner," Raul said.

"It does," Herb assured Raul, "but it's been empty for a while, so we had it shut off. Let me get it going for you." He flipped a switch on the wall and a loud humming and clanking immediately began from overhead.

"That's just the swamp cooler motor kicking in," Herb said. "It'll quiet down once it gets up to speed."

"Swamp cooler?" I echoed.

Herb explained that most of the locals used swamp coolers instead of refrigerated air. "Don't cost but half as much and works just as good," he said, as he led us outside for a look at the square metal contraption perched on the roof of the trailer.

"You see that there box," Herb pointed. "Well, there's a fan inside and it blows across a pan of water that's piped into the bottom of it. When the air crosses the water, it gets cooled down and adds a little bit of moisture, and then it blows into your house. Works like a charm."

Herb led us back inside for the grand tour, highlighted by flushing both toilets, then offered to help us unload the truck. He raced up the loading ramp and grabbed a box full of books. He staggered down the ramp and into the living room, where he dropped the box on the floor and pulled a white cotton handkerchief from his back pocket to mop his flushed face. His white hair lay plastered to his head in thin damp strands. Raul insisted that the truck unloading was his job and he wanted to take his time. He stood on the ramp and refused to let Herb back up for another load. Herb finally gave up.

"I got your phone all hooked up for you, since we're quite a piece from town," he said. "That there phone book is a couple years old, but things don't change too fast around here, so I expect most of the numbers is still good, and our number's right there on that paper pad by the phone. If you need anything, you just holler."

After Herb and Retha left, Raul shook his head. "That guy must be almost a hundred years old." He flopped down onto the box that Herb had carried in and wiped his own brow, which was almost as sweaty as Herb's. "And it's still a hundred degrees in here at least."

I found a thermostat but assumed it was broken because it registered 115 degrees. "Well, I guess that swamp thing must take a little while," I said. "Why don't you go ahead and take a shower and cool off?"

Raul stood up and shook his head. "Nope. I'm unloading that truck for you because I said I would." He was out the door and up the loading ramp before he finished talking. For the next three hours, he carted boxes and bags and furniture, stopping just long enough to gulp down a glass of ice water and shake the sweat from his face, puppy style, when it dripped into his eyes. Every time I turned around, he was carrying another large item on his skinny shoulders. For each trip I made, he made three, carrying twice as much I could handle. I kept asking him to slow down, but he ignored me. Once, when I stepped in front of him and insisted that he take a break, he said, "Miss J, I feel so strong. You been feeding me three meals a day for three days, and I got so much energy I could move two truckfuls."

When everything was off the truck except the piano, I went inside to check the yellow pages for a piano company to move it for me. There were only two piano companies in the book, and both said they'd be happy to do it—next week. The truck was due back at the Ryder office the next day.

"I guess I'll just have to pay a couple days' extra rent on the truck," I told Raul, "until we can get somebody out here to move the piano."

Raul put his hands on his hips and glanced around the yard. He pointed to a couple of ten-foot planks by the side of the trailer. "We could make a little bridge with them boards," he said, "and move the piano ourselves. I betcha it ain't that heavy."

"It weighs four hundred pounds," I said. "I weigh one-twenty-five and you weigh ninety-five."

"Ninety-nine," Raul corrected. "I been working out at the gym."

"Okay, you weigh ninety-nine. If we moved it to the edge of the ramp and it started rolling, we wouldn't be able to stop it."

Raul studied the truck and the front door of the trailer for a few minutes, then walked up the ramp into the truck and pushed the piano to test its weight. He moved the piano out from the side of the truck and checked the back of it, then checked the wooden rails that were bolted to the inside walls of the truck.

"Check this out," he said, after some thought. He took a long rope, looped it twice around the piano, and measured the distance to the end of the ramp. He carefully marked the spot on the rope and tied the ends to the wooden railing behind the cab of the truck.

"There," he said. "Now if it rolls too fast and we can't hold it, the rope will stop it right at the end."

I hesitated. It might work, but if it didn't, the piano would crash into the cement step outside the front door.

"You're always saying I'm smart," Raul said. "If you really think I'm smart, then you should believe me once in a while. I'm telling you this will work."

It worked. The piano trundled down the ramp, Raul on one side, me on the other, and promptly stopped at the end of the ramp, poised for the last leg of its journey. Raul untied the ropes and we pushed the piano across the planks and into the living room.

"It worked! You're a genius!" I hugged Raul. "I'm so proud of you. I'm sorry I doubted you."

"I don't blame you," Raul said. "I didn't really think it would work."

"Then why did you insist on doing it?"

"I figured we should at least try it. I bet those guys would've charged you a hundred dollars to come out here and move it. You could buy a lot of food for a hundred dollars."

It didn't cost one hundred dollars, but it took a lot of food to fill Raul that night. We ate at Cattleman's steak house, a few miles back down Main Street toward town. After two baskets of bread, a sixteen-ounce T-bone, a baked potato, and a double order of strawberry shortcake, Raul finally announced that he was full.

Meanwhile, back at the trailer, we had forgotten to turn out the lights. When we walked into the living room, I couldn't believe it. The walls, floor, ceiling, windows, and furniture were covered with bugs. Flying bugs. Crawling bugs. Wormy looking bugs. Bugs with giant wings. Bugs with antlers.

Normally, I'm not squeamish, but after three days of driving almost nonstop, I was close to the edge, and the bugs drove me over. I grabbed a box and started swatting at the bugs, screaming hysterically. Raul switched off the lights inside the trailer, turned on the back porch light, and propped the back door open. Then he pulled me out the front door.

"The bugs will go out back where the light is," he said, "and we can just sit out here and look at the stars." I was still crying and screaming about the bugs. Raul put his arms around me and rocked me until I stopped crying, then he climbed up on the hood of the truck and patted the space beside him. I climbed up and we both lay down on our backs, our hands locked beneath our heads. The sky dropped right down around us and the stars floated so close that they seemed close enough to touch.

"I never seen so many stars," Raul whispered. Then, for a long time, neither of us said anything. We were lost in the stars and the wind sighing softly across the desert. From time to time, a coyote would cry out, and the sad note would drift on the wind to where we lay listening. At one point, it was perfectly dark and silent. Not a sound broke the stillness.

"Listen," Raul said.

"What?" I didn't hear anything.

"You can't hear any sirens or gunshots."

"Do you usually hear sirens and gunshots?" I asked, thinking he was joking.

"Every night. The sirens aren't too bad, but when we hear the gunfire, everybody gets down to their special hiding place so in case the bullets come in the windows, we don't get shot. I go into the bathroom with my two little brothers. My sisters go behind the stove, and my mother and grandma gets by the washing machine. My father and my other brothers get behind the couch in the living room, but it isn't really a very good place because it's right by the front door and sometimes the gangs crash in the front door and take your TV and stereo if you got one."

I tried to be very quiet, but Raul heard me try to swallow.

"How come you're crying?" he asked.

I couldn't tell the truth. I couldn't say, "I'm crying because you have lived twenty-one years on this earth and have never laid down in your bed and slept without worrying about being murdered in your sleep. I'm crying because you were never allowed to be a child for one moment in your life."

"I'm crying because it's so peaceful here," I said.

"Yeah," Raul said. "Maybe someday I'll move out here, or someplace away from EPA. It would be hard to leave all my friends and stuff, but I don't got no kind of life back there. Every time I get paid, my dad takes half my money and spends it on gambling or drinking. Do you think I could get a job someplace like this?"

"I'm sure you could."

"I'm gonna think about it," Raul whispered. "I'm gonna lay here a long time and just think about it. Them stars make me feel like thinking."

We stayed out there on the hood of the truck for a very long time, surrounded by silence and stars, thinking.

Chapter 21

Hasta la Vista

Miss J, wake up," Raul whispered so softly that his voice drifted into my dream.

By the time the bugs had gotten tired of waiting for us and left in search of other tourists to terrify, and the cool desert breeze convinced us to retreat into the trailer, we were too tired to assemble bed frames and lug mattresses around, so we just tossed a couple of mattresses on the gorgeous pea green living room carpet and waved good night to each other. I immediately dove into an exhausting dream where I was driving a giant truck on an endless freeway, making no progress, while a swarm of huge, ugly bugs hovered just above the windshield. In my dream, Raul was in the passenger seat, yelling, "Hurry up, Miss J, hurry up!" So when the real Raul urged me to wake up, his voice blended into the dream, until he touched my shoulder. I opened my eyes to find him squatting beside my pillow, his face barely visible in the moonlight that filtered through the uncovered windows. He was staring into the darkened doorway that led to the kitchen.

"What?"

"There's something out there," he whispered.

I turned over and raised up on my elbows to take a look. Nothing.

"You're probably having a nightmare," I said. "No wonder, with all those bugs—"

Raul drew in his breath sharply and his eyes widened so that the whites were visible in the semidarkness. I trained my eyes to follow his gaze and squinted into the night. Again, nothing. Just as I was about to flop over onto my back and tell Raul to forget it and go to sleep, a movement caught my eye. Something was moving slowly, silently, across the floor toward us. It was about fifteen feet away, and it was too dark to tell how big the thing was, but anything that is big enough to see in the dark from fifteen feet is too big for me.

"Let's get out of here," I said.

Raul didn't respond.

"Come on," I said, carefully sliding out from under my blanket. "Let's get out of here."

"Wait!" Raul put one hand on my arm. "It's a big bug or something." He shook my arm. "Where's that flashlight? Remember that one that I was messing around with in the truck and you yelled at me to stop messing around with it? Where is it?"

"I don't know where anything is," I said. "I don't even know if we took it out of the truck." Raul was up and out the door in an instant, returning with the flashlight. He knelt beside me again and aimed the flashlight at the mystery bug. Nothing happened.

"Damn!" Raul smacked the flashlight against his palm a couple of times. "You were right. I broke it. Shit!" He whacked the flashlight against the floor, cracking the plastic handle. "Sorry," he said. "Now I really wrecked it." He poked me in the arm. I jumped and yelped. "Sorry," he said. "I didn't mean to scare you, Miss J. And I didn't mean to break your flashlight, neither. You want me to turn on the light?"

I wasn't sure I wanted to see what was crawling out of the kitchen, but it was headed straight toward my mattress, and at the rate it was moving, I would find out soon enough. "Okay," I whispered, as though the thing were listening. Raul tiptoed across the floor behind the mattress. I could hear him running his hand over the wall, searching for the switch. Suddenly, the overhead light flashed on, and I was lying on my stomach, eye to eye with a hairy, black tarantula that was bigger than my hand.

Spiders are not my favorite animal. I don't go out of my way to smash spiders, especially outdoors, which is technically their territory. But when one makes the mistake of trespassing on my turf, I can't rest until the little sucker is squished and flushed down the toilet. I always watch, just to make sure it doesn't come back to life and swim out of the bowl with revenge on its creepy little mind. The tarantula in my living room was too big to squish with a tissue or a paper towel, even if I had been brave enough to try.

"What are you gonna do?" Raul hissed from behind me. He stood with his back plastered against the wall, staring at our spider.

"I'm going to squish it. I'm just trying to decide what to squish it with." A glance around the room at the stacks of cardboard boxes and plastic bags offered nothing in the way of spider-squishing utensils.

"How about one of them dumbbells?" Raul pointed at a pile of dumbbells that were sitting just inside the front door where we had dumped them: one pair of twelve-pound white plastic, one pair of twenty-pound cast iron.

"Good idea," I said, still whispering so as not to alert the tarantula, which had stopped and was watching us. I could tell. I suspected that it was trying to decide whether to go for it and try to rush over and bite me to death or make its break and go hide under my bed or in my closet where it could lurk around and pounce on me at a later date.

"You do it," I urged Raul.

"Me?" he squeaked.

"Please."

Raul drew a deep breath, sneaked across the floor, and picked up one of the white plastic dumbbells. He started toward the tarantula, which sat unmoving until Raul was about three feet away. Then, suddenly, it reared up on its hind legs.

"*Aiih!*" I screamed. I couldn't help it. Raul panicked and pitched the dumbbell at the spider, which promptly started crawling back toward the kitchen, taking the dumbbell along with it for a few feet, until it managed to dump it off. Then it stopped.

Raul had retreated to the far wall. It was up to me. I tiptoed over, picked up one of the twenty-pound cast-iron dumbbells, and held it behind my back where Mr. Spider couldn't see it with its beady little eyes. I felt the steak dinner and the strawberry shortcake stirring below, threatening to revisit me, as I stalked the spider, slowly, from behind. When I was about five feet away, before it had a chance to charge, I leaped forward and brought the flat, round end of the dumbbell down squarely on its back. Its legs flayed wildly, and it took all my self-control to stand still and keep pressing the weight into the carpet. After what seemed like an hour, the legs finally stopped wriggling. Carefully, I lifted the weight a few inches and took a tentative peek.

"Geez," Raul said. "I never seen a spider that big. What are you gonna do with it?"

"I don't know. It's too big to flush, don't you think?"

"I've flushed bigger things than that," Raul said, "but what if it got stuck or something?"

After a brief discussion, we decided to take it outside and put it behind one of the truck tires and then run over it to make sure it was dead. When it was flattened into a black hairy blob, we both sat down on the cement step that served as a front porch, laughing and slapping each other on the back. Soon our shouts of laughter turned to hysterical sobs.

"I'm sorry I messed up your flashlight," Raul blubbered. "I'm always wrecking things because I'm so dumb."

"If you don't stop calling yourself dumb, I'm going to smack you," I said. "Your brain doesn't know the different between fantasy and reality. If you tell yourself you're dumb, you'll believe it, and what you believe is what you are."

"I forgot. I know you already told me that a hundred times. I'm sorry I keep saying I'm dumb."

"And quit saying you're sorry all the time."

"I'm sor—" Raul clapped one hand over his mouth. He loosened his fingers and tried again. "I don't know why I'm so du—" This time, I clapped my hand over his mouth. Surprised by my sudden move, Raul ducked and fell off the step. As I reached down to pick him up, I noticed a funny looking little creature, about three inches long, scurry away into the shadows.

"Did you see that?" Raul said. "I think it was a scorpion."

"No."

"Yeah. I seen pictures of them in that guidebook I was reading in the truck. I recognize that curly little tail thing, the stinger."

"Great. Tarantulas inside. Scorpions outside. Bugs everywhere. I'm about ready to get back in that truck and go right back to California."

"For real?" Raul said, clearly delighted at the thought.

"I can't, honey," I said. "I have a new job lined up here, and I resigned my old one. They already hired somebody to take my place."

"Yeah. But I wish you'd come back."

"You already graduated. I wouldn't be your teacher anyway."

"I know. But if it wasn't for you, me and Gusmaro and Victor and Octavio and German and lots of other guys would just be messed up. We wouldn't be doing as good as we are now, going to community college and working at good jobs and stuff."

"But you're doing fine."

"Yeah. You were there for us. It was like you was holding our hand and leading us through the darkness or something. I wish you was still there because now I'm all alone and I got nobody to hold my hand."

"Then you'll just have to hold your own."

"Yeah," he sighed. Then his sense of humor returned. It spread across his face, the sun peeking from behind a cloud. "Lucky I got two hands, huh, Miss J?"

After daring each other for fifteen minutes or so, we held hands—not as a symbol of togetherness, but because we both wanted to make sure the other one didn't chicken out and run off—and did a quick walk-through, checking to make sure Mr. Spider hadn't left any beneficiaries behind. Satisfied that we were alone, we built a barricade of boxes around our makeshift beds and went back to sleep.

We saw two more tarantulas during the next few days, one in the backyard, heading away from the trailer, and one walking alongside the road.

"There's a lot of stuff I never seen in the world," Raul said thoughtfully, during the last day of his visit. We were driving back from the animal shelter, where I had adopted a puppy, at Raul's insistence. He said he wouldn't be able to rest if he knew I was living in the middle of the desert with a bunch of bugs, all by myself, with nobody to talk to. Raul named the puppy Punkin, one of the affectionate nicknames I had often called him.

"Look at all the stuff I seen just this week," Raul said. He held Punkin up so she could see out the window as we bounced along the dirt road, shooting stones and dust showers every which way. "Like them cactuses and spiders and streets with Spanish names and dust devils and tumbleweeds, and the Rio Grande River. I read about it in my geography books, but it didn't seem like a real place. And there it was. I even threw a rock in it. It was real nice of you to let me drive out here with you, and feed me for a week, and let me ride your bike to town and everything."

"I really enjoyed your company," I said. It was true. I had invited him along as a favor, to give him a chance to see something of the world outside of California, but he had turned out to be excellent company.

The day before Raul's flight back home, he raced into the house with a letter from Isabella Carrillo.

"Look!" he said. "This was in your mailbox down by the road. Open it."

Even without the return address, I would have recognized Isabella's precise, feminine handwriting. I opened the letter, which had been addressed to me in Woodside and forwarded to Las Cruces. Raul peeked over my shoulder, whispering the words under his breath as he read.

Dear Miss J--

I am sorry to hear that you are moving to another place from California, but I am hoping that you are doing fine. I am fine. I will start school in two more weeks. I will be taking chemistry, pre-calculus and health education.

I always think of you, and I want you to know that I am very grateful. How could I ever forget you or all the things you have done for me? Miss Johnson, you will maybe think I am exaggerating, but you are like a star that illuminates my life. Before I met you, my life did not have any meaning. I had feelings of emptiness. I never received love from anyone, not even from my mother because they took me away from her. And my father never worried or cared about me or any of my sisters because we are girls. Thank you for filling that empty spot in my heart and thank you for loving me as you do.

Isabella

"I guess that's why you like teaching, huh?" Raul said. "Because you got a lot of people to love you all the time, even if you live all by yourself. I bet that's why you never get lonely." He looked out the window, suddenly thoughtful and quiet. I asked him what he was thinking about and he shrugged and said, "Nothin'." A little while later, he asked if he could borrow my bicycle and go for a last ride.

"It'll give you a chance to get used to me not hanging around all the time," he said. "And besides, I want to take another look at them weird cactuses so I can remember exactly how they look in my mind."

Raul's grin looked especially mischievous and suspicious that day, but when I mentioned it, he accused me of making up things because I was bored and suffering from heat stroke, so I let it slide.

The following day, Raul asked at least six times during breakfast how long it would take to get to the airport in El Paso for his flight home. Between the heat and the smell of puppy pee from the accidents that neither of us was fast enough to intercept, I lost my graciousness.

"It takes an hour," I said. "One hour. Is that too hard to remember? I know you can count to one."

"Could we leave early, just to make sure?" Raul asked.

At that point, I was ready to get rid of him. "Let's go right now."

Raul didn't seem the least insulted, but he took me literally. A few minutes later, he stood near the door, with his backpack slung over one shoulder and his baseball cap perched backward on his head. He said it would be perfectly all right with him if I just dropped him off at the airport and left him to play video games and eat junk food for a couple of hours before his flight left. I assumed that he was simply tired of being a house guest and was eager to get back to his family and friends and familiar terrain.

Raul was unusually quiet in the car, until we were about five miles from the freeway entrance for I-25. As we passed the new high school, an ultramodern shopping-mall-style campus with a giant white canopy running down the center, Raul suddenly sat up straight.

"Let's go look at that school," he said. "We got time."

"You want to look at a high school?"

"I just think it would be neat to see a school that doesn't have holes in the ceiling and broken windows and tags all over the walls. Parkmont was the only school I ever got to see, you know." He checked his watch. "We got plenty of time, don't we?"

I pulled into the visitor parking lot in front of the building, which was beautifully landscaped with a natural desert motif. As we walked up the sidewalk toward the main entrance, Raul checked out the landscaping and chuckled.

"Hey, Miss J, do you remember when you told the principal why is he painting the railing and planting them trees when they closed half the library, and you said, 'Is that so your illiterate students can stand in the shade?' He got so pissed at you, but you was always fighting for us, Miss J, because you got a big heart. I think you was born to be a teacher."

I did remember how I had pitched a fit about the budgets and wrote letters to everybody I could think of, demanding that they reallocate them with the students as first priority. I was still lost in my reverie when I realized that we were inside the building and Raul was leading me straight down a hallway, as though he knew where he was going. When I asked him where he was headed, he stopped short, glanced quickly from side to side, thinking fast.

"I just figured the office would be over here," he said, as he turned right and stopped in front of a bulletin board outside a glass-walled office.

"What's *developmental* mean?" Raul asked, his eyes on a vacancy announcement posted on the board for a teacher of developmental English.

"It probably means kids who need some extra work on reading and writing," I said.

"Kind of like the Academy, huh?" Something in his voice tipped me off. I glanced at him and realized he was looking at me, not at the bulletin board.

"Probably nobody wants to teach them developmental kids, huh? Cause they probably don't know how to act. They'll probably get some mean teacher and they'll do real bad and get in trouble and flunk out of school and stuff."

He checked his watch and pretended to be surprised. "Come on, Miss J. I don't want to be late. You gotta get rid of me or you'll be stuck with me maybe forever."

I expected him to bring up the teaching job on the way to the airport, but Raul didn't even mention the high school, as though he had forgotten our visit. He kept up a running commentary on the scenery, the dairy farms outside Anthony, the race track at Sunland Park, the view of Mexico across the river.

At the airport, Raul checked in at the ticket counter and asked me to help him find the departure gate for his flight. He insisted that he'd be fine, reading magazines and playing video games, and I should just get back on the road to Las Cruces, but I stayed with him until his flight was called.

When the attendant announced preboarding, I made sure that Raul had his ticket and enough cash for the trip, and my address and phone number. He thanked me again for letting him make the trip. Then he opened his mouth, as though a sudden thought had occurred.

"Hey, Miss J, remember that bet you told me about with Mr. Bernard?" I had mentioned it to Raul when we were trading life stories during the long drive across the Mojave. I nodded.

"Let me know if you need to borrow the money to pay him. I won't even charge you any interest, since you didn't charge me any."

"But Mr. Bernard's bet was that I'd go back to teaching high school," I reminded Raul. "And I already have a job lined up teaching at the college."

"I know all that," Raul said. "But I know some other stuff, too." He tapped his index finger against his temple. "I'm smart, remember? And handsome and charming and lovable. At least that's what you always be telling me. You weren't lying to me, were you?"

"No. You *are* all those things."

"Right," Raul nodded. "So, like I said, let me know if you need to borrow the money. I won't even make you sign a IOU. A handshake will be good enough for me."

He held out his hand. I started to shake it, but at the last second I changed my mind and swooped him into a hug. I squeezed him until I realized he was gasping for air. When I let him go, he said, "I was just thinking abut them Transparentalists."

"What?"

"You know, we read them essays by them guys. I forgot their names. They had weird names like Henry David Waldo or something weird like that."

"Oh. You mean the Transcendentalists. Henry David Thoreau and Ralph Waldo Emerson."

"Right. Them guys. Remember that one thing we read where the guy said say what you gotta say with hard words, but don't be afraid to say some different hard words the next day because it's okay to change your mind?"

"Yeah, I remember. Why?"

"I just wondered if you remembered, That's all." Raul held my gaze for a few seconds, then strolled over and cut into the line of passengers filing onto the boarding ramp. Just before he stepped onto the ramp, he turned and grinned at me.

"If you decide to take that job at the high school and it don't pay as good as the one you got at the college, don't worry. You just send me your pay slip and I'll pay you the difference." His grin faded and his black eyes took over his face.

"*Hasta la vista, Maestra,*" he whispered. See you later, Teacher.

I blew him a kiss. *"Hasta la vista, Estudiante."*

He waved once, jammed his ball cap down hard on his head, slung his backpack over his shoulder, and disappeared into the waiting plane.

I did teach freshman composition at the college for a year before I finally admitted that Justin and Raul know me better than I know myself. I'm back in high school now, teaching developmental English literature and composition to kids who would rather undergo major surgery without anesthetic than read a book or write an essay.

I held out for a year, so I figure I owe Justin one hundred dollars. And I owe Raul Chacon about a million.